Silent Partner

Antonio Commisso

First published by Dog Ear Publishing
4010 W. 86th Street, Ste H
Indianapolis, IN 46268
www.dogearpublishing.net

ISBN: 978-1-4575-1737-2

Printed in the United States of America

For Angie and Chris,
who were there during the dark days.
And Muffy.

Chapter One

December 1984

A knock interrupted the dream I was having. I tried to bring it back, but it floated off. My room was still dark. A faint light came through the slats in the blinds. More knocking then slippers flip-flopping across our hardwood floors. I sat up and blinked to read the clock. Seven twenty-nine a.m. *My father. He forgot something. Or car trouble. It was snowing when I went to bed.* Then my mother's voice called from downstairs.

"Frank."

It didn't sound like her. She had never called to me like that. Something was wrong.

When I got downstairs, I saw two policemen. My mother stood to the side, not moving; she was looking down. Spasms of adrenaline rose within me.

"This is my son." She spoke so quietly I could barely hear her. She looked at me. Her eyes were blank and staring. "Frank, your father—"

One of the men interrupted. "Frank D'Antonio?"

"Yes."

He shifted his weight and looked directly at me. "Sir, I'm sorry to inform you... your father's been shot."

"Shot? Where?" I looked at my mother. "When?" My voice sounded odd to me. I wondered if they had heard me.

"We don't have all the details, Sir. The Brooklyn precinct called us. He's at Methodist. There was another man. A black man. He was shot too."

We exchanged stares. My throat tightened. I tried to clear it.

"That's Reggie, his driver," I said. "Are they okay? Is it serious?"

"Sir, we don't know. Maybe you should be there." They apologized again and wished us well. The door closed behind them. The silence engulfed us.

"I have to get dressed," my mother said. Her face was strained. She was speaking with effort, one word at a time.

"Ma, I can't wait. Tell Angelo and Carman to get you—no, I'll call them. I'll tell them to come." I ran upstairs to finish dressing.

***

The sliding-glass doors opened and I stepped into the emergency room. In the corridor, people waited along the walls in stretchers and wheelchairs. A voice burst out on the loudspeaker, paging a doctor. I looked everywhere for my father but dreaded to see him. At the nurses' desk a man and woman were checking a clipboard. They wore white coats and green pants. The woman looked up. "Can I help you, Sir?"

"I'm Frank D'Antonio."

The man lowered the clipboard and looked at me. "You're looking for Joseph D'Antonio?"

"Yes."

"You can see your grandfather but just for a minute."

"He's not my grandfather. He's my father. How is he?"

The man raised his eyebrows and looked more intently at me. I was used to these looks of surprise. The gap in our ages always amazed people.

"His condition...is critical." My stomach tightened. I stared at him.

"He has multiple gunshot wounds. We're preparing him for surgery now. You must be quick. Around the corner. Number three."

I rushed down a short corridor, dodging stretchers. Cubicles were separated by white curtains. I couldn't find any numbers. I counted to three and pushed aside the curtain.

My father lay still. His eyes were closed. A plastic tube was in his nose. From two plastic pouches above him, a clear liquid was flowing into his arm.

I moved toward the bed and stared down at my father. I put his hand in mine. It seemed to have no strength, but it was warm. I looked down at those familiar hands. His middle finger was bent slightly from that night he caught the ball at Yankee Stadium. I was seven. It had been so exciting. The ball coming at us. Straight at us. I hadn't learned about his pain until later. He hadn't wanted us to know.

I was there, holding the same hand. My father's hand. It looked so alive. So normal. Not like a hand that belonged to a dying man. There was no wound. No sign of trauma. I clung to it, aware I could not squeeze though I wanted to. I wanted to take his hand and walk with him out of the park and go home.

As if by the intensity of my thoughts, he opened his eyes. He looked at me and made an effort to smile. His mouth didn't move, but I could see the smile in his eyes. I felt a slight squeeze of my hand. When he let go, I held on.

"I'm here, Dad. Everything's gonna be all right."

Tears stung my eyes. *Everything's gonna be all right*. That's what you say. But how did I know? I really didn't know anything. I didn't want him to see me cry. He opened his mouth but no sound came. He tried again. There was a hollow sound, as if he had no breath. I leaned close to him.

"We've...come a long way, Son." He lifted his hand slightly off the bed, as if the movement would give more power to his words.

"We got a long way to go, Dad." I didn't know what I meant. It just came out.

"Make sure—" His eyes closed briefly. "Make sure you go the right way. You are my son. I love you, Frankie."

There was no keeping my tears away,

"You're gonna be okay, Dad. You're gonna be okay." My voice

sounded more urgent than reassuring.

Suddenly his hand tightened.

"You're a good boy, Frankie. You got a good name. Don't let anybody change that."

"Please, Dad, don't worry. I'll take care of everything."

He squeezed again and his eyes flickered with pain or confusion. I couldn't tell which.

"Take care of yourself!"

The curtain moved behind me and a woman's voice startled me.

"You'll have to leave now, Sir."

Her voice was not quite matter-of-fact, but it held no possibility of compassion. It was her job to get my father to surgery. After work she could go home—have a drink or watch T.V. Maybe I was being unfair, but I couldn't go home.

Suddenly I remembered my mother and brothers. I took his hand again. "I'll be waiting outside, Dad."

I watched my hand slip away from his then stepped outside. The doctor with the clipboard met me.

"Is he gonna be okay?" I asked.

"I don't know, Sir. How old is your father?"

"He's... eighty-one."

"He's not a young man; he's lost a lot of blood and his heart is weak. We don't know what the bullets did to him." I nodded. I didn't know what to do next.

"We'll call you as soon as we know more."

Doctors always say that. "As soon as we know more." But nobody knows it all. And anyway, I wanted to know now. I wanted him to save my father. But I said only, "Thanks."

The doctor disappeared into my father's cubicle. I walked toward the waiting room. The same nurse was sitting in front of a computer at the nurses' desk. I stopped, suddenly remembering Reggie. "Excuse me. Reggie Reid. How's he doing?"

"The black man that came in with your father? If you're not a relative, we can't give out any information." She paused, gave me a sympathetic look then said. “He’s doing okay.”

“Thank you,” I said and kept walking.

The waiting room was next to the sliding doors. I sat down and leaned over, holding my head in my hand, grateful for the silence that blocked out everything. Where were Angelo and Carman? And my mother? I looked up to see them walking through the door. My brothers rushed toward me. My mother hung back, afraid of asking, afraid of knowing.

“How is he?” Angelo asked.

“They don’t know. He’s shot up pretty bad.”

“Can I see him?” My mother was holding her hands in front of her. When she spoke, she made massaging motions, one hand on the other, comforting herself. Otherwise she looked frozen, paralyzed. I moved toward her.

“They’re rushing him to surgery, Ma. You can’t see him now.” She started to weep quietly. I put my arm around her. I couldn’t stand to see her cry.

“Where’d it happen?” It was Carman speaking. There was no emotion in his voice or his face. He looked directly at me.

“I don’t know. Who would want to shoot Dad?”

Angelo looked at me, then at Carman. His eyes were wide. “It’s gotta be a mistake or accident or…” His voice trailed off.

A nurse with a clipboard appeared. She asked my mother about my father’s doctors and what medication he was taking. As she turned to leave, my mother started to follow. I caught hold of her and led her back to a seat.

It had been eight fifty-five when I asked about Reggie. A small, black clock hung from the wall behind the nurse. Another clock, black and much larger, hung over the sliding doors. It was hard to keep my eyes away from the minute hand which moved in small forward jerks. We waited. No one spoke. We took turns pacing. Angelo picked up a magazine and opened it. In a moment he let it drop onto the table. A man and woman sitting in the corner chairs quickly looked up and as quickly looked away.

It was ten o'clock when the doctor appeared. Just over an hour. My throat tightened. It seemed too soon. The doctor's eyes were heavy as he looked down at the four of us, concentrating mainly on me.

"I'm sorry," he said. "We lost him on the table. His heart just gave out."

My mother put her head into her lap. She made long wailing sounds and rocked back and forth in her chair. Angelo jumped up, his hands over his face. "Oh God, Oh God," he kept saying. Carman stayed seated, his face hard and staring. I sat silently. I don't remember how long we stayed, but as we left I noticed the bright rush of clean winter air and the greasy fragrance of lunchtime on the streets.

When the news got out, our phones both at home and the office were constantly ringing. It was too much for my mother, so I listened to a steady stream of sympathetic and shocked voices ask me what happened. I really didn't know. Between phone calls and making funeral arrangements, the next couple days kept me busy, but I did make a call to the hospital to check in on Reggie.

***

The funeral gave me the first of many insights I would now have about my father, the kind of man he was. A man who lived both his business and private life governed by loyalty, honesty and respect. It showed on that sharply cold day. Snow had fallen the night before, as it had the night before my father's death. But that didn't stop over two hundred people from paying their respects.

There were hundreds of cards, countless flower arrangements, and many tear-filled faces that seem to blur together today, though a few still stick out in my mind. Alfred Lewakowski was one of them.

When my father was doing electrical work for the Rossetti brothers, he was sent one day to Johan and Vera Lewakowski's home. Like many immigrant families at that time, Johan worked as a laborer and Vera stayed home and took care of their son Alfred. Money was tight, so Vera helped subsidize Johan's meager income by selling her homemade chewing gum for pocket money.

They needed a new fuse box which my father installed then made up a bill and handed it to Vera. They knew that electrician house calls didn't come cheap but the sight of the price made her gasp. She gave my father a concerned look and then disappeared into another room. A moment later she returned with the cash, counting out each bill into my father's hand. He thanked them and was about to leave when Vera stopped him. She grabbed his wrist and led him into their bedroom. She walked across the room to the dresser, picked up a small lamp in one hand and with the other grabbed the end of the cord that was missing a plug. "How much to fix?" she asked.

He looked at her, thought about his pressing schedule. "I have other calls," he said. "I'll have to call my boss."

She gave him another concerned look and my father knew what she was proposing. If my father called in to his boss, it might be billed as another service call. What could it hurt to help the lady with such a minor job? He didn't have the proper plug on his truck, and he couldn't take the time to get one then.

"I'm too busy now," he said. "But I'll come back tonight."

Her face lit up. "Thank you." She led him to the door.

Later that day, after his shift was over, he returned to the Lewakowski house with a new plug and repaired her lamp as she looked on. The job took only a few minutes. With the new plug in place, he bent over and inserted it into the wall outlet then pushed the switch and the lamp lit up.

"There you are," he said with a smile. She returned his smile with a look of gratitude then her expression tightened.

"How much?" she asked.

He looked at her. "That's okay, Mrs. Lewakowski."

She exhaled slightly. "Thank you." She said and walked him to the door. “Wait. Please.” She disappeared into the kitchen. A moment later she returned with a small box. “Take. Please. My gum. For you.”

“That’s not necessary,” he said and tried to give it back, but she insisted, so he took the gum and left.

While driving home he tried a piece of the gum and was surprised at how good it was. They became good friends and Vera eventually got my father’s home phone number. Occasionally, when she needed work done, she’d bypass the Rossetti office and call my father directly. He never ran out of chewing gum.

The years passed and Alfred decided to capitalize on his mother’s chewing gum. He opened up a small store in Brooklyn. He remembered my father and how kind he’d been to his parents, so whenever he needed electrical work done, he called him. Business was good so Alfred always paid with cash, but he always included a box of gum.

Eventually Vera and Johan passed away. Alfred had married and, after their first child was born, decided it was time to get out of the city. They moved to the Poconos, an area that was getting a reputation as a honeymoon resort. Alfred opened up a store specializing in gourmet candies and especially his mother’s chewing gum. Business boomed for a while but, before long, Alfred’s luck began to turn bad. He and his wife had three more children, one of which was born with a disabling muscular disease. Her condition put a strain on the marriage. His wife began to drink and, to make matters worse, the Pocono region’s popularity had run its course. Business was dropping.

By that time, my father’s days as an electrician had ended. He invested wisely in New York real estate. By the sixties, he was big time. One weekend my father decided to get out of the city. He’d never been to the Poconos and knew that Alfred had opened a business there. He drove out and finally located the store. He was surprised to find the place and Alfred rundown. Like his mother, his face lit up when my father entered the store.

My father said, “I miss your mother’s great gum, I’ll take two boxes.” He pulled a fifty-dollar bill from his pocket and said, “Ring this up, Alfred.”

Alfred hesitated. He gave my father a look that showed part embarrassment and part gratitude. They talked a while and Alfred eventually divulged his situation. “I think I’m just gonna sell.”

“What will you do?” my father asked.

He gave him a concerned look. “I don’t know.”

My father thought a minute then said. “How about if I buy the store? How much do you want?”

Alfred was too proud for a handout and almost took offense to my father’s show of charity.

“It’s not charity,” my father said. “We both know that your mother has always been the best gum maker in the world. It’s good business. Of course I think I’d make some changes and I will need someone to run things. I’m too busy in New York.” The two men looked at each other then my father said. “What do you say?”

Alfred agreed and, just like many of my father’s other deals, they sealed it with a handshake. My father provided the capital and, through some New York consultant friends of his, they transformed the gum store into a small factory. Then through a well-planned advertising campaign, they promoted the gum as “gourmet.” The combination worked and Alfred began doing well again. My father assured him that they would be partners as long as Alfred wanted.

Once things were set up and running, my father seldom got involved. They kept in touch by phone and Alfred would send him reports a couple times a year. Every Christmas, my mother would get a huge box of gum with a card that expressed his perpetual gratitude to my father.

The other person I recall was Sol Novak. He and my father grew up together in Brooklyn. Sol started out in the deli business in Manhattan. After many successful years, he sold the deli and invested in a resort hotel in the Catskills. It was a seasonal business that was virtually dormant in the winter months.

For a while business boomed. But when the New York State Thruway was created, it cut off most of the traffic coming out of the city to the older side routes. Sol's and many other businesses began to suffer.

He did some research and found a large piece of oceanfront property in Miami, but he'd lost a lot of money in the Catskills. He called my father and asked for his help. Again with just a handshake, they became partners.

My father knew nothing about the hotel business, so he provided the funding and let Sol oversee everything. That was how the Regency was created. Like with Alfred, my father put his trust in Sol, only occasionally visiting the site. Sol would give him a tour of the facility, but the part my father really enjoyed was sitting in the Piccadilly Bar and talking to Gus the bartender. My father would have his usual cup of black coffee and chit chat with Gus, subtly picking his brain about what was going on around the hotel. When he was done, he always left Gus a twenty-dollar bill.

When Sol and Alfred heard about my father's death, they were the first to call and tell us that they were on their way. Gus couldn't afford the trip or the time off but he sent flowers and a card with a long note expressing his sympathy and telling us about the coffee sessions, the money, and how my father always made him feel secure about his job.

There were many others like Alfred, Sol, and Gus that my father had helped over the years. That was the way he was. His success, in a way, had humbled him. He knew that hard work and dedication were not enough. Sometimes a helping hand and a little luck were the difference between success and failure.

Harry Hellman, an up-and-coming real estate tycoon with a reputation for being both tough and honorable in business, had put his trust in my father and given him his first big opportunity. My father had never forgotten it, never let him down, and always credited Harry for his own success. So when small entrepreneurs would come to my father with big ideas but short on money, he would always listen. It was his way of giving back. He had a knack for reading people. He'd notice their demeanor. How they walked, their posture while they sat in front of him, the tone of their voice.

"If a man is sincere, he'll speak with conviction and look you in the eye when he does." If he liked their idea and they had a good business plan, he'd take a chance with them. In return for my father's money and contacts, he would get a share in their business. He helped them get started and, as long as there were no problems, left them completely in charge. It was a casual business arrangement based on trust. He didn't do it for the money; real estate was his business. He even gave them the option to buy back his investment though I don't recall anyone ever did. The people my father helped liked being associated with him. They felt comfortable knowing he was there if they needed him. But it wasn't easy becoming his partner. It was strictly word of mouth.

***

After the funeral, we tried to make things appear normal. Or perhaps I alone was trying. My mother didn't want to leave home. She had her own timetable for grief. Angelo took over my father's office. That bothered me. It seemed too soon. I didn't want it touched. But it wasn't long before he and Carman had buried me in work. It felt strange to be working alongside them, but I welcomed the distraction.

The police concluded mistaken identity in a drive-by shooting. Mistaken or not, it was impossible to accept and more a torment not to know. Meanwhile, Reggie wanted to come back to work. His wounds had not been serious. We kept him on to drive me into the office and to run errands for my mother.

***

On our first commute together into Manhattan, a billboard came into view. It showed a man with a cane. He was tipping his hat in a way that made me think of my father. The question burst out: "What happened that morning, Reggie?"

Reggie was eager to talk. He had gone over the entire day step-by-step so many times that each detail seemed memorized.

He recalled turning our black Lincoln Town Car into the driveway on Long Island, pulling up in front of the house, hearing the snow from the night before crunching under the tires.

"I remember the guy on the radio saying it was twenty-two degrees at six twenty-seven cause I remember thinking I got three minutes before you and your father come out. I been picking up Mister D at six thirty on the nose for—I don't know—ten years." He glanced at me. "And you. Since you started working last year. When I heard there was no hang ups on the LIE, I shut the radio off and waited." Reggie went on, speaking rapidly, seeming to be relieved to be telling his story.

He remembered staring at our wraparound porch in the dim morning dawn, trying to count the inches of snow. At exactly six-thirty, the door had opened and my father appeared. Nothing about those moments had given any hint of what was to come. My father was dressed in his usual attire: gray overcoat and fedora. Reggie had watched as my father grasped the porch railing, taking each step one at a time down to the car.

"I thought I ought to get out and help him...but then I see he was doin all right on his own." Reggie was quiet for a moment then laughed briefly at this memory.

"He got into the front seat," he continued. "He always sat up front with me. That is, till you started riding with us." It was a detail I had not known. I had pictured Reggie driving as the chauffeur. But my father made it look like two men going to work together.

"Yeah, but I had to get out and get the éclairs and coffee."

Reggie laughed again. "Well, you was the new man in the car pool." I was silent for awhile. It was a good memory.

"You didn't come out. That surprised me. I asked where you were. Your father said you was out late closing the deal on the San Maurice. He was letting you sleep late."

It was the first time I'd let that detail about the morning sink in. *I hadn't been there.* My father had wanted me to sleep.

"He said you was gonna drive yourself in later." Reggie paused and was quiet for a while. "He was real proud of you, Frank. We all was. How you put the whole thing together. Those Japs are tough businessmen."

"And big drinkers," I said.

Reggie said my father had been unusually quiet that morning. He had made his customary effort at small talk, but my father had seemed distracted. Except for their morning ritual.

He continued, "I said to him, 'The city's gonna be a mess with all the snow. Maybe we should forget the coffee and éclairs.' But Mister D had his routine. He had something else on his mind, but snow wasn't gonna change that."

It was true. We'd had a tradition. I hadn't realized it until I lost it. Since we'd moved to Long Island, my father had commuted to his Manhattan office every day by way of the Napoli Bakery in Brooklyn. He and Reggie always picked up coffee and éclairs to go. The area had changed over the years. The middle class of the previous generation had moved to the Island or Uptown, turning the once owner-occupied brownstones into low-rent housing. Italians, Jews, and Irish were replaced by blacks and Puerto Ricans, but the Napoli Bakery on Court Street endured all these changes, making donuts and éclairs for the drug dealers and prostitutes and everyone else on the street.

Reggie had been concerned about my father. "Something wrong, Mister D?" Reggie remembered thinking his question had startled my father, who hadn't answered right away. "'I'm just thinking.' That's all he said. I asked him if he was worried about you and the San Maurice deal. When the Casbar deal closed, he acted the same way—funny. You know, strange. He said it wasn't you he was worried about."

I looked over at Reggie. He glanced back at me.

"That's what he said."

Maybe that meant he really had been worried about something. Worried enough to tell Reggie only what it wasn't about. I felt unease rising in me. The same I'd felt before: when the police said *mistaken identity*. But I wanted Reggie to finish his story.

From the Brooklyn-Queens Expressway, they had taken the Tillary Street exit. At the first traffic light, there was one car ahead of them.

"When the light changed," Reggie continued, "the car ahead didn't move. I honked the horn. Then I see a car behind us. The car in front moved a few feet, then stopped again. It looked like he was having car trouble. I was gonna go around the guy but then I see in the mirror the car behind me was right on my ass. I see these two guys come out of the car in front. They had guns. I yelled to your father to get down. Shots fired out. There was broken glass everywhere in the car. After that I don't remember nothing."

We sat silent for a few minutes. I wondered: *Had my father been scared? What had he been thinking that so distracted him?*

"You know, Frank, your father wasn't like a lot of these rich businessmen. He come a long way from them Brooklyn streets and never forgot it. He was a real humble guy, never made you feel low. I don't know if you know this, but I started workin for him back in the thirties when he first got into real estate. Me and him, we'd get up on ladders together. Then he met that Harry Hellman guy and, well, that's when things took off for him. Me? I stayed on doin maintenance, but no matter how busy he was, he would come by and find me, sometimes just to say hello.'

"He seen me one day. I was havin a hard time gettin up a ladder. My arthritis was kickin' up. He knew, too. He told me to get down. He looked at me leanin on the ladder. 'Reggie,' he says, 'I'm lookin for a driver. The commute's gettin to me.' You know that voice of his. Soft, but you know you better be listening. Then he looked me straight in the eye. 'If you know anybody, let me know.' We stood there for a minute. I knew what he meant. He was lookin' out for me. 'Sure, Mister D,' I said."

Reggie stopped talking. He put his head down for a moment then looked up. His eyes looked different. I wondered if he was trying not to cry.

"Climbin up those ladders was gettin to me. Your father knew it. Any other guy woulda just told me to get lost." He turned to give me a long look then turned back to the road. "Your father was different. He just gave me a different job, let me keep my pride. And with a raise to boot! Not bad for a black kid from Harlem. Your father was the greatest man I ever known."

I noticed his eyes begin to fill. "And you just like him," he said finally.

We never spoke about it after that day. He'd pick me up every morning at six thirty to take me into Manhattan. Some days we'd stop at the Napoli for coffee and éclairs.

***

In 1986 I met Harry Hellman's granddaughter Julia Hennings at a cocktail party. A year later we were married. She insisted on a Manhattan apartment, so I rarely saw Reggie after that. He stayed on to drive for my mother when she felt like going to the city.

Reggie's arthritis got so bad, one day he went to a doctor. He learned he had bone cancer. I made sure to visit Reggie then at least once a week. He died six months later. I always wondered if Reggie had left out any of the story, something he didn't want me to know, or something he just didn't consider important enough to tell.

Chapter Two

October 1996

I still had a few minutes before I had to go in. Even with a sunny cloudless sky, it was a chilly October morning in New York City. In front of the Central Plaza Hotel, people were moving through the huge bronze and glass doors, their eyes straight ahead, focused on the invisible task of the day.

I looked at my watch. Ten after eight. Hansom cabs lined up, waiting for people with the time for a brisk trot through the park. Autumn in New York. A cab's busiest time of the year. Odd to think, at thirty-eight, born and raised in the city, I'd never taken a Hansom cab.

The crowds hustling past me brought on a wave of self-consciousness. Was I just another executive, no—divorced executive, on his way to work? It was official, I had lost a lot: wife, money, confidence. I watched people rush by in their suits, briefcases in hand, hurrying to get to their desks. I'm not like them. My face isn't familiar, but my name is a legend here. My name. Actually my father's name.

I guess I should have thanked God for the business. My brothers kept me too busy to think about lunch. Penny, good old Penny, took care of that. Well, not so old—but good, yes, good. She was our "executive assistant." Hell, I didn't even have a briefcase.

In the vestibule, a man wearing a leather tool belt worked on a ladder. I watched him for several moments. He made me think of my father seventy-some years ago, just starting out.

I checked my watch again. I didn't want to be too early and definitely not late. It was time to go in. As I walked past the man on the ladder, it reminded me of a story my father told about Mickey Cunningham.

When my father was first learning the electrical business, he worked side by side with Mickey Cunningham, a veteran electrician and long-time employee of the Rossetti brothers. Mickey taught my father his trade and, over time, they developed a father-son relationship. It was Mickey who instilled in my father many of the values he tried to pass on to us: patience, integrity, discipline, loyalty. Mickey had a wife and three children so, to make extra money, he would moonlight, taking on small jobs on his own. Many times he would ask for my father's help.

They were scheduled to do a job early one Saturday morning. Mickey gave my father the directions to the job site. They needed some supplies, which my father volunteered to pick up, and then they meet him there at seven thirty sharp. He overslept and, in the rush to get there on time, he bypassed picking up the supplies. He finally arrived fifteen minutes late.

"You're late," Mickey said.

"It's only quarter to eight, Mick, what's the big deal?"

Mickey stopped, looked at my father, and pointed his finger at him. "If I tell you seven thirty, I mean seven thirty, not seven thirty-one. Remember that. It might not seem important to you now, but someday you'll understand. Now, did you pick up the things we need?"

My father looked at him. "I was running late, so I—"

"Joe, when you say you're gonna do something, you gotta do it. A man's word is everything. Remember what I tell you. You'll thank me someday."

I pushed open the bronze and glass doors. The lobby was too warm. If I had known where the thermostat was, I'd have turned it down. That made me laugh. Dad would have done the same thing.

The elevator stopped at the third floor, and I headed down the corridor to the conference rooms. Along the way, the elegant mahogany walls gleamed softly under the low lights of the brass sconces. Chandeliers up ahead also gave off a low light. At this hour of the morning, it felt like an approaching coronation. Still, I felt uneasy. Not my coronation; that's for sure.

Entering the room, I saw that everything had been arranged in meeting-room style with a long, shiny table, surrounded by deep red velvet chairs. At one end were six coffee cups in front of six chairs. The smell of coffee permeated the room. I worked my way down the table where the three men already seated greeted me. I knew them well. They spoke first.

"Morning, Frank."

"Morning, Tom." His face gave no hint of tension—as if this was to be a routine meeting. Tom Morton was the chief accountant for our business. The other men, David Cohn and Stanley Schlenker, were our attorneys. Interest in the law was the only thing they had in common.

David was tall, dark, well-groomed, and flamboyant. He was forty-five and dressed in custom suits and monogrammed shirts. He drove a silver Bentley for pleasure on the weekends and commuted to work in a black Mercedes. Every August he vacationed in Gloucester with his wife and children. The annual party they threw for the local hoi polloi made great conversation on the golf course and cocktail circuit.

Stanley, not quite a decade older, started practicing law in the late sixties. Most of his clients had been high school or college grads trying to evade the draft and Vietnam. Radical activities in support of civil rights had made him a celebrity back then. He dressed in faded khakis, tweed jacket with patched elbows, and a mismatched tie. He wore wire-rim glasses and pulled his brown hair into a ponytail held by a rubber band. Except for his hair, which was now shorter and thinner, and the ponytail, he hadn't changed much. His car was a faded green Pontiac Sunbird and he always brought his lunch in a brown paper bag. David, in contrast, lunched with clients at the Twenty-One Club. David fit the role, but the money and the brains came from Stanley.

We exchanged greetings. I turned to the man seated to David's left.

"I didn't expect to see you, Tom!" Tom was the friendliest of the group—slightly stout, always planning trips to some gym but never quite getting there.

When I spoke, he raised his eyebrows. "To tell you the truth," he said, "I didn't expect to be here, myself. Carman only called last night. Do you know what's going on?"

"Not exactly." I took a seat next to Tom. "But I've got a pretty good idea."

"You want to let me in on it? Your brother was pretty closed-mouthed."

"Well he told you to come, so let him tell you, okay?"

"Okay, Frank. Whatever you say."

David adjusted his Rolex nervously. "Yeah, Carman called me and Stanley last night too. Said it was important."

"I guess we'll all know soon enough," I said. "Are my brothers here?"

David checked his watch again. "They were here a minute ago. They should be right back."

We sat down and a waiter in a tux appeared. A white towel hung over his left arm. In his right hand he was holding a silver pot. He approached the table.

"Coffee, gentlemen?"

Stanley centered the cup in front of him. No one spoke as the waiter poured into his cup then moved to David and Tom. The uneasiness I felt seemed to be everywhere in the room.

When the waiter got to me, he paused. "Good morning, Mister D'Antonio. Coffee, Sir?"

"Yes, please." I looked up at him. He had worked for us for a long time. I was embarrassed. Why didn't I know his name? I should know his name. I should know these things. But I had never really been interested in the business, especially in the beginning.

My brothers' tardiness forced the rest of us into awkward small talk.

Stanley took a sip of coffee. It was too hot and he set it down. “Beautiful day in the city! Sun for a change.”

“Yeah,” I said. “I saw those cabs out there—nice day for a ride. Any of you ever go for a ride in the park?”

Before anyone could answer, the door opened and Angelo and Carman walked in.

“Good morning, gentlemen.”

Everyone stood and shook hands. Angelo turned to me in his usual polite way: “Morning, Frank.”

“Angelo.”

Our eyes met. The deep lines around his eyes and forehead were new or maybe just more noticeable. He seemed apprehensive. His cheeks were pale and blended into the gray hair around his temples. He was older; today he looked really old. I glanced at Carman. He looked the same. My stomach tightened.

***

Angelo didn't waste time. He took his seat at the head of the table. He was the oldest of the three of us. After my father's death, Angelo had claimed his position, but filling my father's shoes was difficult for him.

My father had been sent one morning into Manhattan to do an estimate for man named Harry Hellman. The Rossetti brothers got the job, and my father supervised the entire project. That’s how Harry and my father became good friends.

When the job was completed, Harry mentioned a new venture and said he was looking for investors. All my father did was express interest, and Harry brought him in. With a single handshake, my father had become one of the investors in the Empire State Building.

During the next two decades he acquired the Central Plaza, the San Maurice, and the Metro Tower—our landmark—a glass high-rise on Fifth Avenue. By the time of his death in 1984, he had added two casinos, a high-tech plant in Seattle, a factory in Chicago and one in Pennsylvania, the Regency Hotel in Miami, and a Caribbean cruise line.

Angelo's voice brought me back. “Well, everyone's here. Let's get started.”

The waiter refilled our cups and left.

Angelo sipped his coffee then stood up. “Gentlemen, I know you're wondering why Carman and I called you here. As you know, we have a lucrative business—a worldwide business. No one knows mine and,” gesturing to me and Carman, “my brothers' affairs better than you three. The fact is Carman and I are getting on in years and our health, at least mine, isn't what it was.”

He hesitated then cleared his throat. “We've been negotiating with Holden International, V.T.C. Corporation and Paragon Incorporated to buy out our holdings, and they've made us a very good offer.” He beamed slightly.

The uneasiness I'd felt only moments ago descended into fear and the beginning of rage. I stood up.

“What do you mean you've been negotiating? There are three of us in this business. How could you even consider negotiating without consulting me?” I struggled to stay in control.

Angelo seemed annoyed by my outburst. He made a calming gesture with his hand and looked at me. “We didn't think it was necessary to say anything until we had all the figures together, Frank.”

“Figures? Figures? Are figures the only thing you two care about? Are you thinking of Dad? What would Dad do? Would he want this?” I turned toward Carman, but I saw right away he would speak in Angelo's defense.

“Frank, you're young. You're twenty-five years behind me and Angelo. Look, if this deal goes through, you'll have all the money you need and the best years of your life to enjoy it.”

I put both hands on the table and leaned forward. “Do you

realize I have devoted the last twelve years of my life to this company? How could you negotiate this without at least asking what I think?"

I raked my hand through my hair. "And where's your business sense, anyway? It's a bad time to sell. Anybody with half a brain knows that. In four or five years the market will be better. Then we make our move. You're both saying we'll have all the money we'll need. What you mean is you'll have all the money you'll need!"

I pushed away from the table and got up. I had surprised myself with the vehemence of my own speech. "You're right. You've got twenty-five years on me. The money may be enough for you. You don't have to look as far down the road as I do. You're thinking of yourselves. This so-called offer you have...is it in writing? Or did you just call each other and agree on everything?"

"It's in writing, Frankie," Angelo said. "Calm down."

"Well?" I taunted. I could feel my eyebrows rising. I sat down.

***

Angelo and Carman were teenagers when their mother, my father's first wife, died. His busy schedule left him little time to spend with them. When it came to making shrewd business decisions, my father had no equal. But as a young parent he thought with his heart and not his head. As my two brothers matured, to his disappointment he realized that he had taken the wrong approach. His two sons had developed values and instincts different from his. Unlike most parents, he was given a second chance at parenting, which I believe explains the diversity not only in years but in views between me and my brothers.

He had tried to compensate for his absence by giving them things. They dressed in the latest fashions, for their sixteenth birthdays they both got new cars and a credit card. They struggled through high school, showing little interest in education and lacked the discipline that came from parental supervision. They ran up enormous charges on their credit cards, which my father simply paid, blaming himself for their irresponsibility. My father enrolled them in college, but they each only lasted a semester.

Realizing that education was a waste of their time and his money, he brought them into the business. He set them up with their own offices next to his and began grooming them. They came to work each day dressed in custom-made suits—not too bright, not very motivated, content just holding down a job.

They sat through private sessions while my father explained the different aspects of the business. "Honesty, integrity, and friendship are everything. Friendships, like the foundations of these big buildings we own, have to start from the bottom and go up. Every man is important, even the one who sweeps the floors."

He tried not to show his exasperation observing the two of them: Angelo subtly rolling his eyes and Carman gazing out the window.

"You are my sons," he continued. "You represent me. When you do something or say something, people watch and listen." He tried to teach them humility and prudence. Neither son, however, seemed to heed his advice.

Angelo was insecure and, despite my father's instruction about prudence and discretion, was too quick to act in a situation. That caused him to make errors in judgment. One day my father walked past Angelo's office and overheard him giving a tongue lashing to someone on the phone. He paused outside the door and listened. Angelo was berating George, the parking garage attendant, because someone had parked in his space. He pushed open the door and gave Angelo a piercing stare. The sight of my father instantly quieted Angelo's tantrum. He quickly ended the conversation and hung up.

"Angelo. Don't talk to George like that," my father said in a gentle but curt tone.

"But my—"

"But nothing. That's no way to talk to him. I told you about jumping to conclusions. Screaming at him for something so trivial will create animosity, and that's unproductive. You're wasting time over a parking space. Don't you have anything better to do? Now call George back and apologize for losing your temper. And don't let it happen again."

During business hours and in my father's presence, Carman was a dutiful and loyal son. He was short, unlike Angelo and my father, who both stood close to six feet. He saw the disappointment and frustration on my father's face as he tried in vain to deal with Angelo's lack of business savvy. But where Angelo's view on business matters often disagreed with my father's, Carman gave no opinion.

This lack of force came from a combination of things. Carman was in awe of our father and wanted so much to please him, but was intimidated by his powerful presence. His uncertainty made him apprehensive to voice his opinion. Whenever he did attempt to give his view, Angelo usually cut him off, dismissing his input as ridiculous. This fueled Carman's insecurity. His pent-up anger and frustration came out after business hours.

As first a small business man then—with time—a real estate mogul, my father managed to life a satisfying life devoted to his business and his family. He had no vices that I could speak of. His personal life, in contrast to his hugely renowned empire, was low key. While other New York tycoons enjoyed seeing their names in the business section and society columns of the paper, my father enjoyed a quieter, more subdued existence.

To his disappointment, Carman was completely opposite. He was addicted to all the vices: gambling, women, drinking, and, many times, all three at once. He was a regular at several all-night high-stakes card games where the players loved him for two reasons: he always paid his debts before he left, and he almost always lost.

Although he was a frequent participant, Carman's card playing skills were mediocre at best. To make things worse, he never heeded the first rule that any good player learns, gambling and booze don't mix. His drinking clouded what little card savvy he had, making him a predictable and unwise player.

When he wasn't playing cards, he was chasing skirts. The booze gave him a sense of confidence that in a sober state he lacked. But he was a bad drunk, creating scenes wherever he went. He'd walk into a night club or restaurant virtually unnoticed, but after a few drinks he would make his presence known. He'd buy drinks for strangers at the bar saying to the bartender, "Tell them it's on Carman D'Antonio." This usually drew peoples' attention. They'd acknowledge his generosity with impressed looks. If our name didn't ring a bell, he'd mention a city landmark by saying, "You know the Metro Tower? I own it."

People were quick to reciprocate by buying him drinks in return. But more than the drinks, exposing who he was drew attention from women. He basked in his self-promoted celebrity, exchanging looks with beautiful females, usually plucking one of them up by the end of the night.

Out of respect for my father, he wouldn't dare to take a suite in Central Plaza, so he'd check in to any one of a number of posh hotels in Midtown. Everyone knew him, from the bell men to the G.M., and they all stepped over themselves to pamper him with whatever he desired, knowing his reputation as a big spender and tipper.

But there was always some sort of disagreement with a bartender short-shotting his drinks, or a waiter's lack of attention, or a steak overcooked or undercooked. Eventually the episodes found their way back to my father who, at first, reprimanded him then just threw up his hands in defeat.

But what infuriated my father beyond control was Carman's defiant attitude with the law. He'd pull up to some afterhours club and park wherever he wanted, showing little regard for parking restrictions. If he caught the police issuing him a ticket, he'd snatch it from under his windshield wiper and say, "Thanks, I'll add it to my pile." The next day he'd be on the phone with a local committee man, demanding that he take care of the ticket. This worked until one day the committee man called my father. In a tone part apologetic and part complaining, he said, "Mr. D'Antonio I'm starting to get heat from the chief downtown about the tickets."

"What tickets?" my father asked.

"These parking tickets that Carman keeps getting. Maybe you should tell him to be a little more careful."

My father was furious. He called Carman into his office. That's where my father gave full vent to his rage. "You waste valuable favors with our committee man over parking tickets because of your irresponsibility!"

Carman's face turned red as he tried to speak.

"Shut up and listen," my father said. "I didn't work my whole life cultivating friendships so that you can take advantage of them over triviality!"

"It was only a couple—"

"I said be quiet. Now you're gonna go downtown and retrieve whatever tickets you gave him to "fix" for you and you're gonna pay them. And if I ever get another call like this, I'll deal with you myself. Now get out of my sight."

Carman continued his bachelor life style through his early forties. Though he kept an apartment in the city, Carman spent a lot of time at home with us. By the time I'd reached my teens, Carman and I developed a close relationship. At first my father was pleased. Carman took me everywhere with him. We'd go out to dinner and he'd tutor me on restaurant etiquette. He'd take me to his regular watering holes and introduce me to everyone. Because of the gap in our ages, many times we were mistaken for father and son.

Our relationship was actually a bit like a father and son. He was proud of me and he respected me. I think he saw many of our father's characteristics in me. As the years passed, many times he would subtly ask my advice. We came to confide in each other, neither one of us comfortable turning to my father when we had problems.

It wasn't long before my father's contentment turned to concern. He'd blamed himself for the way Angelo and Carman had turned out, but he was determined not to let it happen to me. He started keeping a tight rein on me. On my sixteenth birthday, I asked for a car. My father listened to my request, thought a moment then said, "How do you intend to pay for it?"

I gave him a puzzled look. "I don't know. I'll get a job."

He left me to figure out my dilemma. I worked a summer job but, by September, when it was time to return to school, I was still short. He surprised me by making up the balance himself. It was a loan, he said, so every weekend I worked it off by doing odd jobs at his office.

I had no credit card till I went away to college. If I needed money for anything, I had to ask him and, before he'd turn over a penny, he'd interrogate me about what I needed it for.

My father was well-aware of my relationship with Carman and, although he wanted us to be close, he didn't want me picking up Carman's bad habits. He never made blunt accusations, just subtle remarks. One day he walked into my bedroom and noticed a small pile of tens and twenties on my bed stand. "Where'd you get this money?" he asked.

"I don't know, Dad, I just had it."

"Are you gambling?" he said with a piercing stare.

The question caught me off-guard. I tried to hide my discomfort. "No," I said feebly.

"You know I don't like gambling," he said and then walked out.

The fact was that a couple times Carman had taken me to the card games and sometimes at home, when my father wasn't around, he showed me how to play. Like my father, I had a knack for reading people and ironically it was his lectures about watching people's mannerisms that helped me become quite good at cards.

I went through the woman-chasing years but not to excess like Carman. Finally, to my father's delight, Carman met a girl and got married. That didn't stop his flamboyant lifestyle; it just curtailed it a bit. And as time passed, Carman's reputation seemed to haunt me. The mention of my name would continue to raise eyebrows, sometimes for the wrong reasons.

"Are you related to Carman D'Antonio?" they'd ask.

"He's my brother," I'd say.

There was always a remark. "He's a tough man" or "Are you sure you're brothers?"

I never asked why. By then I knew what they meant. He was my older brother and I loved him but, like my father, it made me furious that he could soil the family name.

Eventually I reluctantly entered the business. That first summer job, the challenge and the struggle to earn the money to buy a car, gave me a sense of satisfaction. It was a good feeling that never left me. I saw how my brothers slipped into positions created by my father. They were content coasting along on a trail carved out by him. I was different. I needed a sense of self-accomplishment. I wanted the challenge of making my own deals. I wanted to show my father that I had what it took to be a player independent of his influence.

Instead, for whatever reason (maybe partly to please him, maybe partly my own insecurity) I gave in and joined our firm. I was frustrated and resentful at first, thinking I'd fall into a position controlled by my father, never having the opportunity to make my own way. I sat in on all the sessions, listening to and observing my father and two brothers. I began to see them not as family members but as businessmen.

As I listened to my father's views on business, to my surprise I not only agreed with him but couldn't understand why my two brothers didn't. I was overwhelmed by his wisdom and ability to analyze facts and numbers along with a keen intuition about people and relationships. But Angelo always seemed to disagree and Carman almost always stayed neutral. As the months passed, I would occasionally express my opinion and it usually coincided with my father's. He was encouraged by this and suddenly we found ourselves exchanging ideas.

Prior to my entering the business, my father had set up the corporation, designating himself as president and CEO, owning fifty percent of the total assets. The remaining fifty percent was divided equally between my two brothers. Being left out didn't bother me. I wasn't contributing to the business then and from that standpoint, I figured Angelo and Carman earned their shares. But as the relationship between my father and I got closer, the gap between Angelo and I widened. He seemed to resent the fact that my father was beginning to let me make decisions. Things even changed between Carman and me. There was never any friction like with Angelo, just a slightly distant regard.

As my role in the business became greater and it was clear to my father that I was there to stay, he informed us that as long as he lived, the shares in the company would remain the same but upon his death his shares would be divided between the three of us, each owning one third equally.

I thought about Dad as Angelo passed around five blue folders, each neatly holding papers about the proposed sale. The room was silent as we studied the details. Everything was there. The Vegas casinos, the Manhattan real estate, our holdings in the Midwest factories, the Seattle high-tech plant, even the Caribbean cruise line and the Regency Hotel. A lifetime of my father's hard work and twelve years of mine neatly listed and priced.

I glanced over at Tom. He looked at me, his eyes soft as a spaniel's. What was he thinking? I studied the numbers and tried to calculate mentally. Off the top of my head, the figures seemed impressive. Fair market value, maybe a bit more.

From that standpoint, it seemed a good offer, but my mind quickly focused on other aspects. There were taxes, bank notes, other liabilities. What would we net out? The profit still seemed substantial. My thoughts shifted. My father's face and words came to me. What would he think? Would he be delighted with what Angelo and Carman had negotiated, or would he be furious?

My mind was racing. Alfred Lewakowski and Sol Novak's faces flashed in my mind. My father had given his word to them that their investments would be secure. Would the new owners honor that? Would there be provisions made for Alfred and Sol and some of the other ventures my father had negotiated out of friendship, or would they be on their own? New ownership usually means changes and loyalty isn't part of normal corporate world.

Unless Angelo and Carman provided for our smaller partnerships, they'd get pushed out. Honesty and integrity meant everything to my father. Would this tarnish his name? Were my brothers going to turn their backs on those people who had believed in us? Again visions of Alfred, Sol, and my father came to me and suddenly I felt ashamed. But maybe they had made contingencies in the sale. I could be jumping to conclusions. I wasn't ready for this, but if they were determined to sell, what could I do?

I set down the report and looked up at Angelo. "I think we're making a mistake. If we hang on a while longer, our debt will be reduced that much more and also we can ask more. Who are these guys anyway? Do they have this kind of money?"

I looked at Tom, hoping for help. "What do you think?"

Tom spoke up. He looked confused, searching for something to say. "Is this going to be a cash sale, or are you getting stock options?"

"It's a total cash buyout, Tom." Angelo said.

"The tax implications will be severe."

"We realize that, Tom," Carman said. "You'll have to figure a way around them. And to answer your question, Frank, we checked them out. I don't think I like what you're implying. You talk like Angelo and I are complete idiots. Maybe you forgot who ran the business while you were off at college, screwing around. And what did you do after graduation? You hung around, still deciding what you wanted to do. You don't have a choice, Frank. We've accepted their offer. You either go along or buy us out."

"Carman, you know I can't come up with that kind of money. What would Dad say if he were here? He'd never approve this."

I looked at my brothers for their reaction. It was Angelo's turn. He looked irritated.

"What the hell do you know what our father would have approved of? I agree with Carman. I don't like what you're implying."

"I know him a lot better than you," I snapped. Angelo and I exchanged stares, but my thoughts drifted back to our father. I recalled those last months together. He was totally consumed by the business and excited that I'd finally agreed to be part of it. We were discussing other acquisitions. Selling anything just didn't come into it.

"The decision's been made, Frank. The deal's going through. You can help us with the transition if you want, or we leave you out. It's up to you."

I felt beaten into silence. Angelo turned to Tom. "Tom, we need you to get the figures together and coordinate the closing. The buyers want a detailed statement no later than mid-November." His voice was calm again, asserting control and confidence.

"We'll have to set up a meeting with their lawyers," David said. "We'll need their names."

"I've got them at the office. I think one name is Kehoe."

"Not Steve Kehoe," Stanley said. "The guy's a shyster, a real piece of shit."

"Yeah, a real nightmare to deal with," Cohn added.

"Well, I'm not sure," Angelo said. "Give me a call. If I'm not there, I'll leave the names with Penny." Their discussion of legal details ended abruptly.

The mention of Penny's name brought me back. What would she think of all this? The business was her life too. She wasn't just a secretary. My father had always liked her. He had treated her like a daughter, and she was like a kid sister to Angelo, Carman, and me.

Well, it was a little different with me. I think my father had visions of Penny and me together, though he never mentioned it directly. He left that to my mother. Over coffee one morning, she had said bluntly, “Your father tells me that Penny's a nice girl. Why don't you ask her out?”

“Penny? Ma,” I said, “I'm not interested in anyone right now.” The subject never came up again. Angelo's voice disrupted my thoughts. “So we'll meet again next month to go over everything and

set a date for closing. Now if there's nothing else, I've got another pressing engagement.”

He seemed in a hurry to leave, quickly stuffing papers in his briefcase. “Thank you all for coming. Stay as long as you want, have some more coffee. Sorry I have to leave. Good day.”

He hesitated at the door. “Think about what you're going to do, Frank. Let us know.”

After he left the room, I turned to Carman. “You really going along with him on this?”

“Frank, it'll be better for everyone.”

“It may be for you two, but not for me. What am I supposed to do, send out resumes?”

“Frank, the transition's gonna take a while, but when it's over you won't have to work at all if you don't want to.”

“Carman, I'm thirty-eight! I can't curl up and die! This company's my whole life! If it's sold, it needs to be the right time and for the right price. How much do you think you’re gonna end up with, anyway? You heard Tom. He’s an accountant, not a magician. After the government and the creditors get done, what’s left? You know my divorce cost me a fortune and most of my savings went into the Atlantic City deal ‘cause you two didn’t have the cash. Remember? If we sell now, I’ll lose all that.”

I paused to collect my thoughts. “Okay, maybe you don’t care about me, but at least think of Dad. He worked his whole life building this business. Selling was the furthest thing from his mind.

And what about the Regency and the gum factory? He'd never sell out without telling Sol and Alfred. Did you? And are they going to be protected in the sale? If you know Dad like you say you do, you know he'd make sure they were taken care of."

Carman rolled his eyes then raised his hand to stop me. "This is business, Frankie! We're not everybody's personal protectors. You can't make deals like this the way Pop did. It's all about business." He paused a moment, then continued. "Look, I know you're disappointed, but in time, you'll see everything will work out for the best."

"Disappointed?" I shouted. "What do you know about disappointment? You always had Dad around to make everything right. After he died, you used me to clean up your messes. Maybe that's what got him killed. Did you ever think of that? Maybe trying to patch up something you and Angelo screwed up. Tell me the last time Angelo made a decision that made us any money. You know what his judgment is like. What about A.D.A. Airways? How much did getting his initials on an airplane cost us? And what about the Casbar in Atlantic City? It wasn't a year since Dad bought the one in Vegas. We had cash flow problems. Angelo nagged Dad. Remember that? Insisting we had to stake our claim in Atlantic City.'

"When Dad died, Angelo dropped everything into my lap. I'm just now getting us out of the red. It's crazy to sell now. Business is picking up, soon the numbers will be up. Then we can get our price plus reap some profit before we sell. Angelo had me up to my ass dealing with the day-to-day bullshit when all the time he was planning this. And you let him. I can't believe this. How could you do this to me, Carman? Angelo's manipulating you. You know that, don't you? You know this is wrong. I have one brother who makes bad decisions and another who can't make any decisions."

It was a long speech, but it hadn't used up all my anger. I stopped, not knowing what else to say. Carman's eyes swept up and down the table, establishing momentary contact with Tom, then the lawyers. I thought I saw his hands trembling. Like years ago, I remembered, when he had sat silently before my father. His head was down, and his hands were shaking. I had wanted to comfort him then. Get him in my room so we could play cards or talk. He looked the same, but this time I only felt contempt. Finally Carman spoke, and as he did, he no longer felt like my older brother.

"I won't listen to this shit, Frank. You heard Angelo. The decision has been made. Live with it." He turned suddenly and walked out.

My anger seemed to subside after he left. I looked across the table at the three men. "I can't believe you could agree to this." I kept my voice low.

Tom spoke first. "Frank, I'm just hearing about this now myself. They never asked my opinion either. If they had, I would have said the same thing you did."

Schlenker followed. "We didn't know anything either, Frank. Besides, selling or not selling is a business decision. We're your lawyers. You pay us for legal advice. And Frank, you may not like this, but legally you've just been out-voted two to one."

I rubbed my forehead. "You're right. I'm sorry." I stood up, put on my coat, rolled my copy of the report like a newspaper, and left. They followed me to the elevator.

No one spoke as we descended to the main floor. Tom touched my elbow. "I'll be in touch with you, Frank."

"Sure, Tom."

"Yeah, us too, Frank. If we need you, we'll call you."

"Well, like my brothers said, you can always talk to Penny."

"Take care of yourself, Frank," Cohn said. I watched as they disappeared into the crowd.

I made my way out to the street. It was colder now, a sharp wind pulled soft white clouds across the sun. I pulled the collar up on my navy cashmere coat. My first impulse was to go to the office, but I was in no mood to face my brothers. They had deserted me. They didn't even feel like family. I was bitter and confused. Besides, Penny would have a million questions and I didn't feel like answering any of them now. Worse, she would be feeling terrible, maybe deserted, too. And I had no comfort for her. I didn’t care about anyone.

Chapter Three

My mood was gray like the January day. It was very cold in New York—the kind of cold that makes your bones ache. The closing had been completed, everyone was gone, and I sat alone in the conference room of my attorney's office. Stanley appeared at the door then walked over to pat me on the back.

"Frank, everything went pretty smoothly. It'll take a few weeks for the banks to transfer the funds properly, but after that you'll be in good shape. You'll have to rough it for awhile. There's a new McDonald's over on Sixth!"

I looked up at him. He could tell I didn't share his effort at humor.

"Oh yeah?" I said.

"Just kidding."

"I don't mean about McDonalds. I mean about me being in good shape."

He leaned back in his chair, glasses resting on his head, hands joined at the fingertips. I watched him mull over what I said. He knew what I meant and he knew I was right. My situation was different from my brothers'. They were on the brink of retirement. I still had my whole life to plan for. Finally he said, in a more serious tone, "What are you going to do now?"

That was my question for three months now. I stared at the rug, unable to focus. I felt his eyes on me, waiting. Finally I looked up.

"I don't know." I kept my voice low and hoped my unease wouldn't be obvious.

I stood and extended my hand. He'd been my father's lawyer

and friend for many years. I thanked him for his honesty and loyalty. Saying anything else would have been too hard. It took a moment, and we moved toward the door. We parted with an awkward handshake. He waited as I walked down the hall.

I headed to the street for a cab back to the office. Penny was at her desk, but her face was blank. For days she had seemed remote, preoccupied. I stopped in front of her.

"Holding down the fort okay, Penny?"

Not once in all the years I'd known her had she cried or shown much emotion. Once a shy kid, she'd become quite a typical New Yorker, always racing with the clock and taking care of some detail of the business.

"Of course I am. Don't I always? There's a lot of work to be done around here. I hope you're not going to leave me with all of it."

She stood as she spoke and turned to file some papers in the gray cabinets behind her. My eyes followed her tall, slender body.

"It's a big change," I said as she fiddled through the cabinet, pushed the drawer shut, and returned to the desk, "but this office is still operating. You'll have plenty of help as we go through the transition."

Standing, head bent down, she shuffled and reshuffled the papers on her desk. I stared at her auburn hair. We didn't speak for several seconds. Suddenly, she dropped the papers in her hands and looked directly at me.

"Frank, what am I going to do?" Her eyes were filling.

"You'll be fine, Penny. Don't worry. I told you. There's lots of work around here. I'll be in and out checking on things."

"I don't want to be fine! I want—" She burst into tears.

I walked behind the desk and put my arms around her. We stood together in the silence. Then she moved against my chest, wanting more intimacy. She was waiting for a sign from me. I knew this moment was coming, one way or the other—had sensed for years that she had feelings for me. I wanted to feel the same. It would make so much sense. I cared for her, but not this way. I pulled away from her.

"Listen," I said. "Put everything away and meet me later for dinner."

When we met up outside the restaurant, her spirit seemed brighter. I faked excitement over the closing, ordering a bottle of Moët & Chandon, and we toasted the end of five-thirty a.m. wakeups. But the levity was hard to keep going. I felt her subdued mood returning. She was pushing pieces of Chicken Francaise around her plate, and she spoke about visiting an aunt Upstate sometime after the transition. Halfway through dinner, she pushed away her plate and poured herself more champagne.

"You hardly touched your dinner," she said, looking at my plate.

"I'm not very hungry."

"You want a doggie bag?"

I frowned then managed a weak smile. "Okay, you got my attention."

"You haven't said three words all night."

"I'm just thinking."

"Well, what are you thinking?"

I stared at my glass. "What am I thinking? I'm thinking about my father. He was already wiring buildings at age thirteen. For the Rossetti brothers. Their trucks are still on the street." A mix of sadness and anger was rising in me.

"You know, by the time he was my age, he was established, successful, focused. Had a family. He started with nothing, not even an education, and did all this."

I was silent for a while, remembering being a kid—his kid. "I'm still floating around, trying to find my place." I looked up at her. She was listening hard. I liked that.

"I'm not saying the business was what I really wanted. It wasn't. But it gave me a sort of purpose, I suppose. A roof over my head too." I watched her for a moment. She didn't speak. "I'm scared, Penny."

"Maybe you shouldn't think about that right now. Take one day at a time. You'll find the answer. That's what I'm gonna do." She sipped more champagne. "So. How long before it's over?"

When I said it would be a while, she looked relieved. She was scared too. We were alike in this: we needed the business for reasons we couldn't quite make clear even to ourselves.

It was eleven o'clock before we finished. Penny looked tired. I was tired too. I pulled up in front of her brownstone.

She began searching through her purse. "My keys. I can never—oh, here they are." She looked at me and hesitated. "Well," she said finally, "I guess I'll see you tomorrow."

"Sure, Penny. See you tomorrow," I said.

"Goodnight."

"Goodnight."

She opened the door and slid out. I watched her climb the steps. She pulled open the front door, glanced over her shoulder, and went in.

I sat there for a moment, thinking about her then drove home.

***

I spent the next few days avoiding the office. Winter had dug in. It was bitter cold and the forecast called for snow. God, how I hated snow. I hibernated in my apartment. Usually I enjoyed fooling around in the kitchen, making up odd recipes with whatever food was around, but I hadn't been in the mood to get out and buy food. So I ordered out. Didn't even get dressed. Except for a couple of conversations with Penny about business, I screened my calls through my answering machine. I pulled the blanket off the bed and slept on the couch. I hadn't turned off the television the whole time.

I used it like a sedative.

After three days of walking through crumpled Chinese food bags and empty pizza boxes, it was time to bear the cold and get some fresh air. One of Cohn's secretaries had called the day before and wanted me to stop by the office to sign some papers. Nothing important—just some legal mumbo-jumbo.

It was eight o'clock when I walked into the firm's office. The whole thing took only a few minutes. Stanley kidded me about my good credit, referring to the time before I got my money. David reminded me I should see Tom Morton about tax implications.

"Yeah, I plan on it," I said.

My mind wasn't on tax loopholes. I left his office, took the elevator down to the main floor, and then walked out to the street. The wind seemed to pass right through my turned-up collar. I shivered. Time to do some banking; get some personal stuff taken care of.

I checked my watch. Half an hour before the bank opened. There was a coffee shop right across the street. Coffee and an éclair. That's what I needed. Through a gap in the crowded traffic I hustled across Madison Avenue into the warmth of the cafe. I unbuttoned my coat, grabbed a table near the front door and waited until a black-haired waitress in brown slacks and a white T-shirt filled the mug in front of me. Funny, she was dressed in the colors of the food she served.

"Do you have any éclairs?" I asked.

"No, Sir. No éclairs. Danish, bagels, and croissants."

"Okay, thanks. Just the coffee will be fine."

I sat there, sipped my coffee, and gazed out into the street. I thought of the settlement. How much I would be getting. I wondered how many cups of coffee it could buy. How many people would it take to drink all that coffee? I laughed.

My thoughts shifted to earlier days and my father. That always brought on a sadness I still couldn't shake. Sure I had, will have, money. But that was my father's doing, not mine. I just picked up the ball after his death, and reluctantly at that. Untimely death was more like it.

I thought back to December 1984. We had grown close just the year before. Both of us, I think, were trying to make up for lost time. We didn't make many connections while I was growing up. Maybe it was the gap in years. He was fifty-five when I was born. I often wondered how he reacted when my mother told him she was pregnant. Probably not the same as how he felt when he was younger. Years change us. Life changes us. He met my mother. They had a wonderful relationship. I think when you marry later in life, you marry for different reasons. Companionship maybe.

That last year made up for everything. *Damn, if only we'd had one more year together*. Why hadn't I ridden in with him that morning? The old question. I ran it through again. I'd worked late the night before, but I could have gotten up. He had wanted me to sleep. Maybe if I had been there—

No, it wouldn't have made any difference. Maybe I'd be dead too. It always came back to this: my father's love for me had saved my life.

The police report said it was a homicide. Gang violence. There was a lot of it back then. Drug gangs. Territory disputes. Sometimes innocent people got in the way. It was believable; I could see that. But not for me. Only my father and Reggie knew the truth. It's so clear to me even after all this time. And the images: the emergency room, my father in his bed, his last words. I had held his hand and tried not to cry.

"I'll take care of everything, Dad."

"Take care of yourself!"

I took another sip of coffee. Julia's face came to mind. My wife…ex-wife now. The sale would have made her happy. For a while we could have gone to all those stuffy parties she liked. Of course the loss of income would soon have made her furious. She had a good lawyer. He wouldn't settle for a lump sum payoff. She'd get her monthly check, no matter what. What a mistake our marriage had been. Two people so…different.

When I first saw her was at that birthday party for Harry Hellman, I thought she could have doubled for Cindy Crawford.

"Who's that," I asked as I watched her work her way through the crowded room.

"That's Julia Hennings. She's Harry Hellman's granddaughter."

Whoa! I thought. Gorgeous. And related to Harry. After my father died, Harry became my mentor. If I needed advice on a business deal or had problems with my brothers, I'd go to Harry. We also confided in each other about our personal lives, sharing some innermost secrets.

Harry was humiliated and infuriated by the bad publicity his wife Lydia's behavior generated. She was an obsessive, demanding snob who verbally and sometimes physically abused everyone in her path. There were so many incidents that people started referring to them as "Lydia Hellman moments."

On one particular afternoon, Lydia's limousine had pulled up in front of one of Harry's hotels. Lydia got out and made her way toward the canopy-covered front door. The head doorman was busy checking in a new arrival and neglected to acknowledge her. She stopped just past his stand and said, "Didn't you see me?"

"I'm sorry, Mrs. Hellman. I was busy with a guest."

She swung at him with her purse, hitting him in the face, and screamed, "Next time, pay more attention!"

When she got to her office, she called the hotel manager and demanded the man be fired. Finally the union had to step in and threaten a strike to save his job. She wasn't happy with the result, but there was nothing she could do against the union.

I mingled in the crowd, waiting for the right moment to meet Julia. Finally, I caught her talking to her grandfather and moved in. "Happy birthday, Harry." I said, extending my right hand.

"Thank you, Frank. How's things?"

"Good."

"How's your mother?"

"She has her days. She misses my father."

"So do I. He was a good man."

We stayed silent a moment then Harry said "Frank, meet my granddaughter." Then he turned to Julia and said, "Julia, say hello to Frank D'Antonio. His father Joe was one of my partners."

"How do you do?" I said.

She looked at me with her dark, chestnut-colored eyes. A smile passed over her lips "Nice to meet you." she said.

Immediately I sensed chemistry between us. Harry and I exchanged small talk until Lydia pulled him away. Then I turned to Julia. We spent the rest of the night together talking. By the end of the evening I'd asked her out and she accepted.

We dated for a year before I asked her to marry me. I thought that Harry's personality and character had rubbed off on Julia. I was blinded by her beauty and refused to see that she was more like Lydia. There were so many little signs that I ignored.

Once, when we were first dating, I was on my way to a business meeting with Harry. I called her and suggested a late dinner after the meeting. The meeting took longer than I expected and I was late picking her up. When I arrived, she blew up at me, screaming that she was starving and how could I treat her like that. I tried to explain that I was helping her grandfather with something, thinking that would cool her off.

"Let him take care of his own business!" she screamed. "You should have told him I was waiting and you had to leave!"

Here I was helping *her* grandfather and she was acting like a nine-year-old who wasn't getting her own way.

By the time our wedding day had arrived, I realized she wasn't the woman I thought she was. Still, we were married and I hoped married life and her love for me would change her. It didn't happen. The fights started at our reception. After we cut the cake, the band continued to play and I suggested we take the opportunity to make the rounds and thank everyone for coming. Before we were halfway through, she insisted we leave. We had airline reservations the next day for Bermuda.

"What's the hurry?" I asked.

"I'm tired." she said.

"We can't say thank you to just half the guests. What will the other half think?"

"I don't care what they think, I want to go."

"Well you can go sit down if you want, but I'm going to finish this."

"Fine," she said and rushed off.

I continued making the rounds but, before I could finish, Penny approached me. She put her mouth next to my ear and whispered, "Julia's in the ladies room crying. She said you're mistreating her. What's going on?"

I raised my eyebrows, pulled myself away, and told Penny to tell Julia to come out. It was the first of many embarrassing situations I would endure during our short marriage.

After the wedding we settled into married life. I dove full-force into the business and Julia continued as Assistant Director of Public Relations, a position created by Lydia. Basically it consisted of a lot of society luncheons.

Marriage gave me a new burst of energy. I was excited about taking our business and my personal life to another level. My future seemed bright and full of promise. Little did I know how bad things would get.

Despite the constant friction and Angelo's poor business sense, business was still doing well. Married life was another story. I wanted a life like my parents. After working hard all day, I looked forward to spending quiet dinners at home with Julia but she had us committed to cocktail parties and black-tie dinners practically every night.

I went along for a while, but one day I'd had enough. She was dragging me off to some Broadway show premier. I'd had a hard day at work and I was tired. I was changing shirts while she stood in front of our bedroom mirror, brushing her hair.

"We gotta cut back on this socializing, Julia. I don't want to be out every night."

She finished brushing her hair then turned and looked at me.

"What do think I'm gonna do, stay home and bake cookies?"

"I'm not asking you to bake cookies, but it would be nice to have a home-cooked meal once in a while."

She sucked in her cheeks, shifted her weight, and gave me a piercing stare. "I'm not your mother," she said and walked away.

I tried my best to hide my resentment and found myself using work as an excuse to avoid going home. We stopped fighting and simply drifted apart. She continued making personal appearances without me. Finally, one night, I came home and found a note. She had moved out. Eighteen months later, our three-year marriage was over.

For a while I was ashamed to face Harry until one day a business meeting forced us together. I didn't know what to say, so I decided to say nothing and try to carry on business as usual. It was awkward for both of us. When our business was completed he got up and fixed us two scotches with ice and handed me one.

"How are you doing?" he asked.

I sipped the scotch and looked at him with a slight quiver. "I'm doin okay, Harry."

"You know," he said, "Julia is my granddaughter and I love her." He paused a moment then continued. "It was both your faults. But I know how Julia can be and I know you. She was more at fault than you."

I felt my chest tighten and my eyes began to fill. I took another sip. "Thanks, Harry," I said. The combination of Harry's words and the scotch lifted the tension, and I was grateful that our relationship had survived.

But that was in the past. Brooding was giving me a headache. I had to think about now and the future. The waitress refilled my cup. What was I going to do? Money certainly wasn't the answer. I had my whole life ahead of me, and I had to do something with it. I needed to know that at the end of my life I could look back and like what I'd accomplished.

A city bus passed by the window. The marquee caught my eye. Two beautiful, long-legged women in bathing suits lying on a sunny beach. The caption read: “Bask in the sun with us in Florida. Get away from it all!”

Florida. My old winter stomping ground. As eager customers pushed open the door, a draft sent a chill up my pant legs. The marquee came back to mind. Florida. Why not?

I reached into my pocket, pulled out a couple of bills, and walked to my waitress who was now manning the register.

“All set, Sir?” she said.

I thought I’d appeal to her sense of humor and ask if she could break a million, but she looked busy and stressed. I just handed her a ten. She grabbed the money and quickly made change. I dropped what I figured was close to fifteen percent on the counter and left.

I pulled up my collar and leaned into the cold. Out on the street, I began to plan. What would I need? Plane tickets. Penny could take care of that. I'd call her from my apartment. The bank—I'd need money for my trip. Who knew how long the transition would take. Lawyers never rush to pay out money.

I had a great relationship with our attorneys, but on the whole I hated lawyers, especially after my divorce. Besides, Frick and Frack already planted the seed at our first meeting, referring to Steve Kehoe as a piece of shit and a nightmare to work with. When things go wrong in the legal profession, it's always the other lawyer's fault. Luckily I had some money saved, and I didn't expect to be in Florida for very long. Maybe a couple of weeks or a month.

There was a bank branch office down the street. I walked down and entered. The bank had just opened and it wasn't crowded. I approached the first teller: a chubby, Italian-looking girl with

Shirley Temple curls.

“Good morning. I'd like to cash a check.”

I had a ten thousand dollar balance in my checking account, but if I decided to stay in Florida awhile, I thought I'd better take a little more. I wrote a check for nine thousand and asked for five of it in cash and four in traveler's checks. The teller looked up when she read my name.

“No problem, Mr. D'Antonio, but I can't give you the traveler's checks here. You have to go to the desk for them.”

She directed me to another woman across the room who took my request right away. We exchanged smiles while she made out each check. The V.I.P. treatment was flattering but unnecessary, I thought. I hadn’t done anything to earn it. It took her a few minutes to get the checks together. I had her transfer ten thousand dollars more out of my savings into my checking account.

Everything went smoothly. In twenty minutes I walked out with my finances in order. I was excited about the trip. I needed only to pack and hope Penny could get my plane tickets. I'd have to pay more on short notice, but what the hell. I'd be rich soon. I hailed a cab and headed for home. I half-ran into my apartment building, punched the five in the elevator, and entered my apartment. I was on the phone before I’d gotten my coat off.

“Penelope Anderson.”

“Penny.”

“Frank, listen. Tom Morton called. He wants you to drop by his office to discuss your personal finances. He's going on vacation next week. He said you'll have to get there by Friday or you'll have to wait till he gets back. And Paul Richards called. Paragon's sending him here next week to meet with you. He wants to take a walk-through of the New York properties. Do you—”

“Penny, Penny, listen,” I surprised myself with my own urgency.

“What?”

“I want you to get me airplane reservations to Miami. I want to go tomorrow, not too early, but get whatever you can. It might be tough this time of year."

"Frank! Miami? Now? We've got a ton of work here and you're going to Miami?"

"Carman's here. So's Angelo. Let *them* take care of things. Besides, I won't be gone long—maybe a week."

I didn't want to say two weeks. Time was another thing I had a lot of, and as far as the business was concerned, Angelo said I could help *if* I wanted to. I didn't think they wanted me around anyway, knowing I was against the sale. Penny said she'd call me at home when she got the reservations.

I pulled a small suitcase out of the closet. Whatever I could fit in would go. It took about ten minutes to fill it. I was just about done when the phone rang. It was Penny with the news that she'd booked me on the eleven o'clock flight out of Kennedy.

"Okay, good. Next thing: can you run me out there in the morning?"

"Only if you take me with you."

"Then who'll babysit the two negotiators? They'll need you when Richards gets there. You know more about the operation than they do. They'd be lost without you."

"They won't like it—you taking off right now," she warned.

"No, they'll be relieved. I won't be looking over their shoulders. Besides, it's probably better I don't see what they're doing."

"Okay. I'll take you. Be ready at eight-thirty. You have to be there an hour before your flight leaves."

"Make it nine. I'll see you in the morning."

We hung up, and I finished packing.

Penny was double parked. I threw my small green suitcase in the back seat and jumped into the front.

"Christ, it's freezing out this morning!"

"Oh Frank, it's not bad. Besides, in a few hours you'll be on some beach. Is that the only suitcase you're taking?"

“Yeah. I told you I probably won't be staying very long. If I need anything, I can get it down there. Come on. Let's go. Traffic will be a bitch getting out there.”

The only conversation in the car came from the radio. Two popular morning disc jockeys were going on about organized crime running the disposal business in the city. I didn't have to ask why Penny was so quiet. She joked some about coming along, but I could tell she was annoyed by my last-minute vacation. A getaway to Florida with or without me had to be better than dealing with my two brothers. I was glad the radio filled the silence for a while.

Finally I decided to break the silence. “They're just finding out about that? The mob's been running the garbage business for years!”

“I can't believe you're running away from all this.” We were not in the same conversation.

“What?”

“You're leaving and I have to put up with your two brothers.”

“I'm not running away. I'm just taking some time off. What's the big deal?“

“The big deal is with you gone, those two will be dumping everything in my lap. They'll tell me to deal with that guy Richards from Paragon. I don't really feel like playing tour guide to somebody who’s probably gonna can my ass.”

“He’s not gonna can you. The fact is my brothers were made an offer and they accepted it. It's as simple as that. Richard has got nothing to do with it. He's just a guy doing his job.”

“Yeah, that's just it. Your brothers were made an offer. Carman and Angelo purposely didn't tell you about it because they knew you'd never approve. They know you're a better businessman than both of them. They hated the fact that you were always one up on them.”

“Looks like they were one up on me this time, Penny.”

“Did you tell them you were going to Florida?”

“No.”

"Well, what if they ask me? What should I say?"

"Tell them you think I went away. If they ask where, tell them you don't know."

Penny stared out at the traffic-clogged expressway, her hands tight on the steering wheel. Then she sighed. "Call when you get down there."

"I will. I wonder if Gino's down there. I haven't seen him in years."

For a moment, my old friend Gino's face came to me. I thought of a memorable night years ago. It had made us friends for life.

Gino was hired as a troubleshooter by his father, Albert Dallo, a long-time union guy. When there was a disagreement between the union and a hotel, picket lines would appear. But before the union could demonstrate, they had to check in with the local precinct. The police had to know where and when and who was being picketed and by how many participants.

Some hotel owners paid off the police to go to the scene and use their authority to discourage pickets by harassment and provocation. Any altercation was excuse enough for the police to disburse the pickets. The union had a list of the hotels that paid off and when they picketed one of those hotels Gino would be sent to make sure no one got out of line.

Lieutenant Jack Ryan was a big Irishman with acne-pitted boozer cheeks and coarse, red hair with graying sideburns that hung next to fleshy earlobes. He had a boxer's nose—flat and slightly bent—and eyes that always looked bloodshot. In other words an on-the-take bully who used his position to take a cut from any money-making enterprise, legal or illegal. Gino had gone to a picket scene and found Ryan harassing the pickets.

"Hey! What's going on here?" Gino said.

"Who the fuck are you?"

"I'm with the union, officer. What's the problem?"

"Your pickets are causing a disturbance. They've been harassing people trying to get in and out of the hotel."

“That's not true, Gino.” One of the members broke away from the line. “This cop's been busting our balls. He threatened me.”

Gino glared at Ryan. “I'm gonna hang around and see that no one gets harassed.”

“You better get your ass outta here before I take you in for obstructing justice.”

“How much is the hotel paying you to break our picket, Lieutenant?”

“Why you wise-ass fuck! That's it! You're under arrest.”

Ryan had Gino arrested. One call to his father and Gino was out in two hours. Gino swore he'd pay back Ryan for what he had done.

Late one night about a year later, I'd been gambling in one of the downtown clubs and there was a disagreement over a card game. I sensed there might be trouble and decided to call it a night. It was an after-hours place, and I had parked out back. I left through a side door and followed an under-lit alley past dumpsters and garbage cans out to my car. It took me a moment to fish out my keys and pull the door open. Suddenly a hand from behind me slammed it shut. I turned and came face to face with three bruisers. One of them was Ryan.

“What do you want?” I said, feeling my body stiffen.

“You think we’re gonna let you cheat our friends out of their money and leave?”

“What are you talking about?”

The back of Ryan’s hand smashed across my face. “Shut up,” he leered. “We don’t like punks like you comin around.” He gave me a smirk. “Gives the place a bad name.”

I leaned against the car door. I felt blood on my lip. “If your friends can’t afford to lose, they shouldn’t play.”

Ryan drove his fist into my gut. My knees buckled. It was hard to breathe. He raised his fist to hit me again. A voice from the alley interrupted. We all turned and saw a man appear from the dark. It was Gino.

“Hey! I don’t think I like these odds,” he said.

Ryan turned his attention to Gino. “Well, if it isn’t the asshole from the union. Get lost if you know what's good for you.”

“You don't have your badge to hide behind tonight, do you, cop?”

“I'm gonna teach you a lesson, you fuckin guinea. And after I'm done with you, your friend's gonna get the same.” He turned to me. “Comin around playin bigshot with daddy's money. Yeah I know who you are—*Mister* D'Antonio.”

Ryan's gorillas went for Gino. With one blow Gino sent the first man plunging into the brick wall. The second man rushed him. With rhythmic moves, he pivoted to one side, grabbed the man by his waist and collar and sent him headfirst into a garbage can. Ryan caught Gino from behind with a blow to his head. For a second he was dazed. Ryan pulled a knife from his pocket. With a snap of his wrist, the long blade extended. I saw its reflection off the street lamp.

“Gino! He's got a knife,” I warned. Gino turned. Ryan lunged at him. Gino reacted with a kick to his chest. Then one blow to the back of Ryan's head sent him to the ground. Gino continued to kick Ryan's head and body. Ryan tried to squirm away on all fours, but a kick to his stomach sent him toppling over on his back.

Gino was out of control now. Blood was running from his nose and lip. His breathing was long and heavy. His crazed eyes looked down at Ryan's blood-drenched figure. A strange delight came over his face. He was going to finish Ryan off with a blow to his Adam's apple. Cutting off his windpipe would be fatal. He raised his leg.

A dead cop would be trouble for us.

“Gino! No!” I screamed and threw myself at him, knocking him off balance just in time to spare Ryan’s life.

I couldn't believe what had unfolded in front of me. Until that night Gino and I had only been casual acquaintances. It was the first time I'd seen the violent side of Gino though I knew of his reputation. He was ten years older than me and, though we traveled in the same circles, our relationship was no more than a casual hello across the bar. From then on it was different with Gino and me. We became buddies, bonded by the events of that night.

"Well, it's winter. That's when you guys used to hang out down there. Do you have his number?"

"No, it's been so long. Besides, I think I just want some peace and quiet."

"Are you using the condo?"

"The condo? I forgot all about that. No, I wasn't planning on it. I don't know. It depends on how long I stay, which probably won't be long."

"You've got an open return on your ticket. You can come back any time."

After fighting the morning traffic, Penny finally pulled up in front of the terminal.

"Do you want me to wait with you?"

"No. By the time you park the car and everything..."

I felt her eyes on my back as I pulled the handle on the door. I turned to her. For the first time during the trip I looked at her.

"Thanks, Penny, for everything."

"For what? You just better get your ass back here soon."

I got out, opened the back door, and grabbed my suitcase. "I'll call you in a couple of days."

"You better!"

I turned and looked back before I entered the terminal door. She was still there watching me. I couldn't tell if she was crying, but I could see concern on her face. I knew some of that was for me. I entered the terminal and didn't look back.

Chapter Four

“In preparation for landing, please be sure that your trays and seats are in an upright position and your seatbelts fastened.”

I never realized how uncomfortable coach seats were, but one has to take what one can get on short notice. The plane's wheels touched the ground. The downshift of the engines thrust me forward in my seat. I looked out over the wings at Miami Airport, drenched in sunshine. My last memories of Miami were of sun, beautiful women, and night clubs. But that was before my father's death. The responsibility of running the business left no time for fun in the sun. It had been thirteen years.

We had controlling interest in the Regency Hotel, an elaborate, five-star hotel located right on Miami Beach. Don Defeo was the general manager and he ran the hotel until after my father's death. One day, Don and Angelo got into an argument over lobby furniture and Angelo demanded that he be terminated. Sol replaced him with Paul Carroll.

The airline attendant announced our arrival and reported the current temperature at eighty degrees. Suitcase in hand, I flung my coat over my shoulder and stepped out into the terminal. People dressed in flowered shirts and shorts embraced arriving friends and relatives. There'd be none of that for me. No beaming faces. No emotional embraces. Nowhere to go and no particular time to be there.

I had to get a place to stay. I should have had Penny make arrangements for me to stay at our condo, but it was too late now. I definitely didn't want to stay at the Regency. I'd feel like a stranger in my own house. It was too soon. I needed more time to get used to the fact that after all the years of owning it and all the memories, it now belonged to someone else.

Sentiment, trust, loyalty—traits that had scant place in business. Business was assets and liabilities. Only the bottom line mattered. My father had those qualities though. It had worked for him. But it was a different world out there now. An every-man-for-himself world where the only trust or loyalty you had was to yourself. Christ, you couldn't even trust your own brothers.

I stepped outside. The hot air pressed against me. Florida air. In the distance a line of yellow cabs waited. I raised my hand. The first car pulled up. I opened the back door and slid onto the seat. It was cooler inside. The cabbie looked back under a white Panama hat and sun glasses. A big smile revealed nicotine-stained teeth.

"How you doin, man? Welcome to Miami! Where you goin?"

Where was I going? "Take me to the Eden Arms."

"You got it," he said and we sped away.

The cab pulled up and I was greeted by a doorman in pale green. Enormous crystal chandeliers hung over a lobby filled with white marble-topped tables, surrounded by couches and high-back, aqua-blue chairs. On the vast surrounding walls hung large oil paintings and mirrors highlighted by crystal sconces.

The hotel was busy. Guests checked in and out and bellhops pushed brass carts full of luggage. The front-desk clerks wore color-coordinated uniforms, complimenting the overall decor. Thick, royal-blue carpeting hushed the lobby sounds. At the front desk I was greeted by a cheery young woman behind a cream marble barrier separating clerks from guests.

"Good afternoon, Sir. Are you checking in?"

I hadn't made reservations. Instantly I felt unsure of myself. Penny always did this sort of thing for me.

"What's the name, Sir?"

Again she caught me off guard. Should I give my real name? She wouldn't recognize it, but the front desk manager might. He might divulge it to the resort manager, who would then tell the general manager. There would be embarrassing questions. So much for peace and quiet. I had to think quickly. We locked eyes.

"Sir? Your name?"

"Oh, my name. Anthony, James Anthony." I felt my cheeks flush.

"All right, Mr. Anthony, let me check. She scanned the computer. I composed myself.

"I'm sorry, sir. I don't see any reservations under that name."

"Are you sure? I know my secretary made reservations for me."

She was beginning to appear annoyed.

"Do you have any available rooms?"

"Only suites, Sir. They are a little more expensive than our rooms. Would you like a suite?"

"Yes, please," I said. "That will be fine."

As she prepared the paper work, I mentally repeated the name. *James Anthony*. I had just created a new persona. I felt strangely reincarnated as I repeated the name, but this briefly pleasant moment was interrupted by her next question.

"Your credit card, Sir."

"What?"

"I'll need your credit card for billing."

"Oh yes, of course."

I gave her an embarrassed grin as I reached for my wallet. She was working to contain her impatience. I pulled out my wallet and fumbled through it for a minute.

"I seem to have misplaced my credit card."

She forced a smile, mentally assessing me with clusters of four-letter words.

"Are you with one of the conferences here? If you are—"

"No, I'm not. Will you—how about if I pay cash in advance for a week? I'm sure my credit card will turn up."

A line had formed behind me. "I don't want to hold these people up. I don't mind paying cash now. After all, it's my fault I misplaced my card."

She stared at me, visibly flustered by the line of people behind me. And by me, as well. No one paid cash for hotel rooms anymore. Especially in places like the Eden Arms, and certainly not for a week's stay. I pulled out a bunch of bills and held them up to her.

"You do accept cash, don't you?"

"Yes, but…" She glanced over my shoulder. "Okay."

She snatched the bills from my hand and a few minutes later completed the transaction.

"Your bags, Sir? You do have bags?"

I lifted my suitcase for her to see. Smiling confidently now, I said, "I'll just carry it myself."

She gave the bag a look, then me, and forced a smile.

"You'll find your room key in here," she said, handing me the welcome brochure. "The elevators are to your left."

***

The first day on the beach in the Florida sunshine was hypnotic. Changing my name would eventually be a problem for me and my credit card, but I had a week to figure it out. For the first time in a long time, I felt no pressure. No business decisions, no pressing appointments. Here was freedom from the rat race. The sun and waves soothed me.

My evenings consisted of quiet dinners alone. The Eden Arms restaurant had a great wine list; I had them send up a different year each night. After dinner in my suite, I'd pour myself a cognac from the honor bar and watch the moon over the Miami shoreline from my balcony.

But the tranquility of my evenings was always interrupted by the same questions. What was I doing? Where do I go? What should I do with my life? My new name gave me new chance, a rebirth, a cleansing of my past. But it wasn't a real identity.

***

A week passed before I called New York to check in with Penny. I had decided to stay in Florida longer and move into one of the condos we owned. The suite at the Eden Arms was luxurious, but it was still a hotel room. The condo would be more like home. Stanley's three weeks until my money came through would probably turn into three months. Paying the extravagant rates at the Arms wasn't practical.

My conversation with Penny was short. I asked her to find out if one of the condos were available and told her I'd call her back. She asked for my number and where I was staying, but I hopped around her questions. I didn't want her to know I was staying under an alias. She'd understand about staying at the Eden Arms, but the phony name would arouse her curiosity. She'd insist on an explanation. I didn't have one.

***

More weeks passed. Penny had made arrangements for me to use the condo, but I still hadn't made the move. It was a few days shy of March now. March is the height of the beach season in Florida. The population triples. Around four o'clock one afternoon, I left the shore to shower for another evening. On the way I passed the outdoor tiki bar. Laughter and the sound of Jimmy Buffet's “Margaritaville” drew me to the crowded watering hole. It was too early for dinner, so I decided to stop for a cool drink.

I stepped under the thatched roof and edged my way to the bar. I spotted a small space between two patrons where I could get one arm in and hope the bartender would notice. I tried to get his attention but had no luck.

“You'll never get a drink standing there like that. Here, move in closer. It takes a combination of waving and screaming.”

I turned and found myself facing a brown-eyed woman in a red and white tennis skirt and white V-necked shirt.

"Thanks a lot," I said and moved into the space she made.

After two more attempts to get the bartender, she laughed. "You're not having any luck, are you? Wait."

She turned to the bar and waved her white wristband-wrapped arm at the well-built bartender.

"Charlie! Charlie!"

Immediately he turned.

She grabbed my arm. "Quick, tell him what you want!"

"Uh, light beer." I glanced at the bottle of Coors Lite in her hand. "Coors. And one for my friend here."

A minute later the bartender dropped two long-neck bottles in front of us. The woman thanked me for the beer.

"Thank you for getting the bartender," I said.

"My name's Stacy Iseman," she said with a slow grin.

"I'm Jimmy. Nice to meet you."

We shook hands. She was lean and lanky, negotiating the end of her twenties.

"So. Are you on vacation?"

"Yeah, sort of. How about you?"

"No. Just stopped in for a beer after work."

"You work around here?"

"Yeah, at the Regency."

The mention of the hotel struck a nerve. Suddenly I felt a connection with her, a common denominator.

"Checking out the competition?"

"Oh no, I'm the tennis pro at the Regency. Employees can't patronize the hotel, so I stop here once in a while."

"How long have you worked there?"

"This is my first season."

"How is it?"

"I like it so far."

"So, did you play professional?"

"Well, not really. After college I played on a couple satellite tours, but it gets pretty tough when you start competing with the big boys. Besides, I didn't have the money to invest in a trainer and a coach, so I opted to do what a lot of tennis players do—teach. There's no fame in it and the money's not as good, but I still get to do what I love. Anyway, I'm twenty-eight, and in tennis that makes you just about over the hill. I couldn't see myself changing careers, taking a job sitting behind a desk. That's not me."

A combination of her good looks and her story sent my mind drifting. "Yeah, I know what you mean."

"What?"

"No, I mean a lot of people don't like desk jobs." I was fumbling for words.

"So, what's your story, Jimmy?"

"I'm sort of between jobs."

"From New York?"

"Yeah, how can you tell?"

"You got a little accent. So, what are you doing down here?"

"Well, I'm kinda thinking about what to do."

"Oh yeah? What did you do up in New York?"

She caught me off guard. I had set myself up. Now I had to think of something quick. I glanced at the bartender.

"I was in the hotel and restaurant business."

"Oh yeah? As what?"

Casually I turned to her. "Bartender. I tended bar in a couple hotels up there."

"Well, if you're looking for work, I know the Regency is looking for all kinds of help."

"Business must be good, if they need a lot of help."

"I don't know. I haven't been there long, but I hear things. I heard there's a big ad in the paper."

"Well, maybe I'll check it out. Do employees get to use the tennis courts?"

"Management gives some privileges, but the tennis courts and the other facilities are off limits to the regular working people. Why? Do you play?"

"I used to play some."

"Are you any good?"

"I can hold my own."

"Well, if you decide to come to work there, I suppose I could bend the rules for you."

"If I do, I'll let you know."

She sipped the last of her beer.

"I gotta get going. I'll give you my number. Give me a call. Let me know how you made out. I know what it's like being in a strange town, not knowing anybody. I still haven't met many people. Charlie, give me a pen, will you?"

The bartender tossed her a pen and she wrote her home and work number on one of the paper coasters from the bar.

"Here are my numbers. Good luck, and thanks for the beer."

A moment later she was gone. I finished my beer and went back to my suite. The afternoon brew had made me sleepy. I flopped on the bed and dozed off.

I woke at nine feeling a bit bloated. Afternoon drinking wasn't really my thing. I ordered room service and stayed in for the night.

Chapter Five

Warm bright sunshine came with Sunday morning. I rose early, called room service, and treated myself to coffee, éclairs, and the paper. Last night's dinner, a turkey club sandwich, left me famished when I woke. Twenty minutes later a distinguished, gray-haired gentleman rolled my breakfast into the room.

I poured myself a cup of coffee, grabbed the pastry and the paper, and retreated to the balcony. After gulping down my first cup and inhaling a freshly baked bun, I sat back, sipping and nibbling as I read the paper.

The headlines announced the upcoming Democratic Gubernatorial Convention in Miami. One article focused on the extra security needed for the convention, because many high-powered dignitaries would be attending. All major hotels would be beefing up their own in-house security.

A similar article toward the bottom of the page caught my eye. The caption read, "Committee picks the Regency hotel for convention headquarters despite recent problems."

With curiosity, I read on. It reported the accidental death of Pedro Quero, a Colombian dignitary who had fallen over a balcony a few months back. The accident must have been big news at the office when it happened, but I didn't recall hearing about it. But then I hadn't really been paying attention, had I?

Besides, accidents and insurance claims are common in the hotel business. Guests were constantly slipping or falling. Sometimes the accidents were staged and the guests would threaten calling their lawyer. It was an easy way to get their entire stay comped. It infuriated our managers, but comping the rooms was better than risking a lawsuit.

I scanned the feature articles and the sports section. There were some tennis tournaments in the area. I'd love to catch one of them. Maybe Stacy could get me a ticket. It'd be a good excuse to talk to her again.

Finally I turned to the classified section. I gave it a weary glance and was about to put it down when I noticed the Regency's huge ad. Stacy had mentioned they were looking for lots of help, but this seemed unusual. Though I'd never been directly involved with the day-to-day operation of our hotels, I heard our general managers mention the high turnover rate of service employees. I'd never seen such an enormous ad for help. I wondered what was going on. I set the paper down and leaned back, holding my coffee. Then a thought crossed my mind. I shook my head. What I was thinking was absurd.

I grabbed the paper again and stared at the ad. I wondered about the people who took these jobs. When Stacy mentioned the jobs yesterday, I told her I was a bartender, but that was just to conceal my identity. Could I even get a job in a place where no one knew me? The thought of some supervisor screaming at me was comical. But my amusement turned to sincere curiosity about why the Regency needed so many people. And what about Pedro Quero? What was that all about?

I smiled. I knew what I was going to do. I was going to work! Joining the troops! I laughed again, and a sense of adventure tingled up my spine. I spent the rest of the day on the beach thinking about my new challenge.

The next morning I prepared for job hunting. I stood in front of the bathroom mirror and stared at my mustache and beard. They'd been part of me ever since college. I hadn't really changed from those days. Despite my infrequent visits to the gym and tennis court, my six-foot frame was still in good shape. But I had changed my name—I might as well change my image.

With scissors and razor, I got to work. When I finished, I stared at my bare face in the mirror. I looked strange. Who was that staring back at me?

Next, the hair. For that I'd need a barber.

I rushed down to the hotel barber shop. Three barber chairs spaced equally apart faced a long mirror to my right. The first two were taken. The man standing by the third chair bid me good morning. I approached and he asked could he help me.

"I'm not too happy with the way I look," I said. "I need a change." I dropped into the chair.

"Perhaps a trim, Sir?"

I looked up at his conservative cut.

"No. A complete cut. Like yours, I think."

"That would be a drastic change, Sir," he warned.

"Then go for it."

Half an hour later, a new me emerged.

The Regency was as grandiose as I had remembered. It was a huge, cream-colored building with a shiny copper roof. The main building was surrounded by numerous smaller structures that made up the complex. To the east of the main building was a natural-and-man-made swamp that stretched over half a mile and led to the white beach. The swamp had become a favorite spot for tourists, as it was home to some Florida alligators. The large reptiles carried on their lives mostly oblivious of people, occasionally surfacing, making brief contact with the tourists. The guests rode the hotel shuttle to the beach, carrying cameras, eager for pictures.

Along the west side of the hotel, a paved roadway lined with palm trees and finely manicured grass circled around to the rear of the main building to the underground parking garages. The first one was exclusively for guests. I headed for the second one, toward the rear of the property.

Walking the grounds the first day put me back in touch with the place. I took the employees' stairway three flights to the lobby level of the hotel. I passed through two large, gray doors, where I was met by a strapping man in a navy sport coat. He stood behind a Dutch doorway, closed at the bottom. The glass top was stenciled "Security."

"Do you have business in the hotel?" he asked gruffly.

"I'm here to apply for a job."

"Sign in on this sheet," he said, pointing to a clipboard. The journal listed a visitor's name, time of arrival, and purpose of visit. Then he handed me a laminated visitor card.

"Wear this while you're here."

As I pinned the card to my shirt, memories of walking with my father down these same halls rose out of my mind. I reached the Human Resources office, just down the hall. In a small reception area, an attractive twenty-something brunette was perched behind a desk reading. She must have felt my presence.

She looked up. "Can I help you?"

"I'd like to apply for a job."

"What position?"

Immediately visions of Charlie came to me. "Bartender," I said.

Another clipboard. This one had an application on it. She pointed toward a round table in the corner opposite her desk.

"Take this over there and fill it out. Come back when you're done."

Filling out the application was strange. I used my new name and an old New York address. Under employment history, I wrote "self-employed for the past fifteen years." I used the name of a restaurant in Little Italy I knew had gone out of business. For references I gave Penny's name and two fake ones. I knew from experience that they wouldn't check all three for a bartender position. More than likely they wouldn't check at all, especially if they were long-distance calls.

In ten minutes I was back at her desk. She picked up the phone and punched in four numbers.

"Yeah, he's here now," she said, scanning the application with her dark brown eyes, evaluating me.

"Do you want to see him now?"

She released the application from the clipboard and handed it to me.

"Here you go. Take your application down this hall to the elevator. Go up one flight. When you get off the elevator, you'll come to Ted McDounough's office. He's the beverage manager. He'll talk to you."

I started to repeat her directions but was interrupted by the phone.

"Yeah, that's right," she said. "Human Resources, Oh—hi!" She nodded and with a generic smile and rotated her chair away from me. The call sounded important. Probably her latest heartthrob or a girlfriend.

Just as she had said, Ted McDounough's office was right outside the elevator door, one flight up. I walked in and shook hands with a husky man in his forties. His brown hair with a hint of red matched his complexion. He had a high-bridged nose and kind-but-tired green eyes. His appearance matched his demeanor: warm and easygoing.

We had a brief conversation about what the job entailed. "We don't do much with any of the tropical drinks in banquets, he said. "It's mainly your basic cocktails: Manhattans, martinis, scotch and sodas."

Manhattans, martinis, scotch and sodas. I exhaled slightly. I'd had my fill of those drinks, but actually having to make them, well, how hard could it be?

"Can you handle volume?"

"What. Oh sure."

"Sometimes our guests can be pretty demanding."

"That's no problem."

Volume? Demanding guests? We stayed silent a moment, exchanged looks. I wondered if this was a mistake. What was worse, I wondered if he was thinking the same thing. Finally he said, “When can you start?”

“Oh any time,” I answered. “Umm, what about the pay?”

“Oh yeah, I almost forgot the most important part.”

We both chuckled.

“Well, all I have right now is banquet bartender. That means you're on call. When we book banquets and private parties that need bartenders, we call you. You work the party and go home. This time of year especially, we have functions almost every day and, with the convention coming to town, we're gonna be rockin here. If you like it and decide to stay, any full-time spots open up I'll try to get you in. The pay is $3.75 an hour but, of course, you get a tip off the party, which goes into your paycheck. The amount of the tip depends on how much the guest's bill is. You can be guaranteed anywhere from $l8-$25 an hour, including your pay. I think that's pretty good money and it’s easy work.”

“I'll take it.”

“I don't see a phone number on your application,” he said.

“Well, I just got into town recently and I haven't had my phone connected yet.”

“Okay, be here tomorrow, three o'clock. You'll need to get your picture taken for your I.D. card. You use the card to punch in and out. Security will explain all that to you. Then go to the uniform department and get your uniform. Go to security first. When they're finished with you, they'll tell you how to get to the uniform department. When you're done there, come back here.”

We stood and shook hands. “Welcome aboard, James!”

The next day I made the rounds then I reported to Ted's office. He stood amidst several bartenders dressed in black and white like me. They scurried about, preparing for the evening's activities. I stood just outside his door in the work area, waiting for my cue. He noticed me and called me in.

“James, say hello to the crew.”

"Hey, everybody! This is... what do you go by?"

"Jimmy is okay."

"This is Jimmy!"

The first one to say hello was a tall slender blonde standing behind the desk with Ted. She had large eyes, incredibly long lashes, and an hour-glass shape complete with perfect breasts.

"I'm Barbara Griffen, Assistant Beverage Manager," she said, showing rank. Our eyes met. Hers were an amazingly deep shade of blue. She extended her hand and gave me a stiff, short handshake.

A man named Dan Hiller came forward. Portly, thirty-something, with nut-brown hair and a mustache to match, he was a barback: a sort of assistant to the bartenders..

"Nice to meet you, Jimmy. Welcome aboard."

As we shook hands, Barbara spoke up.

"If you want to know anything, just ask Dan. He knows the place like the back of his hand."

"That's 'cause I'm one of the few people that does any work around here." A look came across his face, almost a smile. It made me wonder about their relationship.

Kevin Reedy—a tall, wiry, fair-skinned man—said hello next. "I'm the beverage supervisor," he announced.

I guessed he fit in somewhere among Ted, Barbara, and the bartenders. He whisked by after his brief self-introduction, preoccupied with his work.

One by one, everyone said hello. I remembered most of their names, but that first day I was concentrating more on my new job. I tried to ask as few questions as possible. I wasn't sure of what I was doing, and I didn't want anyone to know it.

Luckily Ted paired me up with one of the other bartenders, John Palmer, a soft-spoken man in his mid-twenties who worked days as a bank teller. As he walked me through the setting-up process, he filled me in about general procedure. I half-listened while mimicking his every move. My first-day status was a good cover for my inexperience.

Once I had my bar stocked, it was just a matter of what to do with what I had. We had half an hour before we started. I used the time to observe the other bartenders, hoping to pick up whatever pointers I could.

Each bartender was professional about his job. Their work reflected their admiration for Ted. It was clear everyone liked him. Hell, I liked him. The system worked well too. The bars were portable. They were set up and stocked with the basic supplies and rolled into the banquet room. When the function was over, each bartender rolled his bar back to the work area outside Ted's office, broke it down, and went home. I hadn't done manual labor like this since my teens when I worked that summer job to buy my first car.

Finally Barbara ordered us to push out. I had the jitters of a rookie pitcher getting ready to throw his first professional ball. One by one, guests approached my bar and ordered drinks. I tried my best not to appear awkward, but I caught glimpses of puzzled stares while I searched the well for the correct bottle.

For the most part, Ted was right: it was your basic scotch and soda, gin and tonic, rum and coke. I knew from years in bars how much liquor to put in the drink. If I over poured, the guests would stop me, saying, “That’s enough.” If they wanted more, they’d remark, “Hey, don’t be stingy” or “Make it a double.”

There was a lot of wine by the glass, which was either the house Cabernet or Chardonnay. And bottled beer. Once I familiarized myself with where everything was, it got easier. Except for forgetting the lime in a few gin and tonics, I only ran into one glitch.

“Let me have a Kamikaze,” one man demanded. Aside from World War Two suicide bombers, I had no clue what a Kamikaze was. I began pulling at liquor bottles, pretending to look for the right ingredient. My fumbling immediately caught the man’s attention. I sensed him staring at me and it made my shirt collar dampen. Finally there was nothing to do but admit I was stumped. “I’m sorry Sir, I—”

Before I could finish he interrupted. “I know, you don’t have any Triple-Sec, right?”

Triple-Sec? Again I was clueless, but I played along.

“That’s right,” I said.

“Well, just give me a vodka gimlet.”

Again I mentally shrugged my shoulders and again he unknowingly came to my rescue. “Easy on the lime juice, heavy on the vodka. I can live without the Triple-Sec.”

I gambled and filled a short rocks glass with ice, a little Roses, lime juice and a lot of vodka.

“Hey,” he said, as I was about to hand him the drink. “I like mine shaken.”

I managed a tight smile. “Sure, no problem.” I dumped the concoction into a stainless steel tumbler. I must not have put its glass counterpart together correctly because, when I tried to shake the drink, the contents spurted out all over my hands. I glanced at the man. He smiled slightly. “Having a little trouble?”

“No not at all,” I said struggling to get the two tumblers apart. “Just a little technical difficulty.”

The backup at my bar must have drawn attention because suddenly Kevin appeared next to me behind the bar. “Jimmy, what’s going on? You gotta move faster,” he muttered then turned his attention to the waiting for guests. “Can I help someone?”

He worked around me, pumping out drinks one by one. His speed was intimidating and there was an abrupt manner about him. There was no, “Good evening, what can I get you?” He just shoved the drinks at people. If they acknowledged him with a “thank you,” he’d ignore it, calling out “Next!”

I knew prompt service was important but so was courtesy. What I lacked in speed I tried to make up by exchanging a few words. He immediately reprimanded me, saying, “Jimmy, just make the drinks and keep moving.” Was this the way to treat guests in a five-star hotel? I could feel the blood rush to my head.

In a matter of minutes the line had diminished. I took advantage of the lull to clean and cool off. As I wiped down the bar, I attempted to explain the holdup. Kevin immediately cut me off, insisting I had to work faster while he helped me restock glasses.

How dare he? I'd wanted to tell him off. Tell him who I was then walk out. His voice interrupted my thoughts, "I gotta go check on the other bartenders. I'll be back later."

Before I could reply, he was gone. The time alone gave me a chance to rethink the situation. Maybe someone complained and he got balled out by Ted, or maybe he was having a bad night. Anyway, I wasn't going to let him get to me. Walking away would admit defeat. I wanted to prove to myself that I could do this. Succeed on my own without the D'Antonio name as a crutch. If I walked away, I'd never know.

My anger at Kevin subsided. I reminded myself that I wasn't Frank D'Antonio, I was Jimmy, a bartender. A bartender whose last name probably wasn't important to anyone. But still it nagged me. Was this the way they treated their employees?

After the initial hit, the pace slowed. Not having to rush took some of the awkwardness out of my delivery and gave me time to make conversation. Two gentlemen came up for refills and lingered over the bar, talking. I could tell from their conversation that they were land developers from Orlando. In the sixties, land was cheap in Orlando and my father had considered buying some for speculation but backed out. After Disney came in, the property values skyrocketed. For years he joked about getting beat out by Mickey Mouse.

"So can you still make some money on land in Orlando?" I asked.

One of the men looked up, "Could I have some more ice please," he said and handed me his glass.

I hesitated, stunned that he bypassed my question. "Sure," I said.

I refilled his glass then they turned and left. A chill came over me as I watched him disappear into the crowd. They seemed irritated that I had tried to make conversation. Again I brushed off the thought.

The party was almost over when an attractive blonde approached. “Give me a glass of wine.” We exchanged looks. I expected a smile or a sensuous stare. I tried making eye contact, but she seemed distracted.

“Uh, Chardonnay or—”

“That’s fine,” she said then began fingering through her purse.

“There you are, Ma’am.”

She looked up, setting a crumpled dollar bill on the bar and picking up the glass.

I was told not to expect many cash tips because the guests knew the gratuity was automatically included in the bill. I thought the extra cash was a nice gesture. “Thank you, Ma’am,” I said.

Without a word, she walked away. Again I began second-guessing myself. Why the cold shoulder? I’d never had trouble meeting women. Many times I had to fight them off. This woman acted as if I was invisible. Was it the bartender’s uniform? If I were standing on the other side of the bar in a suit, would it have made a difference? Had I lost my appeal? Was it my name and money that made me popular with women? Maybe I’d never been appealing at all. Again Kevin interrupted my thoughts. “Pack up Jimmy. Party’s over. Let’s go.”

His pushy demeanor made me furious. Without a word I pushed my bar back and broke it down.

With my first day's work done, I approached Barbara, who was in charge. Ted had gone home for the night.

“I think I'm done, Barbara. Can I go?”

“Uh, yeah. Just mop the floor and you can go.”

I almost laughed. I thought she was kidding, but when she pointed to the yellow plastic bucket on wheels and the mop in the corner, I knew she was serious.

It felt good, actually. Except for my personality clash with Kevin, I felt comfortable with my new job. As on-call bartender, I only worked when they needed me. No steady shift and I could refuse any shift if I didn't want to work. I even got to mop the floor! Talk about starting from the bottom. It was therapy.

I'd added two drinks to my repertoire: a Kamikaze was lime juice, Triple-Sec and vodka. Take out the Triple-Sec and you have a vodka gimlet. I also learned something about people and myself. I wondered what Penny would say if she could see me. I crawled into bed and slept soundly till morning.

When I woke, my legs ached. It was a good feeling. I decided to check in with Penny. Nine-thirty. She'd be in the office.

"Penelope Anderson."

"Penny?"

"Frank! How's it going down there? You had enough of being a beach bum?"

"Well, not yet."

"Where are you, at the condo?"

"No, I'm still in a hotel."

"Why are you paying those rates? I told you, you can use one of the condos."

"I don't know. I haven't gotten around to it."

"You haven't gotten around to it. Oh yeah, I forgot, it must be that tight schedule of yours. That must be it."

"Well, I'd have to see about getting the key, I suppose."

"I already called the super and told her you'd be coming. All you have to do is go over and pick it up. You are so spoiled, I swear. If I don't watch you every minute, I don't know."

"I was thinking maybe I could use the hotel as a write-off. I have to talk to Tom about it. Getting all this money might screw me with taxes."

"You might be right. I'll call him later and ask."

"Okay. How's it going up there?"

"Okay. Angelo left me to deal with that guy from Paragon, and the other companies are sending people next week. So I've been busy with that."

"Have they asked about me?"

"No, not really. Carman asked me yesterday if you had called. That's about it. Are you coming home or what?"

"Not yet. I think I'm gonna stay a little longer."

"Well, after all this bullshit is over with these guys, I may decide to take a little time off myself. So don't be surprised if I come south."

"That'd be great, but right now you gotta mind the store. Don't tell Carman and Angelo I called. I'll call in a few days. If you remember, call Tom and ask him about the write-off."

"Do you have a phone?"

"No, not yet."

"Well, stay out of trouble."

"You know me."

"You're right. I do!"

There was a pause.

"Uh, tell me, are you having a good time...?"

I sensed that she was having a hard time letting me get off the phone.

"Not yet. I'm still just relaxing. If anything big happens I'll let you know. Gotta go."

***

During the next few weeks, I adjusted to my job and coworkers. I wanted to be accepted, but I didn't think socializing was a good idea. As I familiarized myself with the setting-up process, it went quicker. John and I had been working together a lot and he introduced me to the employee cafeteria where we sipped coffee before our shift started. Between subtly picking his brain and the bartender's manual I'd purchased, I was actually getting good at my job.

I stopped by the tennis shop a couple of times, once to tell Stacy I landed a job in the hotel, and once to ask about hitting some tennis balls. She asked why I had shaved my beard and cut my hair. I told her I thought it was better to be clean-shaven for the job. She said I looked better. I didn't think so. She suggested a lesson. Paid instruction was permitted for employees and at discounted rates.

At first I thought she questioned my ability as a player, but I found out giving lessons boosted her income. She was salaried, but she received part of the fee for lessons. But there was something else about her. Maybe the sincerity in her voice. I took her up on it.

I made an appointment late in the day and suggested drinks at the tiki bar afterwards. She said the late time slot would get me some extra instruction. As for drinks afterwards, she'd think about it.

She was good at her job. She had all the qualities that any good teacher should have. Patiently she put me through a few drills and calmly explained basic techniques to improve my game.

I watched as she moved around the court, displaying her fine-tuned physique. Her legs were long and tan, breasts high and firm, large enough to bounce noticeably as she sprinted across the court. Her hair was short and auburn, her face, lean, alert, with a tan matching her legs. Her eyes were almond-shaped and dark brown. She wore little makeup. Didn't have to. She blurted out instructions while punching the ball at me, rhythmically moving back and forth on the court. My mind and eyes, however, were on her.

The hour was up. We played a few games before we quit. I was no match for her. She won each point but encouraged me to try harder, concentrate, and said, if I did, I could win. I felt good after we finished. I was exhausted, sore, and thirsty, but she brought me mentally to a level I'd thought was gone forever. I convinced her to join me for a beer at the Eden Arms and waited for her to close up. We walked out to her car.

"Where's your car?" she asked.

"It's in the employee garage."

"Well, hop in and I'll drive you over."

"Oh that's okay. It's only over there; I'll meet you at the bar."

After my conversation with Penny, I'd rented a car. I needed one to get out to the condo. I didn't want Stacy to see it. Rentals were easy to spot and not cheap. How would I explain how an unemployed bartender could afford it? I wanted to keep my old life a secret and try my luck as James “Jimmy” Anthony and not Francesco D'Antonio.

We parted and a few minutes later rendezvoused at the bar. It wasn't as crowded as the last time, but Charlie was behind the bar again. We ordered draft beers and claimed two bar stools. We talked about tennis and joked about how much work my game needed. After ordering our second round, I asked Stacy about the article in the paper.

“It was a terrible thing. That guy, Pedro, fell over a balcony. I don't remember what floor, but it was way up. The police still come around asking questions. I don't hear too much. It's got more to do with the main building and the people directly involved, although a couple detectives did come around to ask me some questions.”

“Oh yeah? What kind of questions?”

“I don't know, like did I see anything or anyone suspicious around the hotel that day? But I'm more or less on my own at the courts. I do my own thing. I don't really have too much to do with the hotel itself.”

“So did they find out what happened?”

“Well, I heard through one of the waiters that guy Pedro was at a party in one of the suites and there was a lot of drinking going on. He must have lost his balance and flipped over the top.”

“I bet that didn't go over too well with management,” I said, trying to keep her talking.

“I guess the general manager, Mr. Carroll, was pissed. He came down on the beverage department really hard. Ted, your boss, almost lost his job, and they did end up firing someone, but I don't know who.”

I didn't want to hammer away at the issue, so I changed the subject. Something wasn't right about what she said. I knew how those balconies were built. It would be pretty hard to fall over. Even if he were pushed—accidentally or otherwise.

We spent the rest of the time talking about her, and she asked a little about me. Her questions were innocent. She didn't want to know what kind of car I drove or what part of New York I was from. To her I was just an out-of-work bartender and I liked that. We were at the end of our fourth beer when she said it was time for her to go.

Suddenly I realized I couldn't very well leave with her. I didn't want her to know I was staying right there at the Eden Arms.

"I think I'll have one for the road," I said.

"Well, I'm out of here," she said. "Give me a call if you want another lesson."

"Okay Stacy, thanks. I'll be talking to you."

I watched her leave then had another drink with Charlie the bartender and called it a night.

Chapter Six

A couple of nights after my tennis lesson, tending to mop detail after a typical night at work, I overheard Kevin the supervisor talking with one of the bartenders. I caught the last part of the conversation as I asked them to move while I mopped.

"Yeah, I played Ted today. He kicked my ass."

"You're a tennis player?" I stopped and leaned on the mop.

"Yeah, you play?"

"Yeah. Let's get together sometime," I said.

"I'm not doing anything tomorrow afternoon."

"Me neither. Let's do it."

Kevin wasn't one of my favorite people, so the thought of beating him at tennis was appealing. He gave me directions to a park where we met and played. I didn't know if it was the tennis lesson from Stacy or that Kevin wasn't the player I had expected, but I won easily. For some reason I had thought all Floridians were big into tennis. But the fact was most people who live in Florida, especially those in the hotel and restaurant business, come from other parts of the country.

We both enjoyed the exercise and, after the match, I treated him to a soda from a nearby vending machine. I took the opportunity to talk one-on-one with Kevin about the hotel. I wanted to hear an employee's candid opinion about how the hotel was run.

"So, I noticed the big ad is still running in the paper for help wanted. Is everyone quitting or what?"

"Well, not really." He took off his white baseball cap, exposing a thin crop of curly blond hair beaded with sweat. "In fact, we'll all be doing a lot of overtime during the convention." He pulled a towel from his tennis bag and swiped his forehead with it. "Plus, they're beefing up security, so they need more people in that department. Some of the people who've been around a while and are familiar with the layout of the hotel have been transferred to help security, leaving a lot of open positions. And between you and me, there was that problem we had a while back."

"What problem?"

"Well, Jerry Cummings had this private cocktail party on the fourteenth floor—bunch of big shots. Anyway, it went on till after midnight, a little longer than they usually do. What happened was one of the guys in the party had a couple too many and was fooling around out on the balcony and went over and straight down."

"Jesus Christ!" I tried to sound surprised.

"I don't even have to tell you what happened to Jerry. He was gone the next day. Ray Brown, he's the food and beverage manager, Ted's boss. He wanted to can Ted but Mister Carroll likes Ted so he saved his job."

"Why ax anybody? It was an accident, wasn't it?"

"The hotel has a strict policy about bartenders making sure that no one gets over-served. The business is changing. The new laws put a lot of responsibility on the bartenders. If a bartender over-serves someone, or serves a minor or a known alcoholic, and that person has an accident and gets killed or hurt, the whole place is in trouble. The bartender can be fined or sent to jail. The hotel or restaurant can get fined, even lose its license. You see what I mean? It's a lot more serious now."

"Did anyone investigate?"

"Yeah, the cops are still coming around asking questions. But everybody's story seems to point to the same thing—too much booze. To make things worse, the guy who died was some political big shot. I'm not sure who."

Kevin took a final sip of his soda.

"Well, I'm gonna get goin. You're working tonight, right?"

"Yeah, Kevin, see you later."

My New York upbringing made me cautious around strangers. I was surprised how much he opened up to me. After all, he hardly knew me. For all he knew, I could be an undercover detective.

I drove home, thinking about what he'd said. It still didn't make sense. How could anyone fall over those balcony railings?

Back at my suite, I showered and dressed. Not only did the hotel furnish our uniforms, they cleaned and pressed them too. I went to work in shorts or jeans and changed at the hotel. When I finished working, I just threw the uniform in a bin. I found it amusing. The uniforms were elegant and well maintained, but they were very different from my wardrobe in New York. The money I saved in cleaning bills alone could buy a family's groceries for a month.

Friday night in the hotel business was typically busy, so it was bound to be a long one. I didn't mind. I was used to late nights. Back in the city I was usually out late at least four nights a week, entertaining business associates, making sure they got what they wanted so, in turn, I could get what I wanted.

I realized more and more how similar this new life was to my former life. These minimum-wage coworkers of mine were no different than I was in New York, and the guests here were like the business associates I had. In the city I often went to extremes to accommodate clients if it meant closing a deal. New York was an exciting, glamorous town, but it took someone who knew his way around to get to places tour guides couldn't provide. Clients wanted to be wined, dined, and entertained. I saw to it they had reservations at the best out-of-the-way places and, if they wanted, beautiful young women on their arm to escort them. Afterwards, at their plush hotel suites, they could cap off the night in the lap of luxury with a sexy lady who would fulfill their wildest fantasies, all at my expense.

Here the demand was not as great, but the principle was the same. Sending up a complimentary bottle of Dom Pérignon to a guest's suite while he's entertaining a secret lover might mean a twenty or thirty-dollar tip. For me, as for those people, the rewards were different but equally important. Tips were the name of the game in this business, not the minimal pay.

***

The banquet work area was a large room where the ten or more portable bars were lined up like cars in a parking lot. Beyond the bars was a long corridor with doorways on both sides that gave the employees access to the conference area and ballrooms and eventually led down to the kitchen.

Past the kitchen area to the right was another series of rooms. The first one was large and contained an enormous state-of-the-art dishwasher. It usually took four people to operate it: two on one end loading the dirty dishes onto a moving conveyer belt and two on the opposite end unloading the clean ones.

Next came the linen room and finally the silver room where all the sterling silver—pots, trays, knives, forks—were kept. At the very end of the hall was a large freight elevator for transporting heavy items like cars or the displays used in expositions or conventions.

As each bartender completed his setup, he was sent to the banquet room designated for him. I was assigned that night to the Midwest Dairy Farmers Association, which was having its annual convention in the hotel. This pleased me. The worry of being recognized was constantly on my mind. I had been, and still was, a well-known man. If not by appearance, certainly by name. Southeast Florida was a winter haven for many Northerners, especially New Yorkers. Convention packages offered special rates. Independent vacationers paid the full price.

Midwest farmers were a far cry from my "snowbird" friends. I didn't have to worry about running into a familiar face in this group. They were a conservative bunch, a little rough around the edges, but friendly in a homey sort of way. If their mannerisms didn't give them away, their mismatched suits confirmed it. Their drink selection coincided with their taste in apparel. Mostly bottled beer or bourbon on the rocks or with 7-Up or Coke. It was a breeze for me by then and gave me time to talk to them.

I was amused at how intrigued they were with me. My accent usually gave me away, but they always asked where I was from. When I told them, they were impressed and asked me questions about the city. At times I felt like a celebrity being interviewed by some starry-eyed reporter. Overall the evening was entertaining.

By eleven o'clock, only Barbara and I were left in the office. Dan was finishing up in one of the rooms. Barbara was putting together the final figures for the evening's parties and I was busy tending to the mop. It was a task I knew in time I'd tire of but, with the high turnover rate, I wouldn't be the rookie much longer. I was almost done when Dan rushed in the door, carrying a large pan covered with foil.

"Shut the door," he said.

Immediately I swung the door closed. Dan set a full pan of jumbo crab legs, complete with drawn butter, on the desk. It was enough to feed at least ten people.

"Hey, Jimmy! Put that mop down and get over here! I'll bet you never had anything like this before!"

I was amazed at how resourceful my coworker was in acquiring such delicacies, definitely off-limits to the hired help.

"Jesus Christ, where'd you get the crab legs?"

"I have my ways. Come on, eat! We better move to the back of the office. I don't want somebody walking in and seeing us."

We moved to the rear, out of sight. The legs were excellent. As the two of us indulged, I made an inquiring gesture at Barbara, then to the crab legs.

"Forget her," he whispered and gave a back-hand gesture to show his disregard, while he chewed on the succulent meat. "If she wants some, she can get up and help herself."

I didn't pursue it, agreeing. If she wanted any, she could join us.

"So, how'd you get the legs?" I asked.

"Listen, in this place, we do things for each other. Arturo's a great chef. He's also a big boozer. Got fired from the Ritz for drinking on the job. We got this deal. I give him all the Remy Martin he wants and I get whatever I want out of the kitchen. Tonight, it's crab legs. That's what it's all about, doing things for people. It's a great thing about this business. You eat like a king, as long as you take care of the right people."

That was it. Take care of the right people and they take care of you. The unwritten rules of life that no university or book could ever teach.

After the unexpected treat, I finished cleaning, bid goodnight to Barbara and Dan, and left. Barbara reminded me to shut the door behind me.

My new job was teaching me a lot more than I had expected. There was no stress and I had crab legs for dinner. Not bad. I was a bit disappointed, though. A bottle of Louis Latour Pouilly-Fuisse would have gone nicely with the main course. Maybe next time.

Meanwhile I was getting a reputation as a tennis player. Now Ted, the boss, wanted to play me. He made arrangements for us to play in the evening on the hotel's tennis courts. My match with Kevin had proved informative. I hoped this match with Ted would do the same.

Our match was closer than with Kevin, but I won. We packed up and headed toward the parking lot.

"So, how do you like the job so far?" Ted had slowed his pace.

"It's great! You have a lot of good people working for you, Ted."

"Yeah, we're all part of a team. I take good care of them too."

"I can see they all respect you."

"Well, I do my best for them and they know it."

"Say Ted, I heard about the accident a while back. You know, the guy that fell off the balcony."

At the mention of the accident, Ted stiffened.

"Yeah, very unfortunate thing. That's what happens when people party too much. We can't afford those kinds of problems. That's why the big bosses are adamant about responsible service in the hotel. That guy should have been cut off at least two hours earlier."

"How the hell could someone flip over those railings? They look pretty—"

"Listen. The story was checked out by the cops and our security. In fact they're still busting my balls about the whole fucking thing. That guy was screwing around out on the balcony, lost his balance, and fell. End of story."

He stopped, turned and paused a moment, as if catching his breath. "Lookit, I'm telling you this because we got this fucking convention with all these big shots and it's bad enough publicity the accident happened at all. We're all trying to put it behind us. I suggest you do the same. This convention couldn't have come at a worse time. We just got bought out and we're in a transition. That doesn't mean anything to you, but when these things happen the new guys usually bring in their own management. Some of us might go. No one knows who. Now the government's bringing in their own people to help with security and they're gonna bust balls and nitpick. So do me a favor. Don't turn into Sherlock Holmes on me. Just do your job and leave the other stuff to the big boys."

"Sorry, Ted, I didn't mean—"

"I know, Jimmy, I guess I'm just a little edgy. We all are, from Carroll on down. We have to come out of this convention looking good. You know what I mean. I can't wait till it's over."

We had reached Ted's red corvette convertible.

"Great match, Jimmy. Let's do it again."

"Sure, Ted. Let me know."

I watched him drive away then continued to the employee garage and my blue Ford. I had hoped to see Stacy, but it was after hours and the tennis shop had closed.

I entered the dimly lit garage and saw Barbara talking to a well-dressed, dark-haired man in a far corner. I slid into my car unnoticed. A moment later I checked my outside rearview mirror. They had vanished.

Chapter Seven

When I arrived at work the next night, there was a new employee. I started setting up while John Palmer showed the new man around.

"Jimmy, this is Andre. Andre, say hello to Jimmy."

"How you doing?" I said. No response. We shook hands.

"Looks like I'm not the rookie, anymore." I continued.

Andre Haefner was a tall, blond, Arian-looking man. Well built. Narrow, pale eyes. Long, concave cheeks and a pointed chin. A cold first impression. Not your typical friendly bartender type. My rush to judge Andre reminded me of my own mismatched situation.

John sent Andre to gather a couple of basic utensils used to make drinks. I was claiming my own tools and noticed him scanning the shelves.

"What do you need?" I asked.

"A fruit muddler."

I hid a startled look and picked up the muddler from the box right in front of him. The fact that I could immediately pick it out made me feel good.

"Here you go," I said, handing him the miniature wooden club.

"Thanks. Where do you keep the bitters?"

Aromatic bitters came in small bottles and were stored on the shelf just below. I reached for a bottle and handed it to him.

Everyone rushed to set up and get to their assigned rooms. It was just another night on the job until the bartenders returned to the work area to clean up at the end of the shift. There was friction in the air. John wasn't his usual talkative self. Kevin, who usually mingled in the work area while the bartenders cleaned up, went straight to the office, took off his black tuxedo jacket, and flung it against his chair.

"Nobody leaves till every speck of work is done here and every bar is put away. I mean everybody," he bellowed.

Dan excused himself, saying, "I'm going down to check the club."

Barbara sat silently at her desk, apparently engrossed in paperwork. We cleaned up and waited until Kevin decided it was all right to leave. I felt a finger poke my shoulder. It was John.

"Hey, Jimmy, want to go for a drink?" He looked like he wanted to talk.

"Sure, let me know where you want to go and we'll meet."

"How about the Dugout. You know where it is?"

"Yeah, I'll meet you there."

Kevin finally gave the okay and we all left. After a quick change of clothes, John and I headed for the parking garage where we split, agreeing to meet in a few minutes.

The Dugout was a popular spot for hotel employees. It was decorated in a rustic design with dark barn board siding and wooden plank floors. Pinball machines lined the walls. A jukebox in one corner played country music.

In another corner, four people enjoyed a rowdy game of pool. It was noisy and crowded. John ordered a couple beers and we sat, silent.

"Boy, what a night!"

"What happened back there?" I asked.

"Come on. Couldn't you tell everybody was pissed?"

"Yeah, of course, but I couldn't figure out why."

"Why? That new bartender doesn't know his ass from a hole in the ground about bartending. He fucked everything up at his private party. Kevin had to stand behind the bar with him the whole time!"

I recalled my first night. How nervous I was. Kevin had to help me then.

"Well, it was his first night. He'll learn, I suppose."

"That excuse might fly about finding supplies, but Dan said Kevin told him the guy didn't know a Gin and Tonic from a Bloody Mary!"

I wondered what Kevin's analysis of me had been.

"Who hired him?" I asked.

"I heard nobody. Out of the blue Barbara recommends him to Ted and practically begs him to hire the guy. Wait till Ted hears about this. He's gonna hit the roof! That new creep made everybody look bad. All I can say is he better learn fast. The convention's coming up and we're gonna be busy as hell. The governor's supposed to be here with some Colombian big shots."

"How do you know all this?"

"Christ, don't you read the papers? They've been talking about it for a while now. And get this," he turned his chin to my shoulder. "Rumor has it they're here to negotiate some big deal between Colombia, Florida, and the feds. Something to do with drug traffic coming into Miami."

"Well, I wish them luck. They've been trying to stop that shit coming into Miami for years. I don't know if it will ever happen."

The conversation changed to small talk. The hours passed and beers flowed. By two o'clock, only a few customers remained. We were both feeling the brew. With a Marlins mug in hand, John suddenly rotated his stool and faced me, eyes puffy and moist.

"Jimmy, what the hell are you doing here? I don't mean here in this joint. I mean *here*, doing what you're doing."

"What do you mean?"

"There's something about you, I can tell. I'm not stupid. You don't belong here. You're different. And let me tell you, I'm not the only one who thinks so."

"Different? How am I different? What are you talking about, John?"

"I mean, just the way you act. It's not like everybody else."

"Not like everybody else! How do I act different?"

“I don't know, Jimmy, you seem more polite or proper or something. Sometimes I feel like I should be waiting on you instead of working with you.”

“Well, I tell you what, John. The next time we work together, you can set up my bar for me, okay?” We both laughed. “I'm just doing my job, working like everybody else.”

“Yeah? What about your clothes?”

“My clothes! What about my clothes?”

“You think I didn't notice when we were changing? I know expensive clothes when I see them. You didn't get that shirt and pants in Kmart.”

“Oh, come on, John! So what? Is it a crime to own a decent pair of pants and shirt?”

There was momentary silence. Then turning back to the bar he said, “I don't know, Jimmy. Just forget it. I mean you're not some company spy or something.”

“John, I'm just trying to make a buck. Like you. You think I'm double-o-seven or something?”

He turned and gave me a once-over.

“No, Jimmy, you're no James Bond, that's for sure.“

“You don’t think so, John? How’s this?” I attempted a British accent. “My name is Bond. James Bond.”

“Give me a break.” He waved me off with a laugh.

“Come on. What gave me away? I know. I should have ordered a martini. Shaken, not stirred.”

We both laughed again. I threw some money on the bar for a tip, patted John on the back and said, “Come on, let's get out of here.”

We left the air-conditioned pub and walked to John's car. The air was warm and heavy.

“You okay to drive?”

“No problem, only gotta go a couple blocks.”

“Be careful,” I warned and slammed his door shut.

I watched him drive away then headed home. It was late. I was feeling the beers, but John's questions kept turning in my head. Did

I stick out that much? I thought I was acting pretty normal. How was I so different? Whether I'd convinced John or not, he was right. I was out of place. My initial perception of Andre was the same. I wondered if I was right about him.

I made it back to my hotel suite. It was two forty. I was bone-tired. Instantly I was asleep.

I hate anonymous phone calls. My nearly comatose "hello" must have scared the caller. It was clear I was asleep. That was no excuse, I thought.

"Hello," I repeated.

Silence. A click then dial tone. I checked the time. Ten thirty.

I sat up, groggy and hung over. I called room service for coffee. I gulped down a couple cups then showered and shaved. The shaving part still bothered me. I couldn't give the Eden Arms number so I had to call in for my schedule or walk the four blocks to the Regency to find out.

The unexpected call and the coffee woke me. I figured the fresh air would clear my head. I decided to walk. I noticed the transportation booth on my way through the lobby. That's what I needed! A stretch limo to drop me off at the Regency and wait while I checked my hours. It would fit right in with my designer wardrobe.

The elevator door opened on the banquet room level. I heard arguing coming from Ted's office. I paused to pick up the conversation.

It was Dan.

"Where did you get that idiot? He doesn't know shit about tending bar! Ted, did you interview him?"

Barbara cut in. "Now listen, Dan. I interviewed him, Ted hired him, and he can do the job. All he has to do is follow orders and that goes for you too."

"Maybe I can't tell you who to hire, but I'm not working with him!"

"You'll do what you're told. Just remember, you don't make the decisions here, we do!"

"That's right, you do. What about you, Ted? Are you going along with her on this?"

"Dan, I appreciate your concern. You've been here a long time, longer than both of us. But Barbara's my assistant and she says the guy can do the job. Besides, we're short-staffed as it is. I'm backing her on this for now. Let's try to work together. We've got a hell of a lot to do in the next few weeks, so let's stay cool and I'm sure things will work out."

"Well, I hope you know what you're doing, boss, cause this guy is trouble."

Dan stormed out and rushed down the corridor toward the kitchen. I gave it a minute more and tapped on the office door.

They both looked up from behind Ted's desk.

"Hi, Jimmy. Come on in. What's up?"

"Not much, Ted. I just stopped by to get my schedule."

"Sure. Barbara, give Jimmy his schedule. You know, it would be a lot easier if you would get a phone."

"I know. I'm working on that, boss."

Barbara fumbled around with papers on her desk and finally picked up one and said, "Looks like Kevin's got you on Wednesday, Thursday, Friday, Saturday, and Sunday nights this week. Five o'clock.

She seemed hurried, as if trying to get rid of me. She wasn't getting any help from Ted.

"Five days this week! That's pretty good, Jimmy," Ted offered me a big, toothy grin. "I told you we'd take care of you. When's the rematch? I need a chance to get back at you."

"Maybe in a couple days. Just let me know. Thanks a lot, Ted. See you, Barbara."

"Have a good day, Jimmy," she said, ruby-red surrounding her pearly whites. I could almost hear, "It's about time," hiding behind her teeth.

I'd taken care of business for the day and decided to head back to the Eden Arms and relax on the beach. I made my way up the drive, past valets and doormen scurrying about dropping off baggage and cars. In the lobby, an idle desk clerk stopped me.

“Hi, Mr. Anthony. Did your friend catch up with you?”

I halted at her question and approached. “What friend?”

“He was here when you walked out before. He asked me for your room number. I told him we weren't allowed to give out guests' room numbers. I suggested he use a house phone and have the operator ring your room. He said he wanted to surprise you. I told him I couldn't. That's when I noticed you walking out the front door. I pointed you out to him. Then he left. Did he catch up with you?”

I hesitated. Who knew James Anthony and where he was staying?

“Mr. Anthony?”

“Uh. No. Thanks.”

When I got to my room, I checked my messages. Nothing. If someone wanted to surprise me, they did. I blew off the thought and headed for the beach.

The tiki bar was part of my routine. I stopped for a couple cool ones before going back to my suite. It was five thirty. The combination of surf and sun with the brew had given me an appetite.

After a quiet dinner, I left the hotel. It was another beautiful Miami night. A great night for a walk. I had no pressing engagements, nowhere to go, and no one to go with. I strolled along, watching happy couples taking in the moon-lit evening. I passed hotel after hotel, including the Regency. This mile-long stretch of beachfront boasted the most luxurious hotels on the entire beach. I had frequented them all at one time or another. Seeing them brought back memories of my times with Gino.

Gino Dallo was still my closest friend, though we had drifted apart over the last few years. I remembered the Flamingo Club where Gino and I used to hang out together. The food was good, great live music, and always a lot of attractive women hanging around. God, the girls we lugged out of there. And if we didn't get lucky with women, we'd try the tables upstairs. On the third floor—if you knew the right people—was a mini casino second to none. As good as Vegas or Atlantic City.

To the ordinary visitor, it was a rumor. The private casino was off limits to the everyday tourist or club-goer. Gambling was still illegal in Florida.

The clientele was hand-picked by management. The only way to get in the club was to be referred by one of the “members.” An individual already accepted was very cautious about vouching for someone. Though the local police knew about the place, the owner had made sure they wouldn't interfere with business. Money was always the answer.

There were other dangers, though. When big money is at stake, people get mad when they lose. Sore losers might try to expose the operation. The club had to be very selective. Anyone allowed admittance had to have unlimited resources—could afford to lose big and not worry about it. Gino and I were part of that group.

I remembered it was just down the street. I continued on to see if it was still there, maybe reminisce a while.

It was still there. I stared at the pink neon sign over the entrance, deciding whether to go in. It had been so long, it probably had changed. And so had I. Who would recognize me? What the hell, I was here. Maybe I'd get lucky.

I was wrong. It was the same dark room and circular bar. Business was good too. Standing room only in the bar, and the rear dining room was about half full. The decor hadn't changed either. Dark red carpeting, tables draped in white with crystal candelabras in the center. I elbowed my way to the bar and scanned the room for familiar faces. The faces were different, but the clientele was the same.

The bartender noticed me and rushed over. He was in his late twenties, medium-sized but burly with enormous shoulders. His short-sleeve, white shirt revealed hairy Popeye arms and a narrow, black tie hung around his neck.

"What can I get you, Sir?"

"Johnny Red on the rocks."

With a flourish, he plopped down my drink complete with white cocktail napkin.

"Do you want to run a tab, Sir?"

"Uh, no. I'm probably only gonna have one."

I dropped a twenty on the bar, which he grabbed and then returned with my change. After a couple of sips, the man in the seat next to me left. I slipped onto the stool. The high seat gave me a view of the whole bar. I watched guys hitting on women and the women feeling the guys out, trying to find out if their pursuers had enough money to afford them.

I gave the cubes a twirl with my finger and downed my last sip. I set the glass down and hesitated. The scotch was going down good. Maybe one more for the road.

Suddenly I heard a voice from the crowd.

"Frank! Is that you, Frank?"

Instead of turning to check, I let go the second drink and slipped out.

Just at the door a hand, big and heavy, grabbed my shoulder, squeezing it tight. I turned around. It was Gino.

"Gino! I don't believe it! How the hell are you? Gee, it's great to see you!"

"You too, kid. I almost didn't recognize you without the hair! You look beautiful!"

We shook hands. He released me from his bear-hug embrace just in time to get my breath back.

"What the hell are you doin here, Frankie? I haven't seen you since you tied the knot!"

"Well, the marriage ended a while ago. But let's not talk about that now. How have you been, Gino? It's so good to see you! Come on, let’s have a drink.”

We made our way back to the bar. “What are you drinking? Bartender, give us a couple drinks here, please.” He must not have heard my request, because he raced past me and right to Gino.

“Hey, Gino! How's it goin?”

“Hi, Tom.”

The bartender held out his hand and Gino shook it then. Without a word, he prepared two drinks and set them in front of us.

“Johnny Red on the rocks, and your usual, Gino—on the house.”

“Thanks, Tom.”

“No, thank *you*, buddy,” he called back, working his way down the bar.

“You haven't changed a bit, Gino. Still got juice with everybody.”

“Oh, Tommy? Hey, I'm still a regular here. Besides, he owes me. But let's talk about you.”

Gino looked great. He had ten years on me, but it was obvious he hadn't stopped working out. My father had met Albert Dallo, Gino's father, when my father bought the Central Plaza. Albert was the business agent for the hotel and restaurant union in the tri-state area. Over the years they’d become close friends. Fourth of July was our annual family picnic, and Albert and his family were always invited.

Gino was an only child and treated me like his kid brother. He'd made “Kid” my nickname. I had hated it then and even now it annoys me, but who would argue with Gino? He was big and tough with a short temper—when provoked he was dangerous, as I witnessed that night in the alley. We reminisced awhile, joked about old times. I scanned the room again.

“The place hasn't changed a bit, Gino.”

“Yeah, same shit, different faces.” Gino took a swallow of his drink then grinned at me slyly. “Hey, Frankie, remember the night we dragged those two broads out of here and ended up in one of the suites at the Regency?"

"I don't know, Gino. Which time?"

"You remember! The time your old man came down to show off the hotel to some guys from the city. Remember? He knocked on the door cause he wanted to introduce you. We had those young broads in there. They couldn't have been more than nineteen. I was scared shit getting caught by him but you weren't. Remember we took them into the closet and—"

"Oh yeah." I laughed. "The secret door. It saved our asses!"

The architects had suggested to my father that we equip some of the better suites with hidden sliding doors located in the walk-in closets. The sliding doors led to a series of hidden stairways used as auxiliary exits out of the building. They thought it would be a big drawing card to celebrity types. Kind of a special luxury in case they wanted to exit their rooms unnoticed.

"I heard about the sale, Frank. I don't know if I should give my congratulations or condolences. To tell you the truth, I was kind of surprised you unloaded everything, just like that."

I tightened the grip on my glass. Gino was reopening my still-fresh wounds. I turned to him.

"Well, what can I say? It's water over the dam."

I took another sip of scotch and shifted the conversation.

"So what's new with you? What have you been up to?"

"Ah, same shit. I'm still with the union in New York. Following in the old man's footsteps. We're trying to organize down here. Don't think it's gonna happen. How long you gonna be in town?"

"I don't know. For a while."

"How's Penny?"

"She's good, Gino. Don't know what I'd do without her. She's helping us wrap things up right now."

"Hey, Frank, they still have the game upstairs. Let's go up and take some of their money. Just like old times. Whad'ya say? Let's go up."

“Nah, I don't feel—”

“Yes, you do! Let's go. Just for a while. Come on. We haven't seen each other in years. We'll celebrate. Come on.”

I didn’t have the energy to resist Gino, so we left the lounge and took the corridor that ran the length of the dining room. Gino pulled open the dark wooden door marked “fire exit” and we took the stairway on the left to the third floor.

“Hey, you're gonna love taking these guys' money. The stakes are still high, but the clientele has changed a bit from the old days. Most of these heavy hitters are drug dealers and you know how we feel about drug dealers.”

Gino's reference to the clientele didn't surprise me. These were definitely different times, and drugs had made many a street kid with no education a millionaire—at least the ones who lived long enough to elude the law. It was a dirty business and Gino was right, we both hated drug dealers. Winning their money would be fun.

We reached the third floor where a six-foot mountain of muscle in a tuxedo stood by a dark mahogany door.

“Hi, Gino,” he said, eyeing me suspiciously.

“He's okay,” Gino said.

Immediately he pulled the door open and we entered a room packed with people. They hung over crap tables and hovered around card dealers playing Twenty One. It was another world. The rear entrance ensured it was inconspicuous to the regulars downstairs. Located three flights up, all noise was concealed as well. Another “black and white” approached. Like Tommy and the doorman, he gave me a quick glance, then took to Gino.

“Gino!”

“Hi, Artie. Full house tonight.”

“Yeah, we're busy. That time of year, you know.”

“Artie, say hello to my friend, Frank. He used to be a steady customer here.”

“How you doing?” he said. Another handshake.

“Good. How you doing?”

"Great! There's plenty of loose broads here tonight and we always got room for old friends."

Gino crinkled a fifty into Artie's hand. "We're gonna mingle awhile."

"Sure, guys. If you need anything, let me know."

We worked our way into the crowd.

"Well, Frank, where you want to go first?"

"Do they still have Baccarat in the back?"

"Yeah."

"Okay, then."

Gino led the way to the table. One seat was left. We looked at each other. "Take it," Gino said. "I'll play some craps for a while."

The sight of the chips and the cards brought back a familiar excitement. I scanned the other players at the table. A portly bald man was to my right. He wore a seventies-style flowered shirt opened down to mid-chest, exposing a heavy gold chain as gaudy as his shirt. To my left sat an attractive fortyish brunette in a powder-blue knit dress. Nervous eyes.

The man at the opposite end made me do a double take. He was the man with Barbara Griffen in the hotel parking garage.

Close range revealed broad shoulders, late thirties pushing forty, white jacket, red button-down shirt, no tie. His face was dark and narrow with down-slanted dark eyes and wide lips. The eyes were jumpy, sparkling, confident. His hair was combed back, wavy and black. A pencil-line mustache traveled the length of his upper lip. He was flanked by two young bimbos hanging over his shoulders. Our eyes met. Intimidation is a big part of card playing. I returned his stare.

"Marcelle, who is our new arrival? I like to know who I'm playing with."

The dealer turned to me. Before he could ask, I introduced myself.

"Frank. And your name, Sir?"

"Victor," he answered.

“A pleasure to meet you, Victor.”

“Make yourself at home, son, maybe you'll change my luck.” The voice came from the flowered shirt man with a Texas drawl. “Name's Sam.”

The woman in the blue dress pulled a cigarette from a pack on the table and lit it with silver lighter. She took a short drag and exhaled as she spoke. “Nice to meet you, Frank. I’m Vivian.” She took another drag and looked right at me. “Now that we’ve got the introductions out of the way, shall we play?”

I took my seat and had Marcelle draw me five thousand dollars in chips. It took several hands and four thousand dollars until I familiarized myself with the players. I noticed that Sam would pick up his cigar when he caught a decent hand, Vivian fiddled with her lighter when she was holding something, and Victor would stroke his mustache when he drew good cards.

Once I knew the players, it was a matter of biding my time till the cards came my way. By the time the dealer called “last hand,” I’d won back the four thousand and twenty-two thousand more. My good luck didn't seem to set well with Victor. The sparkle in his eyes disappeared.

The cards were dealt. A frigid silence hung over the table. He glanced at me over his cards.

“I should tell you,” he said, as he eyed the piles of chips in front of me, “I am not accustomed to losing.” He slid twenty-five thousand dollars in chips to the center of the table.

“I share your sentiments, exactly,” I said and matched his bet.

“Too much for my blood. I'm callin it a night,” said the cowboy. He stuck the last piece of his round fat cigar in the corner of his mouth and gathered up his chips. “Thanks, Marcelle,” he said, tossing him a fifty dollar chip. A quick nod to Vivian. “Little lady,” he said almost inaudibly. Then to Victor and myself, “Gentlemen. It’s been a pleasure.“

“I’ve had enough too.” The lady followed suit and left. A fifty thousand dollar pot drew attention and a crowd had formed.

Gino stood behind me. Everyone watched while Victor and I read our cards.

“Card!” Victor announced. It was an order.

Marcelle snapped a card down. I tapped my cards, and he silently pushed the next one over the green felt to me. Victor turned his cards. A deuce and two threes. He smirked with confidence. The crowd hummed. I'd need a nine to win. I looked into Victor's eyes and showed my hand. His face turned even colder. Gasps of delight came from the crowd. He stared at the four, deuce, and three.

“Well, when you got it, you got it,” I said, leaning forward to retrieve my chips.

Victor stood, reached across the table, and grabbed my wrist. “I’ll see you again, Frank!”

“And I hope our next meeting will be just as entertaining!” I was grinning.

He pushed his chair back noisily and left with his two dolls. The crowd began to stir, breaking the tension. I stood up, flipped three hundred-dollar chips to Marcelle for a tip, and left with Gino.

“A little beginner's luck, Kid?”

“I guess so, Gino.”

“The other guy didn't look too pleased,” he said with a smile. “He's gonna remember you!”

“I hope so. Come on, let's get a drink. I'm buyin.”

“Good. I lost my ass at the crap table.”

I knew Gino was kidding when he said Victor would remember me. But this second encounter had already made an impression on me. I wondered about him and Barbara. What would a wealthy, high-stakes gambler want with a middle management employee of the Regency?

We elbowed up to the casino bar and ordered drinks. I chucked back peanuts and slugs of scotch as patrons from across the bar blurted out congratulations. Faceless pats on the back complimented me on my win.

“First time you been here in years and you got everybody's attention, Frank!”

“Yeah, just what I need.”

“What?”

“Nothing. Hey Gino, do you know that guy I was playing with?”

“I seen him around, his last name is Diaz. I hear he's a big ass drug dealer.”

Barbara and a drug dealer? I shook off the thought and decided to enjoy my unexpected reunion with Gino. We settled in at the bar, making up for lost time, when I felt a tap on my shoulder.

“Think you can afford a drink with all that money you won?” We turned to find one of Victor's girls behind us. Navy blue clingy dress, black hair, midnight blue eyes.

“Oh, sure! What are you drinking?”

“Screwdriver. Lots of orange juice.”

I motioned the bartender.

“A screwdriver, please, heavy on the O.J.”

I handed her the drink. “So did your boyfriend send you over to find out how I beat him?”

“No! He's downstairs sulking. And he's not my boyfriend. Well, not really. I'm Virginia Sullivan.”

“I'm Frank, but you already know that. This is my friend, Gino.”

“Nice to meet you both.”

“Nice to meet you, Virginia.” Gino swirled his ice. “I don't think your boyfriend's too happy.”

“I said he's not my boyfriend!”

“Whatever.”

She looked at me. “You're an interesting guy, Frank.”

“So's Victor. Gino's right. He looked pretty mad when he left. I hope he didn't gamble away the rent money.”

“Hardly. He hates to lose though.”

“Oh yeah? So, what does he do for a living?”

“Importing. Mostly coffee, but a little bit of everything, I guess."

Yeah, you never know what you'll find buried in those coffee beans.

"What about you, Frank? What's your story?"

"Me? I'm sort of semi-retired." I looked at Gino and took another sip of my drink.

"At your age! Come on!"

"No. Just kidding. Real estate. I'm into real estate."

"Yeah. What? Condos?"

If Vic-baby was into coffee, I figured I'd counter with small-time rentals.

"No, nothing like that. Residential. Nothing big."

I downed my last mouthful of scotch, offered her my hand. "Well, Virginia, it was nice to meet you, but it's past my bedtime. Gotta go."

She seemed disappointed. A hooker, I thought, trying to build up her clientele.

"It sure has been. Maybe we'll meet again."

"We leavin, Frank?" It was Gino. "I gotta stop at the men's room. I'll meet you downstairs by the bar."

"Okay, Gino."

We watched Gino walk away.

"Hey, it really was nice talking to you," I said.

"Thanks." She hesitated. "Wait a minute."

She grabbed a white cocktail napkin from the bar, pulled a pen from her purse, and scribbled her number on it. She glanced over her shoulder then slipped the napkin into my hand.

"Call me sometime," she said.

Before I could answer, she was gone. I looked down at the wrinkled tissue then shoved it into my pocket. I paid the tab, tipped out the bartender, and joined Gino at the main bar downstairs.

"Where you staying? At one of the condos?"

"Uh, well, not exactly."

"So where you goin now? You drivin? You need a ride?"

"Nah! It's a nice night. I think I'll just walk for a while."

I wasn't about to tell Gino I was staying at the Eden Arms. I didn't want any deep conversation about it.

We stepped outside. The warm Miami night enveloped us.

"Okay then, my car's over in the lot." Gino stuck his hand in the inside pocket of his jacket and pulled out a business card. "My number's on there. Call me Frank, okay?"

"I will, Gino. See ya."

Gino headed for his car and I headed back to the Eden Arms. Virginia popped into my head. I wasn't into hookers but she seemed nice and she was beautiful. A dark, wounded kind of beauty. A hooker with a mixed-up past, I guessed.

And Victor. Who was this guy? What was he doing in the garage talking to Barbara? Trying to sell her coffee? Right. Maybe Barbara was doing coke and Victor was her supplier. It wouldn't surprise me. I was glad he hadn't seen me in the garage. No one knew my dual identity. I wanted to keep it that way. I could have told Gino. I'd probably get around to it, but tonight it was just great seeing him.

Chapter Eight

I awoke with Victor's face on my mind. Curiosity about him was getting to me. I lay in bed, glancing out at the morning sun burning its way through the hazy white clouds.

I should have left it alone; instead I dialed Penny in New York. I'd have her make a few calls. If this guy was anybody, Penny would find out. I thought about doing it myself but I didn't want to take a chance nosing around about him. If he was somebody, I didn't want him to know I was asking questions about him. Penny could find out discreetly. She was probably sitting around doing nothing. She'd love it. It would give her something to do.

After the second ring, she picked up. I heard a lethargic hello.

"Penny?"

"Frank! What's going on?"

"Not much, Penny. How is everything?"

"Everybody's been asking about you. Why don't you call Carman or Angelo? I'm tired of making up stories. How are you doing anyway?"

"Everything's good. Guess who I ran into last night?" I paused. She wasn't guessing. "Gino!"

"Gino! I told you he'd probably be down there. How is he?"

"He's good. He said to say hello. But listen, I need you to do something for me."

"Oh oh, here it comes. What do you need?"

"I need you to find out who's big into drugs down here."

"Oh come on, Frank! This transition has me buried with work. Your brothers ask all kinds of questions even I can't answer. Now you want me to look up drug dealers. Why? Are you doing drugs?"

I knew she'd appreciate it.

"Come on, Penny. This is important."

"Isn't it always?"

"No really, come on. Just see if there is a Victor Diaz heavy into drugs down here. Give Harry Woods a call—he should know. If he doesn't, he'll know who to ask. If he questions you, tell him it's confidential. He'll understand. Call me. I'm at the Eden Arms."

"Where?"

"You heard me. The Eden Arms. I'm in suite ten thirty-two and I'm under the name James Anthony. That's between you and me, understand?"

"James Anthony! What the hell are you up to, Frank? What's the cloak and dagger stuff?"

"I'm really not sure myself. Penny, does the name Pedro Quero ring a bell?"

"Yeah, it does. He's that political big shot who died in the hotel. Paul Carroll called up here. Talked to Angelo about it."

"How come I wasn't told anything?"

"Well, it was in the middle of all that stuff over the sale, when Carman and Angelo first dropped the news on you. Angelo mentioned there had been an accident at the hotel. He said he'd talk to the lawyers about it and there was no need to bother you with it since you had your hands full dealing with the sale. What's he got to do with anything?"

"I don't know. Maybe nothing. See if you can get me that information and get back to me as soon as possible. Don't leave any messages. If I don't hear from you in a couple days, I'll call you. Listen, I gotta go. Someone's at the door. Call me as soon as you can. Thanks, Penny."

No one was at the door, but I knew if I stayed on she'd badger me with questions I didn't want to answer. If anyone could get information on Victor, it would be Harry Woods. Before turning night-club-owner, he was a homicide detective on the Lower East

Side. My father helped negotiate the deal for his club and loaned him the money to get started. He never forgot it.

The night before was my debut as Frank D'Antonio, but tonight it was back to Jimmy, the bartender. When I arrived at work, I was scheduled to work with a bartender named Michele Walker. She had arrived early and was already setting up. Dan and Andre were working together and Dan didn't look pleased. From what I'd overheard outside Ted's office, I was surprised to see them paired up. I checked the work sheets. They had the late party. That meant a late night for them and a long one for Dan.

One by one, each of the bartenders filed out to a different private party. Thanks to Michele, she and I were half an hour early. While we waited for the guests, she bent my ear about her day.

"What a hell of a day I've had! My car broke down this morning. Just what I need. I can't afford the added expense right now and besides, I'll have to cab it home tonight. It'll probably cost me more for the cab than I make in tips."

"I can give you a ride home, Michele," I said, hoping if I solved her dilemma she'd shut up.

"Can you? Are you sure it won't take you out of your way?"

"No problem."

"That's great, thanks. So Jimmy, where you from?"

"New York."

"New York, huh? I've never been there. It's a great town, isn't it?"

"Yeah, it's a pretty good town. Where are you from, Michele?" I thought I'd better reverse the conversation.

"Virginia."

"That's a nice place," I said.

"Yeah, it's okay, I suppose. Nothing like New York. You married, Jimmy?"

"No, I was but—"

"Yeah. I know. It didn't work out. Right?"

"Yeah. What about you? You married?"

"No. Never found the right guy. I've dated a lot of guys but most of them are jerks."

"Well, you're a good-looking girl. You'll find the right guy. It always happens when you least expect it."

"Ya think so? I don't know. You're a good-looking guy. I'm surprised some girl hasn't snatched you up by now. So what'd you do up there in New York?"

"Ah...I was, sort of, I—"

"Oh, the guests are coming in, Jimmy. We better get to work."

"Yeah, talk to you later."

I still wasn't used to being asked those kinds of questions. It always caught me off guard. This time the guests' arrival saved me, and I had time to think of an answer. I hoped she'd forget about it.

With each shift my bartending skills were improving. The real challenge was dealing with the snooty guests. The fact that my new bartender status made me less appealing was bad enough, but the demeaning way some of the wannabe aristocrats spoke to me was disgusting.

Tonight the function was a fundraiser put on by the local business community. An attractive brunette in a low-cut dress that matched her hair walked up and ordered a glass of wine. I set a full glass in front of her. "There you are, Ma'am," I said.

She arched her eyebrows, looked at me, and said, "Can I have a cocktail napkin, please?"

I glanced at the pile of white napkins in front of her. My face hardened. I looked at her, tempted to say, "Help yourself." Instead I gritted my teeth, forced a smile, and handed her a napkin.

She snapped it from my hand. "Thank you so much," she said and walked away.

"Thank you so much." That must be the expression of the nineties because most of these women used it.

Ted was mingling with the guests. I watched for a moment as he stopped to talk to the cocktail napkin woman and the man with her.

As they exchanged words, Ted looked at me. A moment later he approached my bar. “Jimmy, what happened with that woman?” he said making a head motion in her direction.

I glanced over his shoulder and caught her spying us from the corner of her eye. “Nothing,” I said. “She asked me for a glass of wine and I gave it to her.”

“She said she had to ask you for a cocktail napkin.”

Mentally I rolled my eyes. “They’re right here,” I said. “I thought the guests were supposed to help themselves.”

“You gotta schmooze these people, Jimmy. If she comes up for another drink make sure you apologize.”

“Apologize?” I said. “For what, not handing her a napkin?”

“Jimmy, these people are paying a lot of money to be here. They want to be pampered. Just do it, okay?” He walked away.

My entire body was trembling with rage. Luckily the guests kept me busy. Before long I’d forgotten about it. Later in the evening the woman’s escort approached. My stomach tightened. I sensed a confrontation and my bartending days over. If he was expecting an apology, he would be disappointed. “Can I help you, Sir?” I said.

“Let me have a scotch on the rocks, please.”

Without a word, I began preparing his drink.

“I hope my girlfriend didn’t get you in trouble.” he said.

I stuck a stirrer in his glass and handed it to him. “No. Don’t worry about it.”

“She’s a bitch, I know. I’m sorry.” He set his drink down and peeled a five-dollar bill from a wad he had in his pocket and set it on the bar. “That’s for you. I’ll put a good word in with your manager,” he said and left.

Put a good word in with my manager, what a laugh. I looked at the bill. Wanted to tell him to use it to buy the bitch a personality. For a while I left it on the bar, but the sight of it made me fume. Finally I picked it up and stuck it in my pocket. Again I thought of giving up the masquerade. What did I need all the aggravation for?

Luckily the party ended early. I just wanted to get out of there. Michele helped me clean up and then we signed out. As we headed for the elevator, I caught a glimpse of Dan and Andre returning from their function.

Michele's apartment was a little out of my way, but I didn't mind. It was another beautiful night and the drive I thought would do me good. Besides, it wasn't like I really had to be anywhere. We pulled out of the parking garage. She started talking.

“I really appreciate the ride. How about if we stop and I'll buy you a drink?”

“Okay. You want to go to the Dugout? That's close.”

She nodded assent and I drove to the Dugout. She ordered a couple of draft beers. As we sipped our beer, I recalled how our conversation ended at the hotel. I decided to shift the focus on her.

“So. You're from Virginia. What brought you to Miami?”

“I've been trying to break into modeling. If you want to get anywhere in the business, you gotta be in New York, L.A., or Miami. I heard Miami was the easiest place to start, so here I am. But until I make it, I have to eat, so I work at the hotel. The money's good. Ted's a great guy to work for and it keeps me off the street.” She paused. “Just kidding.”

She was definitely model material. Michele stood about five foot ten and she was all legs. Her black-and-white uniform had camouflaged her figure. Now her red, faded open-neck T-shirt and tight acid-washed jeans accentuated her features. Pale brown eyes, high cheekbones, gently defined and slightly tanned. Her blond hair, brushed back and silky, was long enough to bounce off her shoulders. She spoke softly with a shy innocence, a timid and sincere nature that wouldn't be much help in the world of modeling. I liked her. She seemed to be someone I could trust.

“How do you like it so far?” she asked.

“It's okay.”

“Been some strange things going on lately.”

“Like what?”

"You'll see. I won't mention any names. All I can say is you better stay on Barbara's good side."

"Does Barbara have a bad side?"

Michelle laughed. "Look what happened to Jerry."

"Who? What do you mean?"

"Well, you wouldn't know him. He left before you started. Anyway, it's history and I don't like talking behind people's backs. There's enough of that going around there as it is."

We ordered two more beers. She seemed to want to talk. I hoped a little coaxing and the brew would loosen her up.

"So, come on, tell me. What's Barbara like? Does she have a boyfriend?"

"Please! Who'd want her anyway? All she's interested in is money. She's too much in love with herself to fit anyone else into her life. If she's with somebody, you can bet she's got a reason, and it's probably not love."

"Sounds like a real sweet girl."

She raked her hair back, out of her face. "Okay, I'll tell you, but, promise you'll keep it to yourself."

"Promise."

"Like I said, Barbara is the kind of woman who's used to getting what she wants. I think she came on to Jerry and he blew her off. But anyway, a few nights later, he does this party and the guest ends up going over the balcony. Well, you know what happened next. Jerry got fired for over-serving."

"Sounds pretty irresponsible, if you ask me. I think he should have been fired."

"That's just it. I saw Jerry about a week later. Get this. He told me the guy who went over the balcony had one drink and did mineral water the rest of the night! That's not all he told me. For two weeks before that night, Barbara made him stay late to do extra cleaning. He told me how pissed he was that she always picked him. He said she kept hinting around about how much money he could make if he played his cards right. He said she kept it up for the two weeks before the party. Jerry couldn't figure out what she wanted, but he knew she was up to no good, and he didn't want any part of her. Then, the night of the party, she calls him in and tells him to make sure to give good service because they were potential repeat customers. You know—the usual bull we get all the time. Then she told him there was going to be a private meeting in their suite. When it started, he was to leave and return when the meeting was over."

"So?" I tried to keep my expression skeptical.

"So?" Michelle frowned at me and tapped her mug with a long fingernail. "You never leave a fully stocked bar unattended. You know that! It's a major no-no. You can get fired for that. Jerry knew it, but Barbara was the boss. He did what he was told. He figured if push came to shove, she'd back him up. But she denied the whole thing. Jerry didn't bother fighting it."

"Why not?"

"The same reason he didn't want anything to do with her big money scheme. Jerry's from Seattle. He did some time in jail up there and he moved here to start over. When he filled out the job application at the hotel, he left out the part about having a criminal record. He said Barbara knew about it. So, he was afraid if he started anything it might cause trouble for him. And he told me when he was leaving the room there was an argument between the guy who fell and two of the other men. He didn't know what they were saying because they spoke Spanish."

"Didn't the cops question Jerry about how much the guy drank?"

"Of course. He told them the guy had one bourbon and water and then changed to Perrier. The thing is, because Jerry left the bar unattended, he couldn't say for sure what happened while he was gone. That's why they tell us never to leave our bars, and that's why he got fired!"

Most of what Michele said made sense, but I had some doubts about the whole thing. She said Barbara hinted around to Jerry about making money. How?

“Did Jerry ever tell you what Barbara had in mind about making money?”

“No. I asked him what it was all about, but he kind of cut me off. Like it was a personal thing and he didn't want to talk about it. I never asked again. Anyway, right after that he and his wife and kid packed up and moved.“

“Where to?”

“Nobody knows.”

I'd liked to have met Jerry and asked him a few questions, but in places like this, people come and go all the time. From what Michele had said, I couldn't blame him for leaving.

I ordered two more beers while Michele used the ladies room. Her tale about Jerry bothered me. Then there was Barbara and Victor in the parking garage. What was that all about?

“Another beer,” she said, slipping onto her stool. “I was supposed to be treating you.”

“One for the road,” I said.

We chatted over our last round and I took her home.

The clock on my dash showed 2:03 when I pulled into the parking garage at the Eden Arms. I cruised slowly up and down the aisles and finally found a space toward the rear. I parked the car and walked between the rows of cars toward the elevators in the center of the garage. The heavy, warm air reeked of stale engine exhaust.

Somewhere behind me a car’s tires screeched. A car door slammed shut. I turned suddenly, sensing someone’s presence. Looked slowly around. Nothing. Odd. No one there. I picked up my pace and continued on. The light over the elevator doorway was shining dimly through the smoggy air. Between me and the elevator stood a massive cement pillar. Tiny drops of perspiration covered my face. Footsteps again. I made an effort to take a step, get to the elevator door, but there was a frozen space between my brain and my legs. I was imprisoned in the warm contaminated air by my own sweat and fear. The cement pillar loomed. I held my breath and started past the pillar. Instinct told me to look back but, before I could, a sharp blow to the back of my head sent me face first to the ground. My hands reached out to break the fall and scraped across the dirty cement floor. A hot stinging sensation flashed up my arm and my forehead cracked as I hit the asphalt. Pain crushed my ribs. I breathed in short and ragged gasps. I tried to get up, but someone stepped heavily between my shoulder blades and forced me down.

"Don't try to get up, motherfucker." His voice was strangely calm, assured, as if he were enjoying his power. "Listen. You are trouble to us, motherfucker, and we can put you away easy."

Another voice came from my right. "Get that straight, buddy-boy?" I tried to look up, but another kick in my ribs knocked me back down.

I heard steps scuttling away. I lay still, afraid to move. The sound of an engine starting and tires screeching flooded me with relief until suddenly I became aware of the pain. It was everywhere. I moved slowly to my feet and leaned against the pillar. Lifting my arm sent pain shooting up my neck. I pressed my fingers up and down my chest. Nothing seemed broken but taking a regular breath made me cry out in pain. Had they crushed my ribs?

I waited to get enough breath to walk. Blood ran down my lip. I wiped my mouth with my hand. The gravelly mixture of blood, oil, and dirt made me gag. I spit out black speckled blood. My hands and face were embedded with the same stuff. I got to the elevator and pressed the button to my floor.

Once in my room, I eased myself onto the bed. I tried to find a soft spot for my bruised ribs. Pain was radiating from my back. The scrapes on my knees were starting to sting. Nothing seemed to be broken. What was that about? How had I made enemies? Should I call the police? No, I can't. I don't even know which one of me someone is after.

Suddenly Miami seemed foreign and sinister. I slept fitfully and intermittently. The pain stayed with me all night. I wished for one of those knock-it-all-out pain killers.

It was around nine in the morning when I first tried to get up. I could tell from the sun. It came through my windows making the world look normal and safe. But everything was different. Someone was after me.

I lay back in bed. There was blood on my pillow. I sat up slowly and carefully touched my ribs. Funny how you don't even know you have any organs until they hurt. Inhaling and exhaling was the worst.

I got into the bathroom and looked in the mirror. The tip of my nose was scraped; my lip was swollen and sore. As long as I cut down on breathing, no problem. I went back and sat down on the bed, trying to recall what happened. *Quit trying to start trouble?* Someone thought Jimmy the bartender was trying to start trouble.

Who knew me as Jimmy? Michele? Impossible. Last night was the first time we'd spoken. Besides, why would she have me beat up? I bought the last round.

John Palmer? He thought I looked out of place, and he said other people thought it too. But he had nothing to fear from me. Maybe the others he referred to did. The others.

Dan? What do I care if the chef lets him stuff his face? You don't get someone beat up over crab legs.

That left Kevin, Barbara, and Ted. I wasn't sure how I felt about Kevin. Based on what I overheard outside Ted's office and my conversation with Michele, I didn't think I liked Barbara. The general consensus about Ted was that he was a nice guy. I agreed. Although he did get bent out of shape when I mentioned Pedro Quero. Maybe someone did recognize me and the remark about keeping my job was just sarcasm. I put my suspicions on hold and decided to call Penny.

"Frank? Is this you? Or James?"

"Spare me the comedy, Penny. Did you find out anything?" My voice sounded groggy.

"Tough night last night?"

"More than you know."

"What?"

"Did you find out anything?"

"Well, I talked to Harry," she said. "There's a guy named Victor, but he's not exactly a drug dealer. His full name is Victor Consuela Diaz. Colombian. He is, or was, Special Assistant to the President of Colombia. Rumor has it, and this is only rumor, he was let go by their government because of his alleged association with Ricardo Blanco."

"Ricardo Blanco. Isn't he the Don of a big drug cartel in Colombia?"

"That's right. The biggest. That's all I have right now. I don't want to ask too many questions. It might get back to Carman or Angelo."

"Yeah. Good thinking, Penny. So. How's the transfer going?"

"It's going. I'm working my ass off trying to get it done."

"Have my brothers been helping you?"

"Carman's been around a little but I really haven't seen much of Angelo."

"How's the weather?"

"Guess! Cold and gray. I'd like to get away myself. If I had a boss who appreciated me maybe I could take a couple weeks off and sit in the sun."

"Well, once this transition's over you'll be able to take some time. By then the Jersey Shore ought to be opened up."

"Very funny, Frank."

We both laughed. I knew what she meant about time off and she knew I knew. I was glad we could laugh about it. If the shoe was on the other foot, I don't think I'd share her sense of humor.

"Well, anyway Penny, see what else you can find out and we'll talk about your vacation when you call back."

"Okay, I'll call when I know more. You take care of yourself."

"Sure. I'll see you Penny. Oh, just one more thing. Our two

condos. Is anybody using them?"

"No. I told you they were vacant. Remember?"

"What's the lady's name who I call?"

"Helen Newman. Hold on, I'll get you the number."

She came back in a moment with the number. "Tell her who you are. Once she knows it's you, I'm sure she'll be counting the minutes until you get there. I don't know why you haven't moved into the condo before this. The rates at the Eden Arms must be murder this time of year."

"The clientele too."

"What?"

"The mattresses. The mattresses here are really bad. Well, maybe I'll take a ride and find this Mrs. Newman."

"Good idea. Nobody's checked them for a while. You can see if she's taking care of them. Anyway, keep in touch."

"Don't worry. I'll talk to you later."

After we hung up I decided to check out the condo. My inquisitive nature had someone worried. Until I found out whom and why, changing neighborhoods would be better for my health. I dialed the number Penny gave me. As she had predicted, Helen Newman was delighted.

I cleaned up and half an hour later was on my way out the door. When I pulled onto the street, sirens blared behind me. I kept to the right and watched as red flashing lights raced past me. Two police cars and a paramedic unit. They turned into the Regency's entrance. I pulled in amidst the chaos. Security guards scattered in all directions. Guests headed for the shuttle ramp that snaked through the swamp to the beach. I worked my way through the crowd to the yellow tape barriers.

"Come on, step back please. Move back, buddy!"

"What happened, officer?"

"There's been an accident. Now please... everybody, step back!"

From where we stood, our view was about fifty yards down the walkway to where the trail took a sharp right turn. The terrain dropped drastically past the turn and a little bridge passed over dense vegetation.

A moment later the crowd stirred. Several members of the rescue squad and hotel security made the turn and approached us. They pushed a stretcher past us and lifted what appeared to be a body in a black vinyl bag into a waiting ambulance. I scanned the crowd hoping for a familiar face. The cop didn't seem to know what happened, or if he did, he wasn't talking. If I saw someone I knew, I could ask what happened. There was no one around.

Probably a swimming accident. Drownings were common around any beach area. Behind me two people were talking.

“Yeah, Paula was watching from her balcony. They pulled it out of the swamp.”

I turned, hoping to pick out the pair, but the police dispersed us.

“Come on, everybody, there's nothing to see. The shuttle service should be operating in about half an hour. Come back then, and they'll be glad to take you all to the beach.”

I split from the crowd and headed to my car. An early morning jogger, maybe. I thought about the victim. The police delivering the news to the family.

I tapped on the screen door of Helen Newman's second-floor condo overlooking a small courtyard where our two condos made up half of the right side. A short, chubby, seventy-some woman came to the door.

“Come in,” she said, giving the screen a push. I walked in. “Come. Sit down please, Frank. Let me look at you. Just as handsome as ever. Spitting image of your father.” She gave my nose a questioning look. “What happened to you?”

“My nose? Uh, just a little accident,” I said and centered myself on a beige couch; a plump pull-out kind. She dropped into a brown recliner to my left.

“You poor dear. Does it hurt?”

“Only when I breathe.”

She gave me another strange look as if to say, What does that mean?

"Oh, I still have your high school graduation picture here somewhere." She pulled a pair of wire-rim glasses out of the pocket of a flowered apron and searched through a cluster of small, framed photos on a side stand between us.

"Here it is. You haven't changed a bit."

"Boy, that was a long time ago," I said.

Two phony antique rockers and a thirteen-inch TV on a white wicker stand made up the rest of the room. A glass-top coffee table centered the room. Seashell knick-knacks at perfect intervals decorated the top. The lamps were mismatched but everything was immaculate. Mrs. Newman went on for almost an hour about how well my father had treated her—details I already knew.

"Did you know he sent me a Christmas card every year with three hundred dollars right up till—" She recovered her composure.

"How's your wife?"

"We split up, Mrs. Newman."

"I didn't know. No one tells me anything. Your father used to call once in a while. These girls today—I don't know. All they want is a good time and no responsibilities. No one stays together anymore. My niece Dorothy, beautiful girl. Divorced too." She picked a photo out of the bunch and handed it to me. Dorothy was either a very young divorcee or it was an old snapshot.

"She's very pretty," I said.

"Smart too. She teaches music up in Greenwich. Comes down to visit every year. How long are you staying, Frank?"

"I don't know."

"Well, I'll just need a day to tidy up your condo. Not that it needs it. No one's been down in a while."

"I was hoping to pick up the key today."

"I only have the one key. Your brothers both have their own keys. Don't you?"

"Well I do, but—"

"Oh, how rude of me, I haven't even offered you a cup of coffee or a soda. I don't have anything else. I don't drink, you know. My husband was a drinker. Do you drink, Frank?"

It was clear she hadn't had a real conversation for a long time.

"Uh, only on special occasions."

"Well, would you like a soda or coffee? I have instant, so it'll only take a minute."

I was eager to leave and I hate instant coffee. I would have accepted a soda, but that would have prolonged my visit. I looked at my watch, "Actually, I have to get going. Thanks."

"Let me know when you're coming. I'll have everything ready. I'm usually up early in the morning. We can sit outside and have coffee together!"

The thought of long sessions with Helen and her instant coffee made me reconsider the rates at the Eden Arms.

"I'll let you know."

"Okay, just call. I'm always here, you know."

I got up without saying a word. A single comment could set off another long monologue. I walked to the door with her at my heels.

"You don't know how happy I am to see you. Next time when you're not so rushed we can visit a little longer."

"Sure, Mrs. Newman, thank you."

I finally liberated myself, made a stop at the pharmacy for some Advil, and returned to my suite. I was scheduled to work that night. My ribs ached. If it wasn't such short notice I'd have called in.

I took two pills and lay on the couch. I thought about the accident at the Regency, the body in the swamp. Another death at the hotel. But the hotel wasn't mine anymore. Why should I care about some unlucky tourist whose vacation turned into a nightmare today? It was a real tragedy and the fact that it happened at the Regency made it worse. But there was nothing I could do.

Maybe I'd wait till the story hit the papers and send an anonymous token of sympathy. I knew the news would be all over the hotel. Once I knew who it was, I'd decide what to do. The Advil was working. My ribs didn't feel so sore. I dozed off.

The pain returned and woke me forty-five minutes later. I got up and prepared for work. While dressing, I realized I hadn't heard from Penny. Why hadn't she called? She knew I was waiting. It didn't matter right now, anyway. I could wait. At the moment, finding out who was pulled out of that swamp was more important.

When I got off the elevator, the usual atmosphere of talking and joking was absent. It was nearly silent. I was surprised, assuming just the opposite: everyone would be talking about the accident. There was a somber aura in the room.

I approached the office door and heard Barbara discussing business with Ted. I waved and continued to the work area.

“We need bar towels!” someone shouted.

“I'll get them,” I said and walked down to the storeroom. Robin Sanborn was in there.

Robin was a brown-eyed, tall, slender redhead with a muscular body. She always wore ruby-red lipstick. From the first time I'd met her, I could tell she was obsessed with her appearance. Our first conversation was about working out.

“I belong to Olympia Gym,” she had said.

Who would say that kind of thing after just meeting someone? I complimented her physique. Instead of thank you, I got her justification for daily exercise.

“Listen. I'm almost forty and when a girl gets to be my age, things can start sagging. You know what I mean? You got to exercise to keep in shape!”

Another time I made the mistake of commenting on her hair. Again, instead of thanking me, she stared at me.

“You think it looks okay like this? Maybe I should have it cut shorter.”

Then she pulled a small mirror out of her purse. Focusing it with one hand, she used her long slender fingers to pull at her curls.

“I was thinking about getting it colored,” she said, checking my reaction. I laughed and told her she looked great.

Tonight, though, she seemed preoccupied as I entered the room. Her back was toward me. I couldn't see her face.

"Hey, Robin, what's up?"

She turned instantly. She looked childlike, vulnerable. Her eyes were red. She had been crying.

"Robin, what's wrong? Are you okay?"

With that she openly sobbed, sinking her face into my shoulder.

"Oh Jimmy, Jimmy, they found him in the swamp!"

"Yeah, I know. Did they find out who it was?"

She looked up, stunned at my question.

"Don't you know?"

"Know what?"

"Jimmy! It was Dan!"

"Dan! Jesus Christ."

Robin began to cry again and I stood dumbfounded in silence. My arms and legs were numb. Even the pain from my bruised ribs seemed to subside. My heart pounded. I tried to compose myself, but the blow must have been obvious. Robin's tears turned to concern for me.

"You okay, Jimmy?" Her eyes focused on my face. "What happened to your nose?"

I didn't answer.

"Jimmy?"

"Does anybody know what happened?"

"There's all kinds of stories. Somebody said they found one of the golf carts on the boardwalk near his body. He may have stopped there for some reason. It probably happened last night while he was working. Maybe he was going to the tiki bar. But he'd have no reason to go out there."

"What do you mean?"

"Well I—it just wasn't part of his job."

"Maybe one of the bartenders called for something. Wouldn't—"

"No, that's not the way it works. That's not it."

For a few minutes, neither one of us spoke. Robin collected herself.

"Dan was the nicest guy in this whole department," she sighed. Her eyes filled again. I pulled her toward me and embraced her.

"Come on, Robin, pull yourself together. We gotta get back to work."

I was giving Robin support, but I needed it myself. I was still taking in what had happened.

"I hope I can make it through the night, Jimmy. That bitch, Barbara, better not give me any shit tonight. I sure wish Ted worked nights instead of that witch."

Robin was rambling about Barbara but I couldn't hear her. Why was Dan back in that swamp? The argument Dan had with Barbara came to mind. What about Barbara and Jerry? Barbara and Victor? Was it coincidence? Barbara seemed to be the common denominator. Was she responsible for my aching ribs? Penny's call was even more important now. I walked back to the work area.

"Hey, Jimmy!" Kevin was all over me. "Come on. Let's get going! We're late getting set up. Barbara wants to talk to everyone before we start tonight."

I hurried back to work. I was anxious to hear what Barbara had to say. I knew nothing about her, only what I got from Robin and Michele. I had a feeling once I knew her better, I'd probably agree with them.

Back at the work area, everyone was just about ready. Robin and I stood near each other at the opposite end of the rectangular room, facing the office door.

Conversation ended when Barbara's slender figure appeared in the doorway. Her snug, navy suit hung just above her knees. She had great legs. I stared at her silhouette in the doorway. If she was as smart as she was beautiful, she could do anything. I had known other women like her and had learned how to deal with her kind. God, I'd have loved to put her in her place, but I was Jimmy the bartender here, not Frank D'Antonio.

She stepped into the room.

"Attention everyone, please." She paused. "I'm sure you all know about the accident last night. I know you're all very upset. It's been quite a shock. Dan Hiller was with us a long time. He was here even longer than me, and he'll be missed. There's probably going to be lots of police around, asking all kinds of questions. We want you all to cooperate with them. It was a terrible tragedy. But unfortunately, accidents do happen. All we can do now is see to it a horrible thing like this doesn't happen again."

I didn't know Barbara as well as Robin did. She wasn't buying Barbara's emotional address.

"Do you believe this bitch?" she whispered to me. "She really sounds broken up. What an asshole."

Barbara did seem matter-of-fact about the whole thing. The more I watched and listened, the more I saw a cold indifference in her character. My thoughts gave way to her speech. I caught her last words.

"Let's try to remember it's business as usual. We still have an obligation to management and the guests. Also, guests will probably ask questions. It's my—it's the hotel's recommendation you say as little as possible. That's all. Push out to your parties and we'll see you at the end of the night."

We filed out. I noticed Andre was missing.

"Hey Robin, where's Andre?"

"He's working the Picadilly Bar for the next few nights."

That was a good idea, I thought. The Picadilly wasn't a busy place these days, and it would give him more time to learn what he needed to know.

It hadn't always been that way. When we first built the hotel, the Picadilly jumped day and night. It was a watering hole for celebrities and high-profile guests. The customers were high caliber, but their tastes and fantasies were the same as anybody else. It had also become a haven for classy hookers.

Back in the seventies, bartenders were often go-betweens for hookers and their clients. Discretion wasn't the most important thing. It was the only thing. Public figures couldn't afford a scandal and the hookers had to avoid the vice squad.

That's where the bartenders came in. They knew just about everyone who went in and out of the place. They'd warn the girls about detectives or some john the girls were hustling who was into kinky sex.

The same with the guests. If a reporter walked in, they'd let the celebrities know.

As the years went by, business slowed down in the Picadilly. The seventies gave way to the eighties, and tougher drinking and driving laws were passed. Americans gave up two martini lunches for mineral water and a noon workout at the gym. The lounge kept its plush atmosphere and continued to attract well-to-do patrons, just not as many. When a guest stepped through the tinted glass doors etched with ‘Picadilly Room’, they saw a circular room. Around the perimeter, which formed the upper level, were booths of red velvet with round glass tables, lit by glass-covered candleholders.

Two sets of steps on opposite ends of the lounge led down to the lower level. On one side was a circular bar. A bandstand was on the other end, and in the middle was a small dance floor dimly lit by a crystal chandelier. It was a perfect place for couples worried about being seen. Booths provided hiding places in dark corners.

Despite its slow business, the Picadilly stayed open late. Andre would have a long night. Last call was always at two o'clock.

I had a hard time concentrating on work. Every time I bent or stretched, it hurt, and all I could think about was Dan. He was such a hard-working guy, dedicated to the hotel and to Ted. He had gone out of his way to help me feel welcome when I first started. I thought about the night with the crab legs, hiding in the corner, stuffing our faces. He didn't know he was feeding his former boss.

I wanted to do something for his family but I didn't know them. I hardly knew Dan, but still I felt bad. I wondered what could have happened to make him wander back to that swamp. As Robin said, it was unusual for Dan to make trips to the tiki bar. So what was he doing back there?

I tried thinking of reasons. Some made sense. But Dan was dead and I was mad. I was determined to find out what happened.

Barbara's voice startled me. “Are they drinking much, Jimmy?”

“Not really.”

“Why don't you give them last call and then close up.”

I looked at my watch. Ten o'clock. I gave last call, packed up my things, and pushed my way back to the work area. By the time I got back, most of the bartenders were almost finished. By eleven-thirty, Robin and I were almost done. I was putting the last of the liquor bottles away when Robin suggested a drink on the way home. I needed one too.

Robin signed the timesheet and handed the clipboard to me. I was just about to fill in my work hours, when Barbara looked up and said, “Everything done, guys?”

Robin sounded indignant. “Yeah, we're done.”

Her tone didn't seem to faze Barbara. “Robin, you're all set. Call in tomorrow for your schedule. Jimmy, I’ll need you to stay a little longer tonight. I need some of this liquor straightened out.”

She pointed to the shelves of liquor bottles behind her. Some bottles were out of place, but it was an ongoing problem. When bartenders are in a hurry to get out, they put the bottles back anywhere instead of keeping the same type of liquor together.

Robin looked at me, then at Barbara, and said, “Uh, okay. Well, good night, Barbara. See you later, Jimmy.”

She made her exit quickly.

I was in pain and emotionally hip-hopping between curiosity and rage over Dan's death. I wanted to get home and call Penny and here I was alone with Barbara. I stood there, motionless, waiting for her to tell me exactly what she wanted done. Thirty seconds might have gone by but it seemed much longer. Finally my patience reached its limit.

"Barbara, what do you need done?"

"Uh yes, well, to start with, I need these liquor bottles straightened out."

Still seated, she pointed to the shelves of bottles behind her desk. The shelves ran the full length of the wall where they met the adjoining wall, made the turn and continued down, forming that half of the rectangular room. I hesitated for a moment. I looked back and forth from the wall of bottles to Barbara's sexy profile.

I walked behind the desk and was standing practically next to her. Casually I began pulling bottles from the shelf and organizing them. I'd hardly started when Barbara pushed away from her desk. Her blue skirt was pushed way up, revealing her thighs beneath her black panty hose.

"I want you to start down here."

She pointed to the bottom shelf and rotated in her chair so her legs were directly facing me. Suddenly I was very uncomfortable. Nonchalantly I bent down on one knee and pulled bottles from the bottom shelf. I was flushed. I wasn't turned on by her seductive manner. In fact, I thought it was comical and clumsy. But I decided to play along.

I pulled out a few more bottles. She had returned to her original position behind her desk, pretending to be engrossed in her work, but I caught her watching me. She'd done this a hundred times. I could tell. A control freak. And it was my move. This was where I was supposed to utter some feeble come-on. She'd realize I was attracted to her. In a matter of a few minutes and a couple words she'd analyzed me and knew where she stood.

I spoke softly. "You know, Barbara."

"Yes, Jimmy?"

I hesitated then said, "These shelves do need straightening out."

Her shoulders dropped slightly.

I continued my chore, trying not to look to my left. She sat poised at the desk. My comment had let a little wind out of her sails. She pulled a towel out of her desk drawer.

“Here Jimmy, wipe that shelf off while you're down there.”

I turned to take the towel, coming eye level with her bent knees. I felt her staring down at me. I reached up for the towel. For a second, she refused to let go. Our eyes met.

The whole thing was a joke. I had all I could do not to laugh in her face, or in this case, her knees. This scenario might have worked before, but this time she was striking out. If she was trying to be subtle about seducing me, she wasn't doing a very good job.

“Thank you,” I said coolly. I grabbed the towel and started wiping the shelf, smiling to myself.

I continued reorganizing the bottles and Barbara went back to her paperwork. Except for the clinking of the bottles and the sound of Barbara’s calculator there was silence in the room. I decided to break the silence.

“That's terrible about Dan,” I said, anxious to get her reaction.

She lifted her head. Her voice was low. “Yeah, it was awful. We were pretty close. Professionally, of course.”

No one could miss noticing that Barbara and Dan merely tolerated each other. So why the performance? Either she was naive or thought I was. I shook off the thought and continued.

“Why do you think Dan would go out by that swamp so late?”

“Like I told the cops, he might have been called down to the bar for something. How the hell do I know? I wasn't here. Besides—Dan was a good worker, but he was no angel.”

“What do you mean?”

“I mean, Dan used to sneak in a few drinks when no one was around. A lotta times he'd wander down to the Tiki and bullshit with the bartenders. They'd hook him up with all the Jack Daniels he wanted. I knew. So did Ted. But Dan always did his work so we never said anything.”

“Who was working the Tiki that night?” I asked.

“You ask a lot of questions, Jimmy.”

“I'm just making conversation.”

“Seems you've been making a lot of conversation lately.”

I gave her a look. “What’s that supposed to mean?”

“Ted told me about your talk after tennis,” she said then added smugly, “Ted tells me everything.”

“He said the hotel's been bought out and some of you might get the ax.”

She continued writing and said, without looking, “Some of us, but not all of us.”

“What about Ted?”

“He's a yes man. But we have new owners now.”

“So, you think Ted will go?”

“Ted's a good guy but not a good manager.”

“You think you could do better?”

She pondered this. “You know, Florida is and always will be a right-to-work state. Which means I can fire you if I don't like the way you comb your hair. You know what I mean. If I were you, I'd make sure I was on the right side of the fence when all the changes happen.”

“And what is the right side?”

“If you want to find out, you're asking too many questions. If you're not careful, you might lose your job or worse.”

We stared at each other. I suddenly realized she never questioned my scraped nose. Maybe Barbara...I bet Barbara knows. I couldn't be sure if she was directly responsible, but I knew then she knew about it. Our conversation was taking a heavy direction I decided to lighten it.

“Who did buy the hotel?”

“Some big corporation.”

“You think the change will be an improvement?”

“It can't be any worse.”

“Really. What do you mean?”

“I mean the previous owners didn't know what they were doing. Personally I don't think they cared.”

“Why not?”

“The previous owner was a closed corporation. A family

business. A father-son thing. I heard the old man was pretty shrewd. He died and left it to his two sons. They're so busy spending daddy's money, nobody's minding the store." Still tapping the calculator, she shook her head in disappointment. "Daddy hands them the goose with golden egg, and they screw it up."

It was strange being analyzed by someone who didn't know about our family, but I had to admit she was right about the Regency being neglected. After my father died, Angelo and Carman had me busy in New York. Who had time for trips to Florida? Forget Carman or Angelo going down. Ask them to break their routine? They'd make an occasional phone call to Sol but usually got Paul Carroll and asked how things were going. He'd tell them what they wanted to hear, and they were happy. I was about to get into particulars when the phone interrupted. The caller spoke briefly, and Barbara responded.

"Okay, I'll get right on it. No problem."

She put the phone down and said, "Okay Jimmy, cleanup's over. Go down to the Picadilly and check on Andre. The front desk said a crowd was headed there, and he might be getting slammed. Go down, make sure he's all right and then you can go home."

I turned to leave.

"Oh Jimmy, we'll talk again. I might be able to help you pick the right side of that fence."

"You seem pretty sure of yourself," I said.

She leaned forward, arms resting on the desk and smiled. "I am."

"Well, I better get down and check on Andre. You have a good night."

"You too, Jimmy."

A ruthless bitch on a power trip. I would have liked to continue our conversation, but the idea of getting out of there was more appealing.

I turned the corner from her office and rushed for the service elevator. I waited impatiently, hoping Barbara wouldn't call me back with a change of plan. Finally the door opened. I entered the elevator and sighed with relief as the door closed, ensuring my getaway. The Picadilly was at the opposite end of the lobby. The elevator door opened and I walked a short way past room service through double doors that opened into the main lobby.

Quickly I headed across the long vestibule, passing small clusters of guests along the way. Two couples were reading the glass-framed menu outside the front door of Club Gigi, our fine dining restaurant, which had closed for the night. In the center of the lobby, guests sat conversing on the couches. Finally, I passed Café Chablis, the casual dining eatery which served mainly breakfast and lunch. The Picadilly was next door.

Six or seven men were standing just inside the door. I tried to get a glimpse of Andre, but he was out of sight. I walked around the bar until I reached the far end where the waitresses picked up their drinks for the tables. My view was much better from this end of the room. I scanned it and found Andre bent over the bar, in conversation with a customer. After what already felt like a long night, all I wanted to do was make sure he was all right and go home. I'd wait a few minutes for Andre to finish his conversation, get his attention, make sure he was okay, and leave.

"What are you doing down here?"

I turned to find one of the cocktail waitresses behind me rushing by with a tray full of dirty glasses.

"Barbara told me to come down and check on Andre. The front desk called and said you guys might be busy down here."

"I don't think we need anything. Everything's covered, but why don't you tell Andre to go home and you stay with us. He's no fun and he's slow as hell. Even Gus was faster than Andre," she said as she stopped to unload her tray on the bar.

The mention of his name brought me back. I thought of the card he'd sent when my father died, telling us about their coffee sessions and the twenty dollar tips. He'd been a loyal employee.

"Where is Gus?" I asked.

"Ask that bitch upstairs," she said. "She decided Gus wasn't fast enough so she replaced him with Andre. I heard from a lot of guests that he'd been here for years and they all say what a great guy he is. We miss him too. Someone said his wife was real sick and he needed the hours. He told me he tried to use his seniority to save his shifts but Barbara and Ted told him seniority doesn't mean anything here. All those years and what did it get him. This place sucks."

Suddenly, I felt ashamed, as if I'd let Gus and my father down. My father loved Gus. He would have kept his word to him and preserved his job. My shame was replaced by my rage. I knew what my father would have done; the same thing I would do if I could: make sure that Barbara, Ted, and even Paul Carroll knew not to bother Gus again.

The waitress was looking curiously at my face. "Hey! What happened to your nose?"

"I guess I must have put it where it didn't belong."

"What?"

"Swimming. I scraped it on the bottom of a pool."

"Oh, one of my guys is looking for his check. I better get over there. See you later."

"Okay, see you."

I watched her speed away. She was a Miami cocktail waitress and looked the part. Her idea of me changing places with Andre was flattering, but the story about Gus was more disturbing.

Andre was still talking. The bartender's toughest job: getting away from a talkative customer. Andre had his hands full. I figured the best thing was to call him and get his attention. Trying not to scream, I called out his name.

As he turned to acknowledge me, his body shifted, allowing a clear view of his talkative patron. The sight left me breathless. Quickly I stepped aside out of the man's view. I stood paralyzed for a moment.

It took a few minutes to compose myself. I wondered if he had seen me. If he had, he'd remember. He appeared relaxed, sipping his drink. I had to get out of there fast. I tried to think of the best way out.

"Hey Jimmy, what do you want?"

Wonderful, I thought. Andre calling me. I didn't answer. I noticed a stream of light coming from the kitchen behind me. Slowly I moved toward it. As I walked away, I picked up my pace until I reached the swinging doors to the kitchen. I pushed open the door and stepped to one side. I peeked out of the diamond-shaped window of the kitchen door. I wanted to get another look, just to make sure.

It was Diaz all right. My heart pounded as I stared at him. What would have happened if I'd gone behind the bar? How would I explain it? The thought was chilling. It made me even more aware of how important obscurity was.

What the hell were they talking about? A waitress burst through the doors.

"Hey Jimmy, what are you doing back here? Andre wants to know what you want."

"I just came back to grab something to eat. I'm starved! Do me a favor. Ask him if he needs me, cause if he's okay, I'm going home. I'm beat."

She returned in a moment.

"Andre says he's okay, so get out of here while you can."

"You got it. See ya."

I wasted no time and left through the rear kitchen door.

Chapter Nine

It was almost two in the morning, but I called Penny anyway. The phone rang twice. She mumbled a hello.

Innocently I asked, "Penny. Were you sleeping?"

"What do you think I'm doing? What time is it?"

"That's not important right now. Did you get the information I asked for?"

"Frank. It's...it's almost two-thirty! Do you have to know right now?"

"Well I—"

"I'll call you in the morning. Go to bed, Frank. I think you're getting too much sun."

"All right, but I'll be waiting for your call."

I squeezed in the last word before she hung up.

I went to bed but didn't expect to get much rest. I don't know what time it was when I finally fell asleep. When the phone woke me, I knew I must have overslept. The sun beamed into my suite from the balcony doors. I fumbled for the phone.

"Frank. Are you awake?"

"Penny?"

"Yeah. Frank. It's me. Don't you hate it when people bother you when you're trying to sleep?"

"Right... well... what'd you find out?"

"Well, the latest on Victor Diaz is that Ricardo Blanco uses him as a liaison between his drug cartel and Luis Martinez."

"Who's Luis Martinez?"

"He's the president of Colombia. Diaz passes Blanco's money

around to the right people and they supply him with whatever information he needs to move dope out of the country."

"Sounds like a good setup."

"Well, I guess it has been until now."

"What do you mean?"

"Martinez is the first president in the last three administrations who's been welcome in the US."

"How come?"

"The last three were known to be directly affiliated with Blanco. Martinez is the first one who's publicly spoken out against Blanco and his boys. Martinez coming to this convention has Blanco and his boys worried. If he cuts a deal with our government, it could cost Blanco a lot of money. Maybe his whole operation. That's where Diaz comes in. Blanco pays Diaz for his contacts with the Colombian government. Diaz is well liked from what I hear, even by Martinez. I think Blanco's hoping Diaz can use his relationship with Martinez and a lot of cash to discourage any plans that could jeopardize his business."

"Great work, Penny. What you're saying makes sense."

"I don't know what you're up to, but you better be careful."

"Yeah, you said it," I mumbled.

"What?"

"I will."

"Everyone keeps asking about you here. You ought to at least call your brothers. They're worried about you. They keep asking me questions. I don't know what to tell them. Tom Morton's been bugging me too. You know how he is. He wants all this tax business taken care of."

"I'll give him a call. Thanks for the information. I gotta get going. I'll talk to you soon. Tell everybody I said hello."

I hung up the phone and buried my head under the pillow, hoping to fall back asleep. After about ten minutes of tossing and turning, I sat up on the bed staring at the phone. Finally I picked it up and dialed Carman's house. Our talk was brief, both of us tiptoeing around each other. He asked about the weather and joked about bikinis on the beach. I asked how things were going. He said they were good. We left it at that. I assured him I was all right and said I'd see him soon.

I decided to throw on some clothes and go out for breakfast. I took the elevator down to the lobby. Directly across from the coffee shop was a gift shop that sold newspapers and magazines. I walked in, picked up *The Herald* then went across the way for breakfast.

A dark-haired man in a cream-colored suit seated me. Immediately I was approached by a thin, Hispanic-looking gent with salt-and-pepper hair cut tightly to his head. His nametag read 'Gene'.

He set a laminated, multi-colored menu on the table. "Would you like coffee now, Sir?"

"Sure."

He poured me a cup and asked if I was ready to order.

I bypassed the menu and ordered a toasted bran muffin. He took the menu back and left. I sat for a minute sipping the java and letting the caffeine clear out the cobwebs. Halfway through my first cup, the waiter returned with my muffin cut in half and toasted to perfection.

"Can I bring you anything else right now?" he asked.

"Just some more coffee."

"Sure."

He left and a moment later returned, pot in hand, and refilled my cup.

"I'll just leave this with you. Take it when you're ready," he said. He placed a brown vinyl booklet containing my check on the table and left.

I ate half the muffin immediately then picked at the rest while I scanned the paper. The front page article hyped the upcoming convention. It mentioned that the hotels were beefing up security, especially the Regency, where most of the dignitaries would stay. There were some other stories, world news, an article about drug trafficking in Florida, and an editorial on the national economy. I skipped over them, searching for a story about Dan. All along I'd assumed he'd drowned, so I looked for a story about a drowning. I found it at the bottom of the page with the headline, "Man Mangled by Alligator in Hotel Sanctuary."

It was a short piece about Dan and his employment at the hotel with some details about the accident. Though vague, the thought of death by alligator left a gruesome image in my mind. My God. What a way to die.

The closing sentence read, "The management of the hotel and the police are withholding comments pending further investigation."

I put the paper down, sat back, and sipped my coffee. My waiter had a table of six sitting next to me: four adults and two children. I watched as he attempted to take their order while the two children pounded on the table whining about being hungry. He scribbled their requests on a small pad then gathered the menus and was about to walk away when one of the women said, "My kids are starving so can you rush it? Oh, and I'll have a Bloody Mary."

"Yes Ma'am," he said. "Would anyone else like a drink from the bar?"

Everyone declined. He raced off to the bar which was located at the far end of the dining area. A few minutes later, he returned with the drink, "There you are, Ma'am," he said, placing the drink in front of her.

The man next to her eyed the drink. "Oh that looks good, I think I'll have one," he said over the brats' chanting, "I wanna eat."

"Right away, Sir," the waiter said as he dodged a flying fork from one of the kids. He bent over and picked it up saying he'd bring a clean one. Instead of an apology, the Bloody Mary woman said, "Could you check on our food, my kids have to get something to eat or they're going to die."

How could he even put their order in, they had him running for Bloody Marys. I looked at the two children. From their butterball figures, it didn't appear that they'd missed many meals. I wanted to get up and grab the woman, tell her if she wanted to know what starving was she should talk to one of the Haitians who cleaned her room or washed the dishes she ate off for minimum wage.

The waiter returned with the second Bloody Mary then immediately sped away to put in their order. After a few moments, he appeared again with a coffeepot in his hand. He approached my table. "More coffee, Sir?" Beads of perspiration trickled down his forehead.

"Sure," I said.

As he poured the coffee, one of the men at the next table called, "Hey, buddy-buddy."

The waiter looked at me. I rolled my eyes. He managed a tight smile then moved to their table.

I listened half-amused, half-furious as they complained about everything.

"Hey, what's the holdup with our food?" the man said.

One of the women interjected. "Yeah, what's taking so long?"

"I'll check on it, Ma'am," he said. "But everything is cooked to order."

When nothing seemed to be to their satisfaction, the manager finally comped their entire meal.

With no expression of gratitude, they walked out. I could tell by their accents they were New Yorkers, probably from Long Island. It made me ashamed to come from the same place. After all that trouble, the house picking up the tab, you would think they'd at least leave a tip. Not a cent.

I finished my coffee and decided to make it a beach day. I opened the brown folder and checked the bill. Four fifty-one. Fifteen percent was only about seventy cents. For a moment I thought of the waiter. Probably a man in his fifties running his ass off for tips. My new experience had been a humbling one. I'd discovered how cruel and demanding people can be. How the pseudo-rich turn up their noses at service employees. I felt guilty knowing I must have acted the same at one time or another. I slipped ten dollars into the booklet, knowing the five dollars and fifty cents cash tip would please him, make him feel appreciated.

By the time I arrived, all the red beach umbrellas were taken. I settled for a small spot near the back edge of the beach. It didn't take long before I felt the sun baking my skin. I decided to go for a swim. The water was soothing and warm. I walked until the water was up to my waist and then squatted down to my neck. The back-and-forth motion of the warm salt water seemed to massage my ribs. After ten minutes of this relaxing therapy, I headed back toward the beach. The surf had soothed me and the breeze blowing against my wet skin invigorated me. I sat on my towel, refreshed, and let the sun dry the sheen of salty water from my body.

I watched couples and children playing on the beach, bobbing in the water and strolling hand-in-hand along the shoreline. How I envied them. They all looked so happy. Unlike mine, their week of fun and sun had no doubt been planned and budgeted all year. To me, deciding to be in Miami was no greater a decision than deciding what to eat for dinner.

Yet my life was in turmoil. I thought of my marriage gone bad and the business that had slipped away. Times when I was disgusted and just wanted it all to end, or at least my part of it. Visions of my father would appear urging me not to give up. I recalled phrases he'd use to encourage me. “Real men don't walk away from their problems, they face them.”

Loyalty, honesty, character. That's what he had hammered into me. He had done a good job because I based my life on these principles and I expected the same from others. That was the problem. Assuming people thought like me.

All I knew was the business had been taken from me like a loved one dying before his time. I wasn't ready to let go and my father wouldn’t have wanted me to. I needed the business. Maybe it was just insecurity. At times I fantasized about the hotel and our other properties. I'd picture them like imaginary childhood friends now pushed aside and fading. Even now, walking the hotel's corridors as a bartender, I felt the walls applauding, happy to see me.

My new job had given me appreciation for the “little people.” As I came to know them, I realized how important they were. People who could hardly speak English, so grateful for the work. They busted their asses every day so the guys upstairs in the Armani suits looked good. It wasn't long ago I was one of those guys upstairs. Like the waiter at the Central Plaza—I recognized him because of his presence over the years, but I had never spoken to him, not even to say hello.

Now it was happening to me. Managers were passing me in the hall, talking, laughing, not once did they say hello or even make eye contact. I wondered if they even knew my name. If they knew who I really was, how would they react? Did I need a title to be somebody? If they knew what I was worth would I be accepted? Maybe both.

My father had started like these workers, and through hard work and good ethics, built an empire. I wondered if he ever felt obscure. Probably not. There was the difference between him and his three sons. He’d started at the bottom. We flew high on borrowed wings, never understanding the way things really were.

I checked my watch. Two-thirty. I decided to stop and see Charlie at the bar before heading back to my suite for a nap before dinner. As usual, the bar was packed. Charlie hustled back and forth. He seemed to be his normal jolly self. The glass gallon jug behind the bar marked “tips” was full of dollar bills—sign of a good day.

“Jimmy! How's it going, brother? Beer?”

“Yeah, Charlie, I'll have a beer.”

Since the day I’d met Stacy, the tiki bar was part of my routine at least a couple times a week. Charlie and I were now on a first-name basis. He dropped a draft in front of me.

“Hey, what's with the nose?” he asked then hustled down the

bar.

"Long story. I'll tell you sometime when you're not busy."

Bars like this were a perfect place to forget troubles. There was always a party atmosphere. I stood pleasantly pressed against the happy crowd of patrons enjoying the island music. It was entertaining just to watch. I was about to take my last sip when a voice called from behind me.

"Hey, Jimmy. How you doin?"

It was Stacy. She looked good. Aside from coworkers, she was the only person I had any personal involvement with. Immediately I summoned Charlie and ordered two beers.

"Hey, you bought last time," she said. "I'll get these."

She pushed a ten at Charlie, but I pushed her hand away and signaled Charlie to put the drinks on my tab.

"I'm working, you know. I can afford a couple beers."

"Well, thanks. I hoped I'd run into you. There's a couple of guests in the hotel looking for someone to play with. They're about your level. What do you think?" Her eyes dropped to nose level. "Are you up to it?"

"Yeah, let me know when."

"You sure? What happened to your nose?"

"An accident."

"Does it hurt?"

"Only when I breathe. But yeah, I'd like to play. Let me know."

"That's just it. I don't know how to get hold of you."

How could I give her my number at the suite? I told her I didn't have a phone yet and I'd call her at the tennis shop.

She didn't question it, but the lies were building up. I was insecure, living as a virtual unknown with a regular job but she seemed glad to see me and that boosted my confidence. Made me feel comfortable. I was attracted to her. We had another round of beers and listened to the guitar player strum the familiar island songs. I could feel the chemistry between us. I decided to test my ability to land a date as Jimmy the bartender.

"So, where you going from here?" I asked.

"Home. Tomorrow's a work day, you know. I have two clinics in the morning—little kids, but they're a lot of fun."

"I'm hungry. Do you want to join me? Nothing special. Maybe a pizza or something."

"Yeah, I could go for something."

"There's a place down the street called Mamma Marie's. I heard their pizza's pretty good."

Actually I knew nothing about the pizza at Mamma Marie's, but they had outside seating, so I could go in my bathing suit. That eliminated having to think of a way back to my suite to change clothes.

"Yeah, I've had their pizza. It's not bad. We can go in my car if you want."

"Sure," I said.

Mamma Marie's was small with six tables outside: three against the glass windows and three were out about five feet forming an aisle. The tables and chairs were white plastic. Bright red and green umbrellas advertising Cinzano bloomed over each table. Only one table was available. A waitress in khaki shorts, white tee shirt, covered by a green and red apron brought ice water and menus.

We ordered wine and the waitress left us with a few moments to study the menu.

I wasn't particular about pizza. It was nice not eating alone for a change. I felt at ease. Stacy didn't ask much about my past. She asked about my job and how things were going, but it was innocent. At first I had to remind myself that to her I was just a guy who had moved from another town and was between jobs.

She asked about my nose again. I was tempted to tell her what had actually happened. I needed someone to talk with. Someone I could trust. I was still confused about it myself. Why beat up Jimmy Anthony, a bartender?

The waitress returned for our order which I let Stacy decide—no extra cheese, no onions, fresh basil.

"So, what about you? No guys in your life?"

She looked inside her glass as if searching for something, took a sip, and smiled.

"Well, I had two guys once."

"Two?"

"It's not the way it sounds. My father was one of them. The other was Brad Grady, my tennis coach. After a while, he became more than just a coach." She went on to tell me how her relationship with Brad turned into a love affair.

Her father, an avid tennis player himself, had hit it big in the advertising business. Early on he had groomed Stacy for success. He had high hopes and spared no expense when it came to improving her game. She went to expensive tennis camps as a child and took lessons every week. Her father dumped a fortune into her training with hopes she'd make it to center court of Wimbledon, The US Open, and so on. She did well at the local tournaments. On the satellite tours she struggled but held her own.

"When you get to the top, it's a different story," she said.

We ordered a second glass of wine.

"Competition at that level is unbelievable. The pressure started to get to me. My father kept reminding me about the money he'd invested in my career. And Brad, who was my coach and my boyfriend, felt free to show his disappointment if I lost. Between the two of them, I broke down. I knew they were disappointed, but I was sure they'd stand by me. At least my father. I was wrong. My father turned his back on me. And Brad, I found out, was using me to advance his own career. That's when I decided to come down here. And to answer your question about guys, I guess I need to trust again. I always believed people who meant the most to me loved me no matter what. It's hard to accept they're not interested in you as a person. You're a commodity, a tool to use for their own satisfaction. So, that's it."

Our waitress brought the pizza. We talked as we ate and intermittently she asked subtle questions about my past. She still gave me the impression it was just conversation, good manners. I was starting to really like her.

We left as soon as we were done. I had her drop me off in front of the Eden Arms. With my towel around my neck, I poked my head into her red Mazda and said good night. I hesitated, wanting to kiss her.

"Make sure you call me," she said.

I could tell it was for the tennis match and not another date.

Back at the hotel everyone was gearing up for the convention. There were new faces everywhere. The human resource office was orienting new employees, escorting them around in small groups.

I don't know if it was Dan's grisly death, Penny's information, or that somebody played Kick-the-Can with my ribs, but I found myself looking at faces and feet. I thought maybe I'd recognize the sleek brown boots that had done the number on me.

But did Pedro Quero, Dan Hiller, and Jimmy Anthony have anything in common? The first two, maybe. Jimmy Anthony just didn't fit. If Ricardo Blanco was using the hotel to carry out some plan, he could infiltrate the hotel with pawns to carry out the scheme. But what did that have to do with me?

Maybe I'd blown my cover and didn't know it. Frank D'Antonio fit into the scheme of things better than Jimmy Anthony.

Anyway, they all looked innocent. Regular people starting new jobs. But what would a criminal look like, anyway? They don't dress in black or lurk in shadows. They come with smiles. Normal, everyday people. Even if there were anything to my theory, if I even had a theory—what could I do about it? I had nothing to back it up. The only way anyone would give me the right time of day would be if I revealed who I really was. Even then, I had nothing more than a theory. The whole thing was frustrating and frightening. But if I kept feeding info to Penny, maybe she'd get to the bottom of it. I returned to my suite that afternoon. Penny had called. I dialed New York.

"Penny, it's Frank. What's up?"

"One of Schlenker's secretaries called. They need your signature to distribute the funds. Should I send them down there or are you coming up to show us your tan?"

"When does he need them?"

"He didn't say, but Carman and Angelo won't like it if you hold up the show."

"Well, I went to see Helen Newman. I've decided to move into the condo. Give me a day to decide if I'm staying much longer. If necessary you can send the form there. But Penny, I need to ask you something. This is important. Did we ever get a report from Paul Carroll about Pedro Quero's accident?"

"I think so. Paul probably has one on file at the hotel."

"Yeah that's right. Okay, Penny, I'll let you know about those papers. Say hello to everyone. Thanks." I was off the phone in a flash. I had to check that report.

The article I had read about Pedro Quero's death was vague. Stacy and the others only had secondhand information. I wanted the official report, but I couldn't go directly to Paul Carroll. Though I'd never met him as Frank, we had spoken on the phone a few times. He'd seen me pushing bars around as Jimmy the bartender. Even chewed me out once.

I was assigned to a cocktail party put on by a large stock brokerage house. The bars had just officially opened and I had my hands full, trying to service the first wave of impatient guests when a gorgeous brunette approached. She ordered a glass of wine which I immediately prepared. She snatched it up and disappeared into the crowd.

As the crowd thinned I continued working but at a slower pace. I caught a glimpse of her in the middle of the room. She must have been eyeing me because just as I looked at her she held up her glass, indicating a refill. Immediately I poured another glass, set it on the bar and gave her a hand signal then pointed to the glass. She pretended not to notice. I set the glass aside, thinking when she was ready, she'd come for it. Five minutes passed and the wine was still there.

Paul Carroll was making the rounds mingling with the guests. He stopped to talk to the woman. I caught a quick glance of them across the shoulders of guests. She made a subtle eye motion toward me. A moment later Paul was at my bar. He glanced at my name tag. "Jimmy. Did that woman ask you for another glass of wine?"

"Well, yes—but—"

"Why didn't you give her one?"

I tried to explain that I was busy and that we'd never been instructed to give individual service. He wasn't listening. Instead he said, "Take her a glass of wine right now and apologize to her for taking so long."

His command made me fume. He waited while I poured a fresh glass then accompanied me to her.

"Excuse me Ma'am," I said. "Your wine."

She and Paul looked at me. I struggled to hide my rage. "I'm sorry it took so long."

I expected a "That's okay," or "Don't worry about it." Instead she turned to Paul and said, "You've got to get faster bartenders."

Paul apologized again and then ordered me back to work. For a moment I bored my eyes into hers then glanced at Paul. I hoped he would back me up by pointing out procedure but he didn't. Finally I returned to my bar.

When I called him as Frank D'Antonio I got a different Paul Carroll.

The PBX operator connected me.

"Paul Carroll's office, Janice speaking. May I assist you?"

"Yes, Paul Carroll, please."

"He's in a meeting right now. Would you like to leave a message?"

"Tell him Frank D'Antonio's on the phone."

"Hold one moment, please." There was a pause.

"Mister D'Antonio! How you doing?"

"Fine, Paul. I hope I'm not interrupting you."

"Oh no, not at all. What can I do for you?"

"I'm calling about the transition. How is it going?"

"Okay, I guess. We haven't heard who's getting the ax yet. Is that what you're calling about?"

"No, I don't know who they'll keep. They will, no doubt, bring in some of their own people, but we've put a good word in for you," I lied.

"Thanks a lot. What can I do for you?"

"Paul, a while back we had an accident in the hotel involving Pedro Quero."

"Yeah. I called your brother immediately on that."

"I know. Did we ever get a formal report on it?"

"Yes, I'm sure we sent you a copy. Honest, Mister D'Antonio I know I—"

"Do you have a copy there?"

"Yes. We—"

"Could you get it? I'd like you to go over it with me."

"Sure, just give me your number. I'll call you back in ten minutes."

There was that damn question again.

"Uh, well, I'm on my way out the door. I'll call you back in a half hour."

"You got it. I'll be waiting."

It was amazing how my two lives constantly had me squirming. I was glad to know that Frank D'Antonio still had clout. I sat back and waited out the time.

I called back twenty minutes later. Janice put me right through. Paul had the report in front of him. I learned that Quero had been attending a birthday party for Diaz in his suite. There weren't many people there at the time. Apparently Quero had had too much to drink and was out on the balcony. No one seemed to know if he had been sitting on the railing or on a barstool.

"Was he over-served?"

"It certainly seemed that way, Sir, but we terminated the bartender immediately. All bartenders are well aware of our policies and he knew he wasn't to leave his bar unattended. Apparently he did."

"Why?"

"We don't know that, Sir."

"Did you speak with his supervisor?"

"Yes. I spoke with Ted McDounough. He's a good man, been with us eight years. He was off that night but his assistant, Barbara Griffen, was working. She said she didn't know why he had done such a stupid thing. Anyway he's gone. May I ask, Sir, why the interest in this particular matter? It has been months, and the police seemed to have closed the case. With all due respect, Sir, with the convention coming up, I don't think it's a good idea to bring attention to this right now."

"You're right, Paul. The attorneys for the new owners questioned it and I need to be able to answer their questions. Was anyone else in the room that night?"

"As I said, I was told there were many people who came and went, but at the time . . . let me see. Ah, here it is. There was Mister Diaz and . . . Mister Quero, of course. A man by the name of Vincente Perez, an Eddie Rodriquez, and two women, Rebecca Baker, and Virginia Sullivan. Jerry Cummings was the bartender. It says here when he left the room, at the guest's request, Mister Quero and two men were in some kind of heated discussion. The police asked him what it was about, but he said they spoke in Spanish—he couldn't understand any of it."

I thanked Paul and tried to sound sincere reassuring him about his job. But my experience with him as Jimmy the bartender made me realize that he was nothing but a ball-less little prick with a Napoleon complex.

He said he hoped the new owners would be as good as we have been. That was nice to hear, but I knew he wanted his job.

Paul had given me a lot to go on. The same people kept popping up. Virginia Sullivan. I had her number. She'd made it easy, had asked me to call her. It would be interesting to hear what she had to say.

Before calling Virginia, I let Mrs. Newman know I was coming. The phone rang once and she picked it up. She was thrilled to learn I was coming and went on about airing out the place. When I asked her to leave the key under the doormat, she balked.

"I don't like leaving keys lying around. Someone could take them."

Who would want our condo keys? There was nothing in there to steal except the furniture. I assured her it would be all right.

"Of course it's none of my business," she said. "But God knows if Miss Penny finds out. Tends to carry on, you know. Talks to me like I'm a two-year-old. Always reminding me about every little thing. I may be old, but I'm not senile."

"I'm sure it will be all right. I'll take complete responsibility."

She hesitated. "Well, I suppose, if you say so. Won't get much sleep though. All right."

We hung up and I set out to find Virginia's phone number. After sifting through the piles of assorted papers on my dresser I found the white, crumpled cocktail napkin with her number. I dialed from the bedroom. After the second ring, a woman answered.

"Hello?"

"Hello, Virginia? This is Frank. Remember? From the club? I won your boyfriend's money."

"Yes! This is a surprise! I gave up on you. I figured you threw my number away."

We made arrangements for dinner the next night.

"I'd like to keep this between the two of us," she said.

"What do you mean?"

"I mean I consider my relationships personal."

"Bad for business?"

"Excuse me?"

"Whatever. I won't tell a soul. What time?"

I know a great place on 79th Street. Why don't I meet you there? Say, seven-thirty?"

She gave me directions to the restaurant and we hung up. I didn't mind meeting her instead of picking her up. Hookers were usually discreet. Besides, I didn't know anything about her. Depending on how the evening went, I might want to make a quick getaway. I could do that a lot easier alone.

It was quarter to eight when I pulled up in front of the Steak Pit. I parked my car and trotted in. There was a small bar to my right. She was sitting alone in a short red dress, her long, slender legs lapped over each other. Her dress barely contained her. I apologized for being late, blaming it on the traffic.

"I've only been here a few minutes," she said. She was holding a glass of white wine.

"Do you want to finish that here or should we get a table?"

"I don't care. Let's go in."

I followed her into the half-full dining room and we were seated immediately.

"I had a really great veal dish the last time I was here," she said.

A waiter in a red jacket and black pants placed two menus in front of us and filled our goblets with water. She gave me a glance.

"What happened to your nose?"

"A little accident. I hear the food here is good."

She seemed to be deciding whether to ask more about the nose. But she ducked behind her menu.

"Can I bring you something to drink while you're looking at the menu?" the waiter asked, straining for an authentic French accent.

I looked over at her and asked what she was drinking. It was Chardonnay and I ordered a bottle.

She was engrossed with the menu. I studied mine. A moment later the waiter was back with our wine. He poured a little for me to taste. I nodded approval and he filled our glasses.

"Have you decided or shall I give you a minute?"

"I think we need a little more time," I said, checking Virginia to get her reaction.

"I'm still looking," she said.

I caught a glimpse of her eyes. They were deep blue. She was stunning. I examined her more closely. Her black hair hung like shiny silk to her soft, pillowy breasts. Red glossy lipstick matched her dress. *Black and red*, I thought. *What a combination.*

"I think I'll order that veal dish again," she said, setting her menu down. I looked back to the menu before she caught my stare.

"That sounds good to me too," I said. I raised my glass to her. "Cheers!"

She joined in and we sipped our wine and gave each other an amused glance. I'd seen her type before. I guessed by twenty she had moved here, drawn by the glamour, sunny days, and romantic nights. Guys like Diaz see her type coming. She's fascinated by good looks, smooth talk, and the expensive cars. He's looking for a sexy young doll to hang on his arm—a good piece of ass.

It's one big party, night after night. She falls in love with him and the lifestyle. Love and marriage are not in his mind. She probably doesn't approve of what he does. He isn't perfect, but he beats the hicks she knew back home.

What she doesn't notice is the years creeping by and she's still hanging around with no commitment from him. When she starts talking marriage and family, he throws her out and replaces her with a new twenty-year-old.

Our waiter brought our salad course, a combination of mixed greens in a vinaigrette dressing.

"I hope you won't get in trouble," I said.

"No, it's okay," she said, poking studiously at her greens. "He thinks I'm out shopping."

"How long you been with Victor?"

"A few years."

"Are you married?"

"Victor? Married?" she had just put a forkful of a combination of iceberg and endive in her mouth. After a moment she said, "Are you kidding? If I was married to Victor, do you think I'd be giving out my number to strange guys?"

"Why did you give me your number?" I leaned toward her.

"I don't know," she said, looking up. "You seemed like a nice guy." Then returning her attention to her salad, she said, "Besides, me and Victor have been fighting a lot lately. I was impressed when you beat him at cards. He doesn't usually lose, you know."

"I got lucky."

She mumbled something. I asked her to repeat but she let it go.

Our waiter appeared with the main course. She continued about her relationship with Diaz. It was what I envisioned. The names and places were different, but the story was the same. She was at the settling-down part of their relationship and just getting the hints that Victor wasn't going to marry her. She rambled. I half-listened and tried to think of a way to focus on Victor himself. It was obvious she was disillusioned, but her loyalty was still with him.

It surprised me how she carried on about being impressed with me. We were barely friends yet. Probably dollar signs in her eyes. She wasn't going to tell me anything she didn't want to, and I wasn't going to force anything.

Money, that was it. I'll offer her some cash. But she didn't strike me as hard core. Besides, she already had someone with money. Victor. Maybe she wanted to change sponsors. She knew I had money. After all, how could I have gotten into that card game? Did I really charm her with my looks, personality, and card playing? Money sounded more realistic.

My worries about how to start the conversation were solved by Virginia. Halfway through the Veal Oscar, she began.

"That night, after you guys were done playing, what an asshole he was. He was moody all night because of you."

"Because of me!"

"Like I said, he doesn't lose very often, but when he does he's in a bad mood all night."

That was my opening. "So does Victor gamble often?"

"Oh yeah, he gambles at the club, but he's always got guys in his suite. Sometimes they play cards all night. I think he likes gambling more than anything, even me."

"So, how do I get invited to his suite to play?"

"He only invites people he knows well to his room, but I know he wants a chance to win his money back."

"So how can I get hold of him?"

"Call the club. They can set it up for you. I'd tell him myself, but I don't think it's a good idea. You know what I mean?"

Carefully I was getting closer to what I wanted: Pedro Quero.

I took another sip of wine and refilled our glasses. "I get the impression Victor's room is kind of a dangerous place to be."

"What do you mean by that?"

My remark had struck a nerve. Suddenly she seemed cautious, defensive. I wasn't surprised. Diaz and Blanco were cautious men. They had to be, and she, no doubt, had learned as well. "Didn't some guy fall over his balcony a while back?"

I waited as I carved at my Veal Oscar.

"I thought this was gonna be a nice romantic dinner."

"It is," I said.

"So why all the questions? Are you a cop or something?"

"A cop!" I laughed. "I couldn't afford to play cards with Victor or bring you here if I was a cop. I'm sorry, I was just making conversation."

"I'm sorry too. Guess I get a little defensive sometimes."

We finished our dinner in the silence. Then she spoke.

"Hey, listen, I don't think Victor's ever gonna commit to me or any other girl, but he treats me good, so I guess for now I'll take what I can get. But, I don't know, there's something about you. When I first saw you at the club, you seemed like a nice guy. Like I said, I guess that's why I gave you my number. I took a big chance by doing that because Victor is very generous, but he's also possessive and has a temper. I know he also has a lot of connections and he's used to getting whatever he wants. He doesn't take kindly to anyone who tries to take what's his."

"So tell me an odd thing. Does he wear nine-and-a-half size shoes?"

She looked at me, wrinkled her nose. "What?"

"Nothing. He sounds like a hell of a guy!" I said.

"Listen, I shouldn't be telling you this either, but I'll say this one last thing. That night you asked about, Becky and me were in the room. I really don't remember much about what happened, but that guy Pedro seemed okay. Him, Victor, Vincente, and Eddie were talking earlier in the evening. It sounded like they were arguing. But you know when a bunch of Colombians start jibber-jabbering it sounds like they're arguing. You know what I mean?'

"Then they sort of stopped and everything was okay. But Pedro didn't seem to be in a very good mood after that. I remember they started playing cards and a woman came in. I think she worked for the hotel 'cause she spoke to Victor for a minute. Then she talked to the bartender. They left together. A little later the guys got up from the table to take a break and Eddie went to the bar for some drinks. Then they started playing cards again.'

"That's all I really know, cause a little later Victor told me to take Becky down to the lounge to listen to the band. It gets boring just hanging around watching them play. We were only down there a little while. When we got back, there were cops all over the place. I asked Victor what happened and he said he didn't know. He said Pedro started acting strange and they all took a break. Pedro went out to the balcony. The next thing he knew, they heard a scream, rushed out, and he had fallen. That's all I know. I personally think he jumped. He was acting so weird."

"What about the other two guys?" I asked.

"They're friends of Victor's. They're with him all the time. I think they're business partners, but I'm not sure. Victor never talks about his business to me."

"What does he do, anyway?"

"Importing, that's all I know."

"Coffee, that's right." Coffee, coke, what's the difference? Virginia wasn't going to tell me anything she didn't want to. But did she really know anything? Sometimes you get a sense if people are hiding something. I didn't think she was. If Diaz was the man I thought he was, he wouldn't let Virginia know his business. I poured the last of the wine and we sat back silent. Then Virginia started asking the questions.

"You want to know so much about Victor. What about you? What do you do?"

I was getting used to these questions and gave my standard answer about being in real estate."

Virginia certainly knew the good restaurants. In the tourist traps, the waiter usually lurks in the corner, waiting to rush you out so he can seat someone else. Turning the tables over meant more money for them and the owner. Tonight, after we finished our dinner, our waiter cleared our dishes and offered dessert. We declined. A moment later he appeared again with the check. I picked up the burgundy booklet with the check inside and slipped in cash, including a twenty-five percent tip.

"Are you ready to go?" I asked. She nodded.

Our waiter gave me a smile and bid us good night.

I knew cash made him happy. Waiters can avoid taxes on their cash tips, and owners always like cash 'cause they can opt not to show the sale.

"I had a great time tonight," Virginia said.

We strolled across the parking lot to her car.

"You're really a nice guy. It's good to know guys like you are still around."

We reached her car, a black Eclipse convertible. She turned and leaned back, resting her back against the driver's side door.

"I think you're nice too," I said. "The pleasure's been all mine. Maybe we can do it again."

Our eyes met. Slowly I pulled her to me. We kissed. Briefly, she responded. My emotions raced. Suddenly she pulled away.

"I can't do this," she said, fingering through her purse for the keys. She saw my quizzical look but without turning back, opened the door and slid in.

"I better go," was all I heard as she slammed the door and disappeared behind the tinted glass. I turned toward my car.

"Hey you!"

I turned. Her window was down.

"Call me again, will you?" Was she smirking?

I smiled back at her.

"Sure," I said. I stood in the lot with my hands shoved deep in my pockets. She drove away.

I thought about calling her again. I had started out for information from her and ended up mesmerized by her kiss. But now my pulse had slowed and now I was tired. One more night in the hotel. Mrs. Newman was probably holding vigil, wondering where I was. The condo was closer than the hotel, and safer. I decided to sleep in the condo.

I crept into the small courtyard and looked up. Light showed between closed blinds. I grabbed the keys beneath the mat and slipped in without turning on a light until I was locked in. I'd deal with her in the morning. I flopped onto the couch by the front door and dozed off.

Chapter Ten

The next morning I was awakened early by Mrs. Newman's humming and the slamming of her screen door at two minute intervals. I lifted my head enough to peer through the bottom of the blinds. She was seated at the little round table sipping her instant coffee and reading the paper, waiting for my door to open. I didn't mind the clattering. I wanted to get an early start. My bill at the Eden Arms was prepaid, but I owed for long distance phone calls. First I wanted to call Penny and let her know I'd moved. The phone was on the end table right by my head. I dialed her number; she answered right away.

"Hello."

"Penny, it's Frank. What are you doing?"

"I'm leaving for work. What's up? Did you decide about those papers yet? Are you coming up?"

"I don't know just yet. I called to tell you I've moved into the condo."

"Oh, that's great! Give me the number there. How's Mrs. Newman?"

I gave her the number and peeked through the blind. She was still there, standing her ground.

"Oh, she's good. She's an early riser. And quite a conversationalist."

Penny laughed.

"Hey listen! I talked to Harry Woods again. He says Diaz and Blanco go back a long way, and Martinez and Diaz are pretty close. Sounds like Blanco might be using Diaz to play "negotiator" with

Martinez, and is probably paying him well for it. Seen the *Times* lately? It ran a story the other day about how pissed off the Colombians are over the bad rep they have as drug dealers. It mentioned Martinez is trying to change that and have quotas raised to allow more Colombians into our country. What a joke. We don't let the good hard-working Colombians in but the drug dealers have enough cash to buy their way in."

"Harry also found out something about Pedro Quero. When he died, he was working for Martinez, his personal counsel. Think about these four guys and their relationships. Then think about this article about Martinez and what he's trying to do for his people. Quero's death could tie into it all. Well, listen, I have to go. Let me know if you're coming. I'm gonna tell your brothers you're at the condo."

"No, Penny, don't tell them yet. Give me a little more time. I'll call you."

I hung up and lay back on the couch, pondering Penny's theory. It sounded like the Colombians were putting pressure on Martinez; Martinez had put pressure on Blanco and his cartel; and Blanco put pressure on Diaz to do something about it. If Quero had been close to Martinez and was advising him, he could be a key for Blanco and Diaz.

Keeping track of the Colombian names was giving me a headache. I pushed the whole thing out of my head and looked around for a clock. I had no idea what time it was. If Penny had left for work it had to be close to nine. I found a digital clock on the bedroom dresser. Nine-fourteen.

I had to be at the Eden Arms before noon checkout. There was time for a shower. Mrs. Newman was thorough. She had all the towels hung out and had even unwrapped new soap for me. All my shaving things were in my room at the hotel so I couldn't shave. I hadn't shaved for years. I hated it, so I was glad. I didn't think one day's growth would offend anyone. The shower invigorated me. Even my sore ribs were feeling better.

I stepped out the door and caught a glimpse of Mrs. Newman, perched on her chair.

"Frank!" She called, catching the outer screen door.

"Good morning, Mrs. Newman! You're up early."

"Early! I've been up since seven. I couldn't sleep, you know. I was worried about someone finding your keys under the mat. Come up, Frank. I've made coffee—"

"I'm late. Sorry, maybe—"

"I've been keeping the water hot all morning. We didn't have a chance to talk the last time."

Just what I wanted to avoid: a visit with Mrs. Newman over steaming hot instant coffee. I climbed the stairs and joined her. She scooped two teaspoons of store brand coffee into a cup and added boiling water. She offered breakfast, which I refused, then went on about her responsibility to the condos and me now that I had moved in. I worked my way through half the cup—all smiles and half ears. How could I avoid these encounters? Finally I stood, made an excuse about errands, and promised we'd talk again.

"If you need anything just knock on my door. I'll be here."

"I'll do that, Mrs. Newman," I said, quickly descending the stairs. "Thanks for the coffee."

I drove to the Eden Arms and thought about my conversation with Penny. The convention. Martinez and the governor would be there. Visions of California in 1968 and Bobby Kennedy came to mind. I was only eight when it had happened, but I recall staring at the reruns on the TV. The media focused on it with each anniversary or whenever Sirhan Sirhan was up for parole.

I thought of going to the police with my theory. They'd laugh me out of the precinct. I thought of going to Paul Carroll, revealing my identity and telling him my story. He could beef up security. Without a definite plan, they'd be no match for Blanco. If he was planning something, only he knew it.

Of course I could be wrong about everything. I pulled into the circular drive of the Eden Arms. I handed the valet a ten and told him I wasn't staying long. I had learned from my coworkers that greasing the valets would give you parking privileges in front of the hotel. I'd always parked in front when we owned the Regency. I never realized a few extra bucks could make anyone a V.I.P.

I approached the front desk and was met by the clerk who had first waited on me. We had struck up quite a relationship. I'd made it a point to deal only with her during my stay. She was aware of the situation and it would save me having to explain every time I paid in cash. She was actually glad to see me now. Maybe my "cash customer" status aroused her curiosity. She looked disappointed when I explained I was checking out. I thanked her for her courtesy and went to my suite to pack up.

I stopped by the tennis shop at the Regency and made arrangements with Stacy to play the guest she'd told me about.

On my way back to the condo, I treated myself to a real cup of coffee. Black, the way I liked it, with a sesame bagel. Sitting by the window in a tiny café, I returned to the Diaz and Blanco situation. It frustrated me. Helplessness and doubt made me furious. I needed advice. Who could I talk to?

Gino! Of course! I could trust him. We'd grown up together in New York; we thought alike. Besides, he'd been coming down to Miami all along while I'd been away. He was respected by his friends and feared by his enemies. He was street smart—big and strong. I'd had occasion to witness just how big and strong.

I finished my coffee and headed home, eluding the ever-watchful Mrs. Newman. I called Gino immediately. He answered after three rings.

"Gino, it's Frank, what are you doing?"

"Hey! What's up, Kid? I was just on my way out the door."

"You feel like going to the beach for a couple hours today?"

"Sure! I'm going to the gym for about an hour, then I'm free till tonight." We arranged to meet at one-thirty.

I couldn't wait to talk to Gino. I'd finally be able to tell someone my story. It'd be good to hear his opinion. I changed into my swimsuit, grabbed my tennis shoes, a towel, and my bartenders' manual and headed for the beach. I had to be at the courts by four.

On the way I stopped at a 7-Eleven and picked up a six-pack of soda and a mini cooler. I parked in the adjoining lot and hopped the shuttle to the beach. The driver, an elderly gent with snow-white hair, apparently appreciated the local vegetation and took the opportunity to point out a bushy tree that was said to be endangered. No one could harm these trees. We needed them to keep us from losing our beaches to erosion.

Later, as we crossed a small bridge, he directed our attention to the swamp far below and the alligators floating around. I had learned about alligators. They were hard to see. Silent and unmoving, mostly. Looked like big, dark logs. I looked hard at one and wondered if he had any sense of me. Was he the one that Dan had encountered that night? Visions of Dan struggling flashed in my mind.

It was one o'clock by the time I made it to the beach. I took a spot just to the right of the entrance, then settled back to read while I waited. Gino showed up at quarter to two in bright orange swim shorts, sandals, and a black "Gold's Gym" muscle shirt. He was carrying two beach chairs.

"Gino! Over here!"

"Hey! Frank. I knew you wouldn't bring chairs."

He was right. I hated lugging beach chairs. It was easier to just grab a towel. "I brought us some sodas instead. How was the workout?"

"Good! Why don't you come with me one day? You should see all the broads over there! Besides, there's nothing like a good workout." He pointed to his nose. "Hey! What happened?"

"I'll tell you in a minute. Anyway, I've started playing a little tennis. I'm playing later today at the Regency. I met the pro there; she's a nice girl. She set me up with one of the guests."

"What happened to the guy pro that you guys—I mean—what was his name? Bob?"

"I don't know. Didn't ask."

"Did you talk to Paul Carroll? How's he doin?"

"I talked to him."

We settled in, covering ourselves with sun block. I wasn't one for umbrellas either, but it was what we needed to stay out for any length of time.

"So, what ya been doin? Why haven't you called me sooner? And what's with the nose?"

"I got jumped in the Eden Arms parking garage."

"You what—? When?"

"Same night I ran into you at the club."

"Know who did it?"

"No. I couldn't get a look at them."

"You got any ideas?"

"That's just it, Gino. I don't have a clue. I know there were two of them and while they were tap-dancing on my chest they said something about asking questions and starting trouble. I'm pretty sure Barbara Griffen knows something about it."

"Who's Barbara Griffen?"

"She's the assistant beverage manager at the Regency."

"What's she got to do with it? You bangin her?"

"Give me a break. She's not my type. Besides, she's, well... she sort of...."

"Sort of what?"

I could feel his eyes on the side of my neck while he waited for an answer.

"She's my boss," I said and turned to him. "I've been working."

"Working! As what?"

"A bartender."

"What'd you say? I don't think I heard you right." He sat up in his chair and dropped his sunglasses to the tip of his nose.

"I'm an on-call banquet bartender at the Regency."

"What the fuck! What the hell you doin?"

"Let me start from the beginning."

"Go head man. I'm listenin. This ought to be good."

I told Gino every detail of my story from the day in my lawyer's office to Dan Hiller's death. I told him my theory. Gino sat silently, slowly shaking his head.

"And that's it," I said.

He sat back, pushed his glasses back, and crossed his arms on his chest.

"I can't leave you alone for a minute without you gettin into some kind of shit. I'm gonna have to keep my eye on you." He laughed. Then he got serious again.

"The guys that gave you the ass-kickin were sending a message. If they knew who you really were, they would have said so. It sounds to me they meant it for you as the bartender. That's how you should look at it. The other thing sounds personal."

"What do you mean, Gino?"

"Well, I don't wanna bring up sore subjects, but you and your brothers sold the hotel, right?"

"Yeah, so?"

"So Frank, it can't be business cause what goes on in that hotel ain't your business anymore."

"Maybe it's not my business, damn it. Maybe it is personal. That motherfucker killed two people in the hotel. I didn't know Pedro Quero, but this Dan worked for us for eight years! He was a good guy. And the sign still says Regency, so call it what you want, business or personal. If that son-of-a-bitch Blanco is behind it, I want to know, okay? Now I'm asking you to help me. If you don't want to get involved, I understand."

Gino gave me a long look. "Is it that important to you?"

"Yeah, Gino, it is."

"Well, if it's important to you, I'm with you. I think you're nuts, but I'm with you."

"Okay, so here's what we're up against, Gino. These guys all work for Blanco."

"Yeah, I heard of that asshole. You start fuckin around with him Frank and you might get more than a bloody nose and sore ribs."

"I know it, Gino. But he's up to something and he's using the Regency to do it. I can't let him get away with that and I can't do it alone. But if you're with me Gino, we can get these bastards."

"You talked to anybody else about this?"

"I mentioned it to Penny."

"What'd she say?"

"Not much."

"She thinks you're crazy, too, doesn't she?"

"She doesn't know much. She's been nosing around when I ask her but she's busy helping my brothers."

"They know?"

"No."

"Well, Frank, thinking something's goin on ain't good enough. We gotta know more about these guys and exactly what they're up to. You can't go around pointin fingers at people without proof."

"You're right, Gino, we have to know more. I'll get Penny to help—I was thinking—maybe you could ask around down here. I've been out of touch for a while, and I can't go to Carroll."

"He probably doesn't know nothin anyway."

We hashed over the details then Gino changed the subject.

"Frank, I want you to know I felt shitty about what happened between you, your brothers, and the business. I know how hard you worked at it. I know you gave up a lot so you could run things after your father died."

"Thanks, Gino. I've thought a lot about you and how you would have handled things the way they came down. You were always tougher and smarter than me."

"I'm not any smarter than you, Frank—been around a little longer, that's all. Maybe gettin involved with your father and brothers was a mistake. I always thought you deserved better. Maybe you should have done your own thing by yourself. If you had, maybe that marriage would have worked out. You ever see Julia anymore?"

My throat tightened at the mention of her name. "No, not really. I heard she's still showing her face at all the right parties."

I reached into the cooler and grabbed two sodas. I handed one to Gino and snapped open mine quickly, downing some, hoping the suds would cool the burning in my throat. I took another sip then forced a cough.

"She seein' anybody?" he asked.

"I have no idea," I said. I couldn't tell if Gino noticed my discomfort. "It wasn't all her fault, Gino, us breaking up. I did spend a lot of time working. But that society bullshit— going to those parties with all those phonies—it just wasn't me."

"I know what you mean. A lot of times I wanted to call you, but I figured you needed time to sort things out. My old man asks about you all the time. I tell him I ain't seen you. He always talks about your father, what a great guy he was."

If Gino wanted a heart-to-heart talk, he sure knew what buttons to push.

"You know, Gino, I wasn't a very good son. All those years me and my father always butted heads. He took a lot of shit from me and always turned the other cheek. I realize now I just didn't understand him when I was young. I don't know if it was his money or his power I resented the most. I never realized what he went through. When you think of it, he really accomplished a lot. Not just as a businessman. He was a good husband and father. He never made excuses for his life; he did what he thought was best for my mother, brothers, and me. I remember all those arguments. He'd talk to me about being honest. How much a man's word should mean. How a man should live by certain rules and codes like loyalty and integrity. I resented him badgering me like that. I thought he meant I wasn't living up to his expectations. But all he was trying to do was to make me understand what was important.'

"I think because I came along so late in life for him, he thought he wouldn't be around too long, so he tried to cram a lifetime of wisdom into a few years. He was disgusted with my brothers too. The way they were—or shall I say, trying to—run the business. He was constantly using up favors bailing Carman out of trouble. He knew how Carman used to bully his way around town, drinking and making scenes, trying to pick up anything in a skirt. Angelo, he was no better. You remember. When the union was striking all the big hotels in the city, Harry Hellman called my father."

"That was right after Lydia slapped one of our pickets," Gino added. "What a bitch. Don't know what Harry ever saw in her. Your father apologized for Harry and we almost had things worked out."

"Yeah, until Angelo stuck his nose in. Yelling and screaming at that union rep your father sent over."

"Yeah, I remember. Your father already agreed to everything. I couldn't understand that."

"I know, Gino. He threw the guy out and told him the deal was off. My father was so pissed. Your father understood and things worked out. But that's what Angelo's like. Who the fuck was he to change deals my father had made?"

I took a sip of soda, checked the sand at my feet, and then turned back to Gino. "I guess me and him just ran out of time. There just wasn't enough time."

We slid back on our reclining chairs and let the afternoon sun bake us. Our talk had relaxed me. I was glad to get so much off my chest. When I looked at Gino, his eyes were closed. I lay back and did the same. The sound of the surf and the warm breeze soothed me. We stayed like that for many minutes. Gino's voice brought me back.

"After all those years, your father gettin on your case about your long hair and beard. I wonder what he'd say if he could see you now?"

I leaned forward in my chair and looked at him. His eyes were still closed. Then he grinned, squinted at me, and we laughed.

"Gino, you think these guys are really up to something?"

"Well, you know Diaz is here. You've seen him. This guy Quero, he's the one who took the swan dive. Right? That was no accident—and Diaz, he's no killer. Quero worked for Martinez. It don't look like coincidence to me. Now Martinez is comin to town. Somethin's goin on, Frank. You can bet on it. What about this Virginia broad? Get anything outta her?"

"No, she doesn't know anything. If she does, she's not talking. Diaz has a suite at the Regency. If we could search it, we might find something. Then we can go to the cops."

Gino was sitting up, rubbing sun block into his already well-tanned arms and chest.

"Yeah, you could," he said. "But how the fuck you gonna get into his suite?"

"I'll give Diaz a chance to win his money back. Let's set up a game at the club."

"That's no problem," Gino said. "Then what?"

"While I'm taking his money again, you can search his room. What do you think?"

"How am I gonna get in there?"

"I'm friends with a couple of the maids in housekeeping. I'll ask them to give me one of the master keys they use when they clean the rooms."

"I don't know, Kid. You think they'd do that for you?"

"Gino, you wouldn't believe what goes on in these hotels. The workers take care of one another. It's like back in New York. You take care of me today and tomorrow I take care of you. And let me tell you another thing. Don't ever believe the managers know what's going on. You want to know something, ask the bartender or a dishwasher or a maid."

"One of the bartenders I work with has been banging one of the room service waitresses. Last week she was working the graveyard shift. He stopped over after getting off at midnight. She called the front desk, found out what rooms were empty, grabbed the key from housekeeping, and they went up, banged the shit out of each other, he went home, she went back to work! And her partner covered for her."

"That's fuckin amazing."

"So Gino, you set up the game at the club. While I'm over there playing, you search the suite. Try to find anything you can about Blanco, Diaz, the convention, and what they're up to. We'll be playing for at least two or three hours, so you'll have plenty of time to search. And Gino, make sure you put everything back exactly like you found it. As soon as you're done get out of there and call the club. We'll meet back at my place later."

I waited for a response from Gino. I needed his help. What would I do if he said no?

"Well, what do you think? Are you okay with this?"

"I'm fine with it, Kid. Just make sure Diaz doesn't take all your money."

"Don't worry, Gino. I haven't lost my touch at the table."

We laughed, held up our soda cans and toasted to our success. I checked my watch. I had twenty minutes until my match. I couldn't wait to see Stacy again. We packed up our things and Gino said he'd call after he set up the game.

He beeped as he drove away, leaving me to put on my socks and tennis shoes in the parking lot.

I thought about our plan. It worried me, but I couldn't think of anyone better to have with me than Gino. He was fearless and tougher than any man I'd ever known. Physical strength, however, was no match for Ricardo Blanco's kind of power. If anything ever happened to him, I'd never forgive myself. We could both be getting in over our heads.

Was it justice or vengeance I wanted? I didn't know. Maybe it was because they were drug dealers. Like my father, I hated drug dealers. Maybe it was an excuse to vent my frustration. Maybe subconsciously I felt obligated to the hotel or the people there or even the city of Miami which, like New York, had been good to my father. Maybe it was loyalty to my family, a need to protect our name so rumors wouldn't blemish what my father had so carefully protected.

As I made the short drive from the beach parking lot to the tennis courts, I tried to settle on a reason. Maybe it was all of them. I couldn't believe how quickly—almost overnight—my life had become so complicated.

Chapter Eleven

I scanned the courts looking for my partner. I didn't see anyone. I was glad. I wanted a chance to talk to Stacy. Maybe ask her for another date. She'd done a great job decorating the cube-shaped tennis shop. I entered through the tinted glass door and walked a short distance. The shelves on both walls were crammed with tennis things: shoes, shirts, shorts, and skirts. Every type of racket hung from the wall behind the glass-topped counter.

I approached a short brunette with long, curly hair. Her nametag read “Adrian.” She was busy stringing rackets.

“Hi Adrian, my name's Jimmy. Stacy set up a match for me with one of the guests.”

“Yeah—Mr. Mills. He just called. He said he'd be a couple minutes late.”

“That's fine. I'll need a can of tennis balls.”

“Sure, just help yourself.”

She pointed to the shelf and I walked over and plucked a can of green Wilson tennis balls.

“Where's Stacy?” I asked.

“She's over there finishing up a lesson.”

She turned her head, indicating the tennis courts visible through the large window at the back wall of the shop. I paid for the balls and Adrian resumed stringing the rackets. I wandered over to the rear window and observed Stacy in the middle of the court as she rhythmically punched tennis balls at her middle-aged male student.

I could see her lips moving simultaneously, offering instructions while strategically moving him back and forth on the court. She seemed so content in her domain—manipulating and encouraging and happily showing her approval when the ball came back at her properly. She fed him the last ball in the basket next to her, indicating that the lesson was over. They exchanged a few words, then she left him to pick up the balls scattered over the court. A moment later she entered the shop.

"Hi, Jimmy! Where's your partner? You have a four o'clock court time, right?"

"Yeah. Adrian said he called and said he'd be a little late."

I wanted to ask her out again. I felt like a teenager asking some girl to the prom. When she moved toward the soda cooler by the front door, I joined her.

"So, did you give him a workout?" I motioned toward the court where her student was still retrieving balls.

"I don't know who works out who." She took a sip of soda. "It's hot as hell out there."

"You feel like pizza again tonight?"

She gave me a look. "I don't think so. I'm beat. I was gonna have Adrian close up for me. I don't have any more lessons, and I'm gonna go home and relax. Besides, you gotta play tennis."

"Well, I'll be hungry after I'm done. What about you? Don't you have to eat?"

"I think I'm just going home, take a hot shower, and relax."

"How about I pick up a pizza when I get done playing and bring it over to your place. That'll give you time to take a shower and relax."

She hesitated.

"Free delivery!" I added.

She smiled. I shrugged trying to let her know it was no big deal. But it was.

"Well, okay but—"

Just then Mister Mills appeared. I introduced myself and told him I'd meet him on court five. He left and I grabbed two white towels for us from the stand by the front door then looked at her.

She looked back then smiled slightly. "I live just over the causeway, off Seventy-First Street. I'll leave the directions for you before I leave."

"Okay! Great! I'll see you later," I said and headed off.

It was almost seven o'clock by the time we finished our match. Two long sets left us exhausted and sweaty. We each won a set and agreed it was too late and we were too tired to play the third and decisive one. We shook hands and I told him to call the shop if he wanted a rematch before he left town. Then I was off.

My plan was to go home, call in a pizza, take a quick shower, and head for Stacy's house. I'd pick up the pizza and a bottle of respectable red along the way. There was a small strip mall on Biscayne Boulevard right near her house with a Big Daddy's Liquor store and a place called Pizza By Dominick.

The dashboard clock showed eight forty-one when I pulled into Stacy's apartment complex. A sign said, "Welcome to Falling Waters." I crossed a small bridge past a manmade waterfall.

She lived on Camelot Court. I checked the directory listing the individual courts with arrows. Camelot was small, and I scanned the court for her car. I picked it out immediately and parked two cars away. I found her apartment and used our beverage to tap on her door.

"You made it. Come on in."

She stepped aside and I entered.

She took the red and white cardboard pizza box and carried it past the kitchen area on the right to a round glass-topped table already set with two cloth placemats, paper napkins, and knife and fork. Behind the table a counter separated the kitchen from the dining and living area. She was shoeless, wearing faded red shorts that hung loosely above her knees and a silky white top which overlapped the shorts.

"So, how'd you do?"

"We split sets. He won the first one 6-3 and I won the second 6-4."

"You didn't play a third?"

"Are you kidding? I didn't realize how out of shape I was." I didn't mention my sore ribs.

"Sounds like you had a good workout."

"Yeah, it was pretty good. You have a nice place here."

"I like it. I don't like renting though, but I'm not sure if I'm staying. Grab these, will you?" She pulled two wine glasses from the kitchen cabinet and passed them over the counter to me along with a wine opener and two plates.

"I'll let you open the wine," she said.

I popped open a Bardolino made by Bolla. I hadn't eaten all day and the beach talk with Gino and the tennis had stirred up my appetite. Stacy looked hungry too. Neither of us spoke. By my third piece, I was ready to socialize again. I asked about her day. She asked about my job. I checked her through the bottom of my first glass. She caught me.

"What's the matter?" she asked.

"Nothing—more wine?"

"Sure."

I refilled our glasses. Being with her was refreshing. A breeze from the balcony doors behind her sent a faint scent of perfume toward me. It was a healthy, clean fragrance. I wanted to move closer to her.

"So now it's my turn," she said. "What about you? No girls in your life?"

For a change I was glad for a question. Suddenly I felt comfortable opening up a little.

"You mean was I married? Yes. Not very long."

"Any kids?"

"No."

"What happened?"

"Well, she came from a well-to-do family. She was into the social scene. She liked the big house, big cars, the cocktail parties."

"And you couldn't afford to give it to her, right? Where'd you meet her? The hotel you were working?"

"Well, not exactly."

I pulled another slice of pizza onto my plate.

"Anyway, I tried to keep the marriage together for as long as I could. One morning in February, I came home and found a note." I forced a tight smile. "She'd left." I stared into my glass then looked at her. "It was tough on both of us. Just two people with nothing in common except a bad marriage."

"Sounds pretty bad. So, would you do it again?"

I looked at her. I almost said yes. "I don't know. I guess, like you, I have to learn to trust again."

We sat for a moment, and I emptied the bottle equally between us. The wine was making my eyes glassy. I looked at hers; they were the same.

"How about some music," she said. "This oldies station I listen to plays what they call Midnight Memories from nine to midnight."

"I love the old songs," I said.

She directed me to the couch. I sat back on the white leather, feeling completely relaxed. She went over to the radio, flicked the button. "Crystal Blue Persuasion." That took me back. Sitting in the back seat of Carman's car on our way to the beach. I must have been about twelve. It was when I started growing my hair long; when my interests shifted from baseball to bikinis.

She began cleaning up. I made a gesture to assist but she told me to sit.

It was one of those evenings when you make last minute plans and they turn out perfectly. "Crystal Blue Persuasion" gave way to "Unforgettable" which was just finishing when she returned and plopped down beside me.

"This is one of my favorite songs!" she said as the DJ played "You and I."

We sat back and listened as the music and wine mellowed us. Any other time or place, my first intention would have been to end up in her bedroom. But this was different. She was different. She was cautious; so was I. I respected her and I wanted her to respect me.

She leaned forward to pick up her glass from the coffee table. Everything stopped for a moment. I'd been here so many times before: wine, music, and the woman. We'd exchange looks. At the right moment, I'd pull her toward me and kiss her. I'd feel her lips responding to mine. My hands would search, caressing her. I'd put her hand on my thigh and the routine would begin. But tonight was different. I felt awkward, unsure of myself. I thought of our conversation about trusting again.

We sat silently for several moments.

“Is something wrong?” she said.

“Wrong? What could be wrong?”

Suddenly I turned her toward me and kissed her. I could feel her start to respond. We fell back against the couch. Then she pulled away.

“I'm sorry,” I said.

“Don't be. I—I want to kiss you, I do. But—”

“What?”

“It’s just—it was wonderful. But I’m not ready. I don’t know how to trust.”

Elvis Presley was singing “Welcome to My World.” We finished the last of our wine.

“You want some more? I think I have some here.” She got up to find a bottle she had in her kitchen. We spent the evening talking and listening. It was one great song after another. It was almost midnight when I left. She walked me to the door. I turned and gently pressed her mouth to mine.

“Thank you,” I said.

“Thanks? For what? You brought the pizza.”

“I'll call you tomorrow,” I said and left.

I woke the next morning thinking about Stacy and the night before. With all the expensive dinners I'd had in all the fancy restaurants with dozens of women, I'd never thought that a pizza, a mediocre bottle of wine, and a radio could make me feel so good. My rage about Diaz, Blanco, and the convention didn't seem so pressing.

I had work at the hotel that night so other than a call to Stacy I was going to relax at home. I had no food in the condo and suddenly it seemed important. I didn't even have coffee. I threw on some clothes and headed to the supermarket. At three o'clock I called Stacy. She was busy with guests. We tentatively planned a day on the beach during the week. After a shower, I was off to work.

I passed the hotel security office on my way to punch in. A notice was posted, announcing special badges to be issued to all employees and worn at all times. It was June already. Three months had passed since I'd begun my new life. Now—with Stacy—it had taken another unexpected turn.

Activities at the hotel were moving along conspicuously toward the upcoming convention in September. The extra security precautions were especially obvious. Every square inch of the huge structure was being checked and rechecked. The heads of security were meeting on a biweekly basis, holding seminars on all kinds of scenarios, making sure the crew was ready for anything.

For me, it was a typical night at work. The excitement of the upcoming convention was slowly overshadowing the recent gruesome events. No one was talking about Dan or the accident anymore. There wasn't much time for talk anyway. Each department was holding its own meetings on procedure and policy. There was tension in the air. Tempers were flaring among the staff and management. The entire hotel was under pressure. The end of the convention couldn't come soon enough.

Politicians aren't known as big tippers. From the banquet department's point of view, it was a straight fifteen percent with little chance that a good-hearted delegate with a memory of waiting on tables to pay for college might throw an extra five dollar bill.

I went right home after work. I'd picked up an answering machine that afternoon and already there was a message. It was Gino saying he'd made arrangements for the game. Diaz was out of town but would return in a few days. The game was set. Tomorrow I'd make arrangements with housekeeping for the master key.

Getting the key, as I suspected, was no problem. I called off at work for the next few days. I spent most of my time with Stacy. Her days were busy, but it was officially off-season so she could slip out early to go to the beach. The warm salty water was restoring my ribs.

On our first afternoon on the beach Stacy surprised me with a gift.

“I brought you something for your scrapes,” she said, handing me a tiny tube with the word “aloe” on it.

“Aloe... what's that?” I asked.

“It comes from a plant. It's magic.”

She leaned back with a smile, her eyes playing with me. I must have looked skeptical, “Trust me, this will help.”

She unscrewed the cap and squeezed a little onto her fingers. “Just lie back,” she instructed, “Don't worry, you'll like it.”

Whether from the aloe, the sun, or Stacy's solicitations, the scrapes on my nose were disappearing. We'd settled into a comfortable routine: evenings at her apartment; home by eleven and a lot of time strolling on the beach, except for Sundays. Sundays were reserved for a kids tennis clinic. I'd assumed it was for Regency guests.

Every week she'd load a bunch of demo rackets and a basket of balls into her car and drive to Manatee Park, an inner city play ground with rusted fences, torn tennis nets, and cracked courts. The baselines were so faded that she'd use white chalk to make them visible. A group of kids would be waiting. She'd put them through drills and coordinate mini matches that lasted till late afternoon. Afterwards, while the kids retrieved the balls and loaded them into the car, she'd pass out cold cans of soda from a cooler in her trunk.

I'd told her about Gino, saying he was my close friend, and left out the important details. I had to explain our getting together Sunday night as a kind of guys' night out.

Chapter Twelve

I looked out the front window into the courtyard. It was overcast and rain seemed imminent. There was no one outside, not even Mrs. Newman. I called Gino and asked him to come over for coffee. I wanted to go over some details about our plans.

While he was on his way over I jumped into the shower. I stood in front of the mirror combing back my hair. The sight of my hairless bare face brought back the heckling I took from my brothers and the look on my father's face when he'd say, "Frankie, when are you gonna get a hair cut and wash your face?"

Well I had a "clean" face and a haircut now, and my life seemed to be taking a better direction because of Stacy. My thoughts were interrupted by a knock on the door. I threw the comb down and noticed the plastic key card.

I stuck it in my pocket and went to the door. It was Gino. I poured us the coffee I'd put on before my shower.

"I haven't been here in a while," he said. "Your brothers come down at all?"

"I think Angelo uses it once in a while."

"What about the other one? You rent it out?"

"I think so, but Penny handles that from New York, and Mrs. Newman takes care of them down here. She lives upstairs."

"That little old lady? She was sitting out there when I came in."

We talked for a while. I told Gino about Stacy. He laughed and asked if she was "the girl of the week."

I knew what he meant. I started to protest but then let it go. He wouldn't have believed my protest either. It was easier to talk about business.

Gino set the card game for eight o'clock. Sunday was usually a big checkout day at the hotel, which meant low occupancy and little staff. It would be easy for Gino to get into the room. All he had to do was slip the key into the slot and walk in as if he belonged there. Who would question him? Even if someone saw him, he could act like one of Diaz's men, waiting for him to return. The plan seemed foolproof, but I was still concerned about letting Gino go through with it. With our plan set, he seemed more determined than I.

"Gino," I counseled, "you don't have to rush once you're in there but don't take all night either. And don't forget to call me as soon as you're out."

"Will you lighten up? We already went over all that! It's gonna be all right...I tell ya!"

"Are you sure Diaz is going to be there? He's not gonna back out, is he?"

"I talked to Artie. He set everything up. He knows what he's doing. If Diaz cancels, he'll let me know."

"Gino, can you trust Artie? He wouldn't screw us, would he?"

Gino stood up, smiled slightly and said, "Artie? He knows better. I'll talk to you later."

I spent the afternoon flipping channels on the TV and staring out the window at the rain falling in the courtyard. Before I knew it, it was quarter to eight. I called Gino and let him know I was on my way.

"You okay, Kid? You sound a little tense."

"I'm okay. I'll call you from the club after I'm sure he's there."

"I'll be waiting. Get yourself a drink before you start playin. Don't forget, Diaz is no fool. If you look real nervous, he might get suspicious, and you'll fuck everything up."

"I'll talk to you soon, Gino."

It was just after eight when I pulled into the parking lot. I walked past the main bar and up to the club. Artie was waiting for me, smiling from ear to ear.

"Hey Frank. How you doin? So you gonna try and take more of Victor's money. He hates to lose, you know."

"So do I, Artie. Is he here?"

"No, not yet."

I handed Artie a fifty which he politely folded in two and slipped into his pocket.

"I'll be over at the bar."

"Sure, Frank. Hey, if you need anything, just let old Artie know, okay? Oh, and I'll let you know when Victor gets here."

By my first sip of scotch, Diaz arrived. He had two well-dressed men with him. One had a scar just below his left ear. Bodyguards I assumed, but they looked like bullies to me. Diaz wore a black suit with a canary-colored shirt buttoned to the neck. No tie. Virginia was there too, looking as gorgeous as ever. She wore ivory. Low cut, short, and stuck to every curve of her body.

Artie directed them to the bar. The two goons went to the table. Virginia and Diaz joined me, arm in arm.

"Good evening," he said.

Virginia smiled at me.

"Honey, you remember...Frank, wasn't it?"

"That's right," I said.

Our eyes met. She pulled at his arm. I offered them a drink, but they declined.

"Why don't we get started, Frank?" he said.

He had a piercing stare. His long face seemed cut from stone under the dim lights. I glanced over at her then downed my scotch. Had she told Diaz about our dinner?

"Artie has a table for us in the back," he said.

They started for the table. I followed. Diaz and I sat down with one of the goons and two strangers. The Croupier drew chips for everyone.

"What about him? Doesn't he want to play?" I said.

"Oh... Frederico, he doesn't gamble."

"Too bad. He's got a real poker face," I said.

"Becky's at the bar, Victor," Virginia said. "I'm gonna talk to her."

"Go ahead, honey. Tell her I said hello." She gave him a peck on the lips and left. He motioned for Freddie to follow her. Then he turned his attention to the table. I knew from our last meeting that as much as Diaz hated to lose, he wasn't a very good card player. Taking his money would be easy.

After fifteen minutes of play I needed a reason to leave the table. I glanced over at Diaz. He was happy; he'd won the first couple hands. We played another hand and he won again. He thought he was on a roll, but I hadn't even begun to concentrate yet.

"I guess this isn't your night, Frank."

"Yeah, maybe you're right," I said. "I think I'll get a drink."

"Don't get up, Frank. I'll have someone bring you a drink."

"That's okay. I want to stretch my legs anyway. Can I bring you something?"

"Not me," Diaz said. "I never drink when I gamble. Hurry back though. We don't want the cards to cool off on us."

The bar was crowded. I looked around for Virginia while I waited for the bartender. She was nowhere in sight.

"What can I get you, Sir?"

"Scotch and soda and I'll be right back. I'm going to the men's room."

There was a pay phone right outside the men's room door. I punched in Gino's number.

He gave me a raspy hello.

"All set, Gino. Call me as soon as you're done."

"No problem. Make sure you don't lose all your money."

"Good luck to you, too." We hung up. I grabbed my drink at the bar and returned to the table.

"I'm back," I said. "Maybe the scotch will change my luck."

Diaz laughed. "You keep thinking that, Frank, and I'll get richer."

With Gino on his way and our plan in motion, I could concentrate on the game. It didn't take long to turn my luck around. Diaz was losing again and not liking it. The two strangers dropped out. First one, then twenty minutes later, the other. That left me, Diaz, and the goon named Eddie.

"You're a talented man, Frank," Diaz said. "It seems I have no luck when it comes to you, or maybe you have more talent than you show."

He thought I was cheating. Why would I have to cheat? He was a terrible player. After watching him for a couple hands, I noticed he'd fiddle with his chips when he was bluffing and instead of checking, he always raised. Real amateur stuff.

"It must be the scotch," I said.

His face turned unfriendly. "Maybe it's the atmosphere," he said. "I suggest we adjourn to my suite and continue our game. Perhaps my luck will change there."

I couldn't believe my ears. He had caught me by surprise. What could I say? I had to think fast.

"What do you say, Frank?"

"Well, I fail to see any reason for moving the entire game, just because you're losing."

"Oh come on, Frank, humor me. I have a suite at the Regency. It's just down the street. It's a nice place. You ever been there?"

"Yeah, I know—"

"After all, Frank, as a gentleman, do you think it's right to refuse me this small request? You're winning. What's the difference? I'm sure you'll find my accommodations adequate. You don't even have to drive. You can come with me and I'll have you brought back when we're done. We can be there in ten minutes."

Ten fucking minutes. Suddenly the room felt too warm. I

glanced down at my watch. It was nine-thirty. Diaz sent Eddie to gather up Virginia and "Scarface." I decided to drive myself and agreed to meet in the parking garage.

We entered the elevator in the parking garage. It was nine forty-five. As we took off, I thought about Gino. What time was it when I had called? If he had left right away, how long would it take him to get into the suite? How long would it take him to search the room? Diaz said something, jolting me back to the moment.

I watched the round, white lights flashing at each floor as we ascended. Any other time we'd be stopping at each floor to pick up more people. Tonight, of course, we went straight up. The door slid open and we walked a short distance down the hallway to his suite. I held my breath. He opened the door. I caught a glimpse of the room as I walked in. The light was on. I didn't like that.

"Come in, gentlemen. Make yourselves at home."

Diaz seemed distracted, not himself.

"Eddie, did you leave the lights on when we left?"

"I don't think so, Victor. Maybe the maids came in."

"Of course, the maids. Why don't you get us a drink, Frederico?"

My chest tightened, I could barely breathe. The bedroom door was closed. Was Gino in there? I watched the door as Diaz approached.

As he entered, Frederico asked what I was drinking.

I checked his jacket for bulges. Was Freddie packing a gun? If Gino was in there...

Virginia left the room. I started calculating. If we were caught, I'd take Diaz. I'd leave the two goons for Gino. Freddie brought my drink. I took a long sip. The alcohol calmed me. I called to Diaz who had just entered the bedroom.

"Hey! I thought we were gonna play cards? Where are you going?"

I turned to Freddie and Eddie who were busy preparing the card table.

"Is that where he keeps his marked decks?" They ignored me. "Just kidding."

I took another sip. The ice cubes rattled against the glass. I wondered if my hands were trembling. My heart pounded as I waited for Diaz to return. My shirt collar felt damp. I took my seat at the card table. Something was wrong. I knew it. I sat staring at the bedroom door. Finally he came out. His eyes were long dark spots. Slowly he came toward us. I tried to read him. He stood behind his chair opposite me. The chandelier over the table blocked my view of his face. His long, veiny fists clenched the back of his chair. I think he was staring at me, but I couldn't tell.

"You look edgy, Frank. Is something wrong?"

"No, just waiting to play."

Sit down, I thought. Gino wasn't in the room. We wouldn't be sitting here if he was. Maybe he'd left some clue. Finally Diaz pulled out his chair and sat down.

"Deal the cards, gentlemen," he said.

It was almost one when I left Diaz's suite. He was right. The new location changed his luck. After each winning hand he gloated about his good fortune and what a good sport I was. It was irritating. I suggested a last hand. He won. We tallied up what I owed. I set twenty-eight thousand dollars on his table, we stood and shook hands. He showed me to the door, smiling triumphantly, "Let's do this again," he said and opened the door.

"Sure," I said. The door closed behind me and I headed down the hall to the elevators. I was irritated about the screw up, losing to an asshole like Diaz, and about the heckling I'd get from Gino. Gino was supposed to call me at the club when he was out of the suite, but I wasn't at the club. I drove there, hoping he would be waiting. I found Artie unwinding at the bar.

"Anybody looking for me?"

"Hey Frank, how'd you do? No, nobody I know of."

I decided to try his condo. I punched the number. He picked up immediately.

“Hey Frank. Where you been?”

“Where have I been? What about you? Meet me at my place; I'm at the club. I'm leaving right now.”

Fifteen minutes later I was home. There was a message on my machine from Gino telling me to call him at home. I was listening to it when he knocked on my door.

“Gino! What happened to you?”

“What happened to me? What the fuck happened to you?”

“That fuckin Diaz decided his luck might change if we moved to his suite.”

“How much you lose?” he asked.

“How do you know I lost?”

“I know,” he chuckled. “One thing, I was there, I heard you. I didn’t wait around. Diaz’s bullshit remarks were getting to me.”

“But Gino. I don't understand. How the hell…”

“Those secret doors your old man put in still work.”

I was speechless. Gino was gleaming. The same closet doors that saved us from my father had saved us from Diaz.

“Those fuckin secret doors!” I said. “I should have known. What’s the other reason?”

“I was talking to Artie when I went back looking for you. He told me the game at Diaz’s suite is fixed. He’s a cheater. That’s how he wins back what he loses at the club. Fuckin guy. He meets the players at the club. If he wins, he’s happy. If he loses, he sets up a game in his suite and wins it back. Artie would have warned you, but he didn’t realize what happened until it was too late.”

“That’s okay, Gino. Win some, lose some. Come on, let’s have a drink.”

I popped open a bottle of Louis Latour Pouilly I had chilling in the refrigerator and Gino told me what had happened from the time he heard the door open and Diaz welcomed us in. He'd found a briefcase under Diaz's bed and was snooping through papers when he heard the door open. He slid the case back under the bed and retreated to the only logical place to hide: the closet.

“That's when I remembered the secret doors. I figure what the fuck, I'll give it a try. You believe the fuckin things still work?”

He explained how he followed the hallway to the stairs and down three flights to the eleventh floor where he took the guest elevator down to the parking garage. He then stopped at the Flamingo, had a drink at the main bar, then drove home and called my place.

“The thing is Frank, I didn't find anything.”

“Nothing?”

“Well, nothing out of the ordinary. His passport, aparking garage

Swiss bank account booklet, some check receipts made out to Friends of Lawrence Dudley. There were at least two checks, ten thousand each. Contributions. But there ain't nothing illegal about supporting the candidate of your choice. I told you you were crazy. Just forget the whole thing.”

He took a last sip of wine, picked up the bottle, and refilled his glass. “I was shooting' the shit with Tommy,” he continued. “He told me Kevin, the beverage supervisor at the Regency was in there the night I ran into you. He asked who I was.”

“So, what about it?”

“He told him I worked for the union.” He gulped down the last of his wine and said, “That might explain why you got jumped.“

“What do you mean?”

“Maybe they think you're tryin to help me organize the place. Union is taboo around here. If the Regency's going through a change, the last thing they need is a union guy tryin to talk it up with the help.”

“Ted McDounough's not the kind of guy who'd have me beat up. I don't think he's got that kind of juice.”

“He may not, but what about that bitch, Barbara? You said you seen her with Diaz.”

“Why wouldn't they just fire me?”

“For what? They got to have a reason with or without a union.

Being an on-call bartender, you're not there fulltime but enough to interact with your fellow workers. Besides, from what you told me, this Barbara sounds like she's on a power trip."

He set his glass down, got up, and said, "It's just a hunch. And it makes more sense than guys gettin pushed off balconies and getting fed to the alligators. Think about it. He paused. "Well, I gotta go. Give me a call tomorrow."

"Okay, Gino. Thanks for everything. I'll call you."

My Diaz theory had reached a dead end and maybe Gino was right about the beating I took. A misunderstanding, a case of mistaken identity. John Palmer had his doubts about me. Ted got awful defensive when I asked about Pedro Quero. Maybe Kevin added it all up with our conversation after tennis. Then the clincher—me and Gino together at the Flamingo. In any case, it didn't matter. They were dead issues and I was relieved. I lay in bed thinking about Stacy till I fell asleep.

Chapter Thirteen

I was about to pick up the phone and call Stacy when it rang.

"Hi Frank."

"Penny. What's up?"

"I need to know what you want to do about these papers."

"Oh yeah, I forgot. Why don't you send them down and I'll sign them. How's everything going up there?"

"It's coming along. One other thing, there was an article in the *Times* this morning about Luis Martinez and the convention."

"Yeah. So?"

"Well it had a picture of Martinez and his guys in it. I recognized one of the men."

"You recognized one of them? Who?"

"Victor Diaz." There was a pause. "Frank? Are you there?"

"Yeah, I'm here, Penny. What do you mean you recognize him?"

"Well, I've seen him before."

"Okay, you've seen him before. Where? Penny, are you trying to tell me something?"

"Okay. I don't know if this means anything, but about two weeks before your father was killed, I remember seeing Diaz in your father's office. He came in with two other men and they had a long discussion with your father."

"Diaz in my father's office? Discussion? About what?" I asked slowly.

"I don't know. The door was closed."

"Were my brothers there?"

"Yeah, they were there. Anyway, I remember after they left, your father was really upset. He told your brothers to leave and then he just stayed in his office for the rest of the day."

"So what are you trying to say?"

"I don't know. It's just that they had a meeting with your father. Then he gets killed. Now after all these years this guy Diaz turns up again."

"You don't have to say any more. I know what you mean."

So there would be no closing the book on Diaz, Blanco, and all the insanity. Here he was again, haunting me. Not a dead end—a detour.

"Penny, you didn't hear what they were saying?"

"No. Why would I be listening? Your father had meetings with people all the time. Besides, how could I hear? The door was closed. I didn't think anything was wrong until after Diaz left. Then your father started yelling at Carman and Angelo, but I couldn't make out anything. After a few minutes the door opened and the two of them left. I walked past his door and stuck my head in. I asked him if he was okay. He said yes and told me to close the door again. That was it."

"How come no one told me about this?"

"I don't know; I just assumed your brothers would have told you."

"Well, they didn't. I wonder what else they haven't told me."

"What do you mean?"

"I don't know. Nothing. Where are you, Penny?"

"At work, of course."

"Is either one of them there? No, never mind. Forget sending me those papers. I'm coming up."

"When?"

"Uh, tomorrow, see if you can get me on a plane tomorrow. After you make the reservations, call me back. If I'm not here, just leave a message. And Penny, don't tell them I'm coming."

"Frank, you have an open return, remember? Just call the airline down there; you shouldn't have a problem."

"Okay, but I also want you to make reservations for me to come back to Florida."

"You're going back down?"

"Yes, I'm only staying a few days. I'll explain when I get there."

I hung up and called the airline. They booked me on a seven-thirty-a.m. flight. Then I called Gino. We met an hour later for coffee at Brueggar's, where I told him about my conversation with Penny.

"You know, there were some rumors going around about your father doing business with drug dealers. I remember my old man was pissed off about it. He didn't believe any of it. I didn't either. He said he was gonna ask your father about it, but then he figured it was none of our business. After your father died, my old man said he wished he'd said something. They could have taken care of that piece of shit back then."

His expression changed. A frightening look I'd seen before. His eyes darkened. They seemed to bore into me. A moment later it was gone. "But the cops investigated the whole thing and ... well ... you know the rest. They came up with a drive-by shooting. You were just getting involved in the business. We thought your brothers would do their own investigating. I guess they didn't."

"Why not, Gino? I always thought that myself, but I'm gonna find out. I'm going up to the city."

"When?"

"Tomorrow."

I told Gino I'd be back in a few days. I had to call the hotel and tell Ted I'd be away for a few days and then I went to see Stacy.

Business was slow in the banquet department. Ted even told me to take two weeks. He said we'd all be working a lot soon enough.

My rental car was becoming expensive. Car dealers were offering great deals on leases. My plan now was to drop off the rental and have Stacy take me to the airport the next day and pick me up when I returned. Then I'd lease a car.

I walked into the shop. She was perched on a stool, stringing a racket.

"Where is everybody?" I said.

"Well, I didn't have any lessons today and occupancy's down in the hotel, so I gave Adrian the day off. Did you and Gino have a good time last night?"

"Yeah. It was great."

"Are you working tonight?"

"No."

"Well, I'll be getting out early. Why don't you come over for dinner?"

"Sure. But listen, I'm leaving for New York and I need to drop this car off before I go. I was wondering if you could follow me to the car rental place, then I'll need a ride to the airport."

"A ride to the airport! When are you going?"

"Tomorrow."

Her head dropped and she went back to stringing the racket.

"Stacy, what's wrong?"

"Nothing," she said without looking up. "Are you coming over for dinner?"

"Of course. I have to pack, then I'll come here, wait for you to close, and we'll drop the car off. My flight leaves at seven-thirty tomorrow morning."

Stacy's drop of spirit puzzled me. Was she losing interest in me or was she afraid I wouldn't return? I decided to believe she wanted me to come back.

We agreed to meet at five and, when I returned, Stacy had already locked up. She followed me to the car rental. I dropped off the car and we went to her place.

Stacy didn't say much during dinner. I tried to make conversation; she wasn't contributing. We'd both finished our Fettuccini Prima Vera and three quarters of a bottle of pino grigio. She put down her fork and replaced it with her glass.

"So, vacation's over. You're going home."

"I'm going to New York, on business. I'll be back in less than a week."

"All of a sudden you have business in New York?"

"Yes, something's come up."

"Wait, let me guess, the hotel you were working at wants to give you your bartending job back and you have to negotiate. Or maybe your wife made you a better offer."

"My wife's not even in New York."

"How do you know that?" she said, pulling the plate from between my elbows and retreating into the kitchen. I followed.

"Gino told me. Stacy, I know this is pretty sudden and I really can't explain it now, but you have to believe me. I'll be back within a week. I wouldn't lie to you, honest."

She was bent over the sink. I reached out for her arms and turned her toward me. I brought my lips to hers. She turned away but I persisted. I kissed her. She squirmed. I kissed her some more, deeper, longer. Slowly she relaxed.

"I don't know why, but I believe you," she said.

"I wouldn't lie to you."

"Will you call me when you get there?" she asked.

"I'll call you every day."

We looked into each other's eyes. I'd convinced her.

We opened another bottle of wine, put on the radio, and listened to Robin Ward singing "Wonderful Summer." We decided I'd stay the night and we'd swing by early in the morning for my suitcase. She retired to the bedroom and I headed to the couch. It had become a pattern.

The seatbelt sign went on and the attendant announced our descent into Kennedy. I had never called Penny to tell her what time I was coming. I cabbed it right to the office. It wasn't quite eleven-thirty when the cab dropped me off in front of our building.

I stood in front for a minute. Summer had come to New York.

The heat hadn't slowed anyone down. I felt insignificant as people raced past me. With suitcase in hand, I went in. I passed a security man sitting behind his desk.

"Good morning, Mister D'Antonio. Nice to see you."

I stopped and looked for a nametag. I didn't see one. "Good morning," I said and approached. "Where's your nametag?" I asked.

My question seemed to surprise him. "Uh, well I—"

"It's okay. I just didn't know your name."

"It's Henry, Sir."

"Henry," I held out my hand. He gave me a puzzled look then slowly extended his. "It's nice to see you too."

I made my way to the elevator and pushed the button. For a moment, I looked back at him. I turned away and waited for the elevator, but couldn't get him out of my head. Was he married? Did he have children? What did he do when he wasn't sitting behind that desk?

The elevator door opened, breaking my thought. I got on and smiled to myself, amused at the whole scenario. Had Miami changed me that much? The elevator door opened again and I shook off the thought.

I stepped off the elevator. Our offices were at the end of the hall. I could see Penny working away at her desk as I approached the tinted glass doors. I opened the door and entered the office.

"Hello, Penny."

"Frank! How are you?" She looked at me with wide-open eyes and a quarter-moon smile. I followed her as she came around and we embraced. I smelled her perfume, like spring flowers.

"I don't believe it! You shaved! You look great!"

"So do you." I said.

"Why didn't you let me know what time you were coming? I would have picked you up."

"I wanted to surprise you. How are things around here?"

"Coming along. We're almost done. Angelo says we're gonna

rent some space here from the new owners and keep a small office operating. I guess I'll still have a job for a while."

"See, I told you there was nothing to worry about. Are the boys in?"

"Carman's in there. Angelo left a half hour ago. He should be back. I didn't tell them you were coming."

"That's good. What are you doing tonight?"

"Nothing."

"Good, let's have dinner. You pick the place."

"Okay."

"Well, I better go in. I'll talk to you later."

I walked down the short corridor past my old office, all the way to the end. I turned the gold doorknob, looked down and held it for a moment then swung the door open. Carman was behind his desk on the phone. He gave me a startled look.

"Let me call you back. Okay?" He hung up the phone. "Frankie! What a surprise! I didn't know you were coming home! You finally did it! You shaved! You look beautiful! Sit down."

I sat down in one of the two chairs facing his desk.

"How's the vacation?"

"It's good. I'm going back."

"You're goin back? What do you mean?"

"I mean, I'm only here for a few days and then I'm going back."

"A few days? What are you talkin about? I want you to come out to the house. You gotta see Ma. She's been worried about you."

"Where's Angelo?"

"He left early. He's not feelin good, Frankie. We didn't know you were coming. He would have waited."

He leaned back, his hands folded behind his head.

"So how's things in Florida? Have you been to the hotel at all?"

"Yeah, you can say that."

"You talked to Carroll? He's pretty worried about his job. I told him we'd put a good word in for him. I don't think it's gonna do any good. These guys'll probably bring their own people in. I would."

"Carman, Penny called me about some papers that need to be signed."

"Yeah, just some last minute legal bullshit. I think she's got 'em out there."

"She told me someone you know made the front page of the *Times.*"

"Really! I never have time to read the paper. Who was it?"

"Victor Diaz."

Carman slowly changed positions, leaned forward in his chair and slipped off his glasses.

"What's the matter Carman? You okay?"

"Yeah, I'm okay."

"Penny says he's been in this office. He came to see Dad. She said you and Angelo were there too. Is that true?"

"Listen, Frank. You forget about him; he's trouble."

"If he's trouble, what was he doing here?"

"You don't understand. I can explain."

"Good, I would like you to."

"Frank, it was a long time ago. Just leave it the hell alone."

"What'd he come here for, Carman? He had something to do with Dad dying, didn't he?"

"Frank, I told—"

"I'm waiting, Carman. Tell me." I could feel my momentum building. So could Carman.

"Calm down, Frank. You don't understand. I tell you what, come out to the house with me. We'll have something to eat. You can relax and we'll talk about it."

"No, I want to talk about it now. I'm not leaving this office till you tell me."

He got up and moved from behind the desk. He stood immobile by the window and stared down at the street, his hands sunk in his pockets.

"Okay. You wanna know? I'll tell you." He turned and faced me.

"Diaz did come to see Pop. Ricardo Blanco, that piece of shit, sent him. He came to offer Pop a deal. He said Blanco had a lot of money to invest and he wanted to buy into some businesses in the U.S. He heard about Pop and his reputation and figured he'd be the guy he needed to help him. He offered Pop a great deal, Frank! No risk at all on our part. All Pop had to do was negotiate the deals. He offered Pop a piece just to put them together and he told Pop if he had any new prospects he would put up all the money. Pop's name could be on everything; he'd be a silent partner. We could have made a fortune!"

"But you know Pop! Stubborn as hell. He wouldn't even listen to Diaz. His mind was made up even before the guy walked in. He told Diaz to get the hell out of his office. Then he told him to tell Blanco if he knew what was good for him he better find another place to clean off his dirty money. He told him if he found out he was trying to do business in New York, he'd be sorry."

"After Diaz left, we tried to explain to Pop. What would it hurt to help Blanco a little? Pop didn't realize what kind of people those Colombians are. He got all pissed off and threw us out, too. Christ, he'll back somebody like Alfred Lewakowski, a broken-down gum maker and that loser deli owner Sol Novak, but Ricardo Blanco comes to him and he not only turns him down, he threatens the guy! We could have been big, Frankie! I mean really big!"

"So you'd do business with a drug dealer, is that what you're saying, Carman?"

"Oh come on Frankie, it's business. We weren't gonna marry him!"

"What about Dad getting killed?"

"What about it?" He moved slowly back behind his desk. "You remember. We called in a lot of favors and had everything checked out." He rested his fists on his desk and leaned toward me. "He was just in the wrong place at the wrong time." He stared at me a moment then moved toward the window again.

He used two fingers to massage the bridge of his nose as if deep in thought. “How many times did we tell him not to drive through the old neighborhoods? Those old neighborhoods had become dangerous ghettos. Now you know that and he knew, too, but it didn't stop him.”

When he reached the window he turned toward me. “You keep putting Pop up on this pedestal. He was a great father and I loved him just as much as you did, but Frank—wake up! Pop had a lot of enemies. He always said about the business, this was what we chose so we gotta take the good with the bad. Do you think we should have started pointing fingers at everyone? We decided it was best to let things slide and forget it.”

“I don't believe this, Carman! Don't either of you have any balls?”

“Frank,” he said, pointing his finger. “Watch your mouth.”

I lowered my tone. “Why wasn't I told about any of this?”

He threw his hands up. “What good would it have done?”

I stood and walked back toward the door. Over my shoulder, I said, “What good would it have done?” My momentum was returning. I turned, pointed my finger. “I was part of the business too. Were you too proud or afraid I could settle the problem? That wouldn't make you look very good, would it?”

He traced his steps back to his desk. “I don't have to listen to this, Frank. You can think whatever you want; it's not gonna change things.” He was waving an outstretched palm toward me. “What's done is done and if you want some good advice, stay away from those guys or you'll be sorry. I know your feelings might be hurt, but I'd rather hurt your feelings than have to cry at your funeral.”

I folded my arms across my chest. “Save the sentiment, Carman.”

“It's not sentiment. We had Mom and our families to think of, in case you haven't noticed. What were we supposed to do, pick a fight with a bunch of Colombian drug dealers! They’d kill us all as quick as you can blink an eye. We'd not only be putting ourselves in danger, but our wives and kids too."

I dropped my arms, rested my hands on my hips. "There were things we could have done, Carman. You should have told me."

"You never wanted anything to do with the family business back then, so we left you out and that wasn't just Angelo's and my decision, but Pop's too. You're so worried about Pop; did you ever think that he could have told you all about it if he wanted? You with your arrogant attitude and your liberal views. You resented everything Pop worked his ass off for. While you were running around enjoying yourself, me, Angelo, and Pop were running the business. So why don't you just forget it and go on with your life?"

Suddenly my argument didn't seem so strong. Carman was right. I hadn't cared about the business back then. But things were different now. Why didn't my father tell me about Diaz? Carman was right about that too. He didn't want to tell me. Why? Was it because I'd hurt him by not showing any interest? Or maybe he just didn't want me involved in a world he could see changing before his eyes. I had been wrapped up with myself. I couldn't see. My father had had feelings too. Everything seemed so confused. I shook off my thoughts and focused again on Carman.

"After Pop died, we figured our total investments would be more than we could ever need to support us very well—you too. Why stir things up? We figured we could coast through with your help then we could sell out to a legitimate company, which is what happened. How can you complain about that?"

"How can I complain? I admit I didn't fall right into the business like you and Angelo did. I wasn't sure what I wanted to do."

His eyebrows arched. "Oh?" He said crossing his arms across his chest then glanced at me over his shoulder. "You weren't sure what you wanted to do? That's putting it lightly, don't you think, Frank?" He turned, leaned against the windowsill. "Tell me, the four years you spent in college, what'd you go for?"

"Business."

To my surprise and my father's delight, I had been accepted at

Cornell University. He didn't say much to me, just "I'm proud of you Frankie." But shy of placing an ad in the *Times*, he let everyone know. When I left for school he handed me a credit card and told me to charge anything I needed. I thanked him and took it, but I decided to use it only for bare necessities.

College was a breeze. I managed to get high grades with very little studying, which left me a lot of free time. For spending money, I worked in the cafeteria and hustled a few bucks playing cards. Before long I'd organized a group of amateur players and realized I could make even more money running the game as well as playing.

The fact that, unlike most of my fellow students who sponged off their parents for spending money, I opted to work in the cafeteria, made me a hit with my coworkers. I'd established myself as a good worker who took a sincere interest in them and my job. I made a hush-hush deal with one of the cooks to supply me with sandwiches for the players at a discount for cash which went directly in his pocket.

My father was pleased to see that there were very few extra charges on his credit card, but how I did it baffled him.

After graduation I had no idea what I wanted to do. My father wanted me to come to work with him, but to me that was a cop out. I didn't spend four years in college to just slide into a position created by my father.

I tried selling commercial real estate but filling out contracts and sales pitches wasn't me. I even pursued an acting career for a short time. I was confused and frustrated. I couldn't seem to find my niche, but I was determined to make it on my own without my father's help. I still hustled cards and occasionally freelanced for my father as a go-between when there were problems with contractors or property managers. Unlike my brothers, who were content coming to work in their suits and sitting behind a desk, I liked being out in the field mixing it up with workers. I learned a lot by listening to their issues.

"And what about the year after, when you decided you wanted to go to acting school? And what about the gambling, which Pop always blamed me for."

"Yeah you're right about all that, Carman, but Dad did bring me into the business. If he didn't want me in, he would have left me out."

"You were working part time—when you felt like it."

"I was learning the business Dad's way. The right way. He didn't keep anything from me and he always said communication was important in business. Remember our weekly meetings? The four of us talking about whatever we wanted? That all ended when Dad died. So maybe I was irresponsible about my life back then, but the fact is I was a part of the business before and after Dad died. You used me to run the day-to-day business when all the time you were planning things behind my back."

He moved away from the window and centered himself on a brown leather couch. I walked across the room and faced him.

"You think you got all the answers, Frankie. Always thinking of you. Did you or anybody think about me? Frankie doesn't want to work in the business, he doesn't have to. Frankie wants to go away to school. Sure. Wherever he wants to go. Frankie wants to screw around in Florida. Why not? I didn't have that luxury. I didn't get to finish college." His volume had increased and his face turned red, veins appearing in his forehead.

"Oh come on, Carman, you didn't finish college because you didn't want to."

"That's cause Pop wouldn't let me go away to school. I had to go to school here so I could spend my time with him learning the business. Did you ever think maybe I might have wanted to do something else? But I never had a choice. Christ! I couldn't go anywhere without him keeping tabs on me. Angelo'd make changes in contracts, piss off some goddamn manager, and Pop would take it out on me. I was the one! Angelo got married young. He settled in with his wife and family. I waited. I was the one out there at night going around buying drinks for people, spreading goodwill for the D'Antonios all out of my own pocket. I never made any decisions. Angelo was the oldest. Him and Pop made them all. Carman was there just to carry things out. Then you finally decide you're ready to take over the family business, so now Pop starts confiding in you. I was passed over, Frankie! I didn't deserve that!"

He picked a half-smoked cigar out of an ash tray on the coffee table in front of him, pulled a match book from his shirt pocket, struck a match and held it to the cigar, focusing on the end till the smoke showed it was lit. He rested his elbows on his knees, pulled the stub from his lips.

"Do you know Angelo is real sick?"

"I know he's not feeling well."

"No, Frankie, he's sick. Prostate cancer. He's dying. If you'd take the time to ask about your brother, you'd know. Did you ever think he might want to enjoy some of his money before he dies?"

I struggled to hide the shock on my face. "Cancer. What? I knew he wasn't feeling good but… Why didn't he say something?"

"What was he supposed to do, put an ad in the paper?"

"Well… Does Ma know?"

"Yeah, but she doesn't know how bad it is."

"What are the doctors saying?"

"He's going for chemo. They're waiting to see how the treatments go."

"How's he doing?"

"Okay, I guess." We stayed silent a moment. He leaned back on the couch and continued. "So we had a chance to sell out to these companies and I made the decision."

He glanced up. I stared back at him.

"*You* did Carman? *You* talked Angelo into selling out?"

"Yeah, I did. For once I made a decision."

"I'll see you later, Carman," I said and turned for the door. He followed.

“Where are you going, Frankie? Wait. We'll go out to the house.”

“I can't now. I have things to do.”

“How long you staying?”

“I don't know.”

I walked out and pulled the door closed behind me. I signed the papers Penny needed and told her to call me at my apartment.

“You okay?” she asked.

“I'm okay. I’m going for a walk. See you later.”

I walked for a while. A mixture of guilt and rage consumed me. A bus passed. The marquee advertised weekend excursions to the Casbar. When I reached the Metro Tower on Fifth Avenue, the tightness in my throat made me panicky, lightheaded. There was a coffee shop on the first floor. I thought I’d go in then decided to hail a cab and go home.

Chapter Fourteen

My apartment was different from those last gray January days. Sunlight streamed through clean, white curtains. The empty pizza boxes were gone, the bed was made, the place was immaculate. I threw myself on the bed and stared up at the ceiling. I'd always looked at my father as a hero. Angelo and Carman were old enough to be my father. They were so protective when I was small. I never stopped to think that they were human too and not perfect. Carman was right. I was always so wrapped up in myself. I thought about Angelo. What he must think of me. His selfish little brother so caught up with himself that no one else seemed to matter. Carman's words kept returning. I never looked around to see what was going on.

Angelo did make a lot of decisions, mostly bad ones, and he was a hothead. My father had to step in and change things he had done and Angelo didn't like it. My father would make promises to people. Angelo would break those promises. When the people would question him, his answer would be, "That's the way it is boys, take it or leave it."

Sometimes my father would pick Angelo's brain, ask his opinion on a certain subject. When my father didn't take the advice, Angelo would scream, "If you weren't gonna do what I said, what'd you ask me for?" The fact was Angelo and my father were completely different when it came to business.

I felt guilty mentally criticizing Angelo in light of his condition, so I turned my thoughts to Carman. He was right about going around town, but it wasn't goodwill he was spreading. Carman would move on anything in a skirt; it didn't matter if she was with someone or not. He only stood about five foot six, but he did everything in a grandiose way. With him it was always big cars, big cigars, and even big women. And he'd pick a fight with anyone who looked at him cross-eyed. Luckily there was always someone around to bail him out of tight situations. He was a big tipper, so he thought he could do anything he wanted.

One time, in Harry's Playmore Club, a known hang-out for New York City cops, Carman had been drinking. He scanned the bar until his eyes focused on an attractive brunette. She was with a guy. It didn't matter. Carman sent them over a drink, which they politely acknowledged. While the man went to the men's room, Carman moved in. He introduced himself. But it didn't take him long before he had his hands all over the woman. She told him her boyfriend was coming right back. "Why don't you tell that asshole to get lost and you and me can get out of this toilet and go somewhere else."

"Listen," she said. "My boyfriend's a cop so cut the shit if you know what's good for you."

"A cop! What's his name? I know almost every cop in the city."

Just then the cop returned. "Hey! What's going on here?" he said.

"This asshole's got his hands all over me. Tell him to get lost."

"You heard the lady, asshole, take a walk."

Carman answered in his usual tactful way: "Fuck you."

That was it. The cop went for Carman. Thank God for Harry Woods and his bartenders. They broke up the fight. Harry Woods cringed every time Carman came into the joint. The only reason he wasn't banned was because Harry and my father were close friends. He'd put his arm around Carman, lead him away and tell him picking fights with the police was trouble.

When my father found out, he blasted him. He reminded Carman he had lived his life free of embarrassing blemishes from sleazy performances like those and if he didn't care about his own name, he should consider his father's. Carman tried to make excuses for what happened, but my father sent him running back to work. These memories were uncomfortable. My eyelids felt heavy. I felt myself falling asleep to my father's last words: “Take care of yourself.”

My phone rang. I checked my watch. Six-thirty. I felt disoriented. I cleared my head and realized I was back in New York.

Penny was on the line. She told me to meet her at Jason's in Tribeca at seven-thirty. I took a quick shower and put on a clean shirt and pants. I called Stacy and got the answering machine. Where was she?

I took the elevator to the street and cabbed it downtown. It felt good to be back in New York. The noise, the people, and the peculiar Manhattan mix of grilled meat and exhaust fumes were like nowhere else.

Tribecca was a former industrial area recently transformed into “the place to be,” with restaurants emerging out of old warehouses. Jason's was one of those places. I entered the typically crowded bar and elbowed and shouldered my way through, searching for Penny. I found her in the middle, wedged between patrons.

She reminded me I was only twenty minutes late. I ordered a scotch on the rocks and we chatted while we waited for a table. Three quarters of a drink later, the maître d' led us across the waxed hardwood floor to a small room with hanging plants and Tiffany lamps. We ordered more drinks and studied the menu. I found nothing appealing. I asked the waiter for advice. He was trim, well-built, and young with a feminine lilt in his voice. He suggested the grilled tuna. I agreed. Penny ordered the same.

“You shaved; I don't believe it. What's the matter—those young Florida girls aren't into beards and mustaches?”

“Well, I wanted a new look. Besides I'm working part time and I need to look clean shaven.”

“You're working? Come on, Frank. Oh—I get it. That's why you were staying at the Eden Arms. You made a deal with Paul Carroll to take a room there and spy on the competition." She laughed at her thought.

"Very funny, Penny," I said.

"So, what *are* you doing?" she asked.

"I'm working at the Regency as an on-call banquet bartender."

She gave me a dubious look. "Cut the shit, Frank."

"No, I'm serious."

The waiter brought our dinner. I ordered two glasses of house white and for a few minutes we both enjoyed the tuna presented picture perfect, camouflaged among the four baby carrots, three asparagus spears, a tablespoonful of whipped potatoes, and a sprig of fresh rosemary. I tried to read her.

"Frank, I know what you've been through with the sale and all but you taking this job, bartending at the hotel—that's insanity."

"Penny, I've learned so much about myself and about people in the short time I've been there. But that's not all. There's a lot more going on in the hotel."

"Like what?"

"Like murder."

"Murder! What are you talking about?"

"Remember I asked you about Pedro Quero?"

"Yeah, and I told you that was an accident. Didn't you talk to Paul Carroll? What's he think about you working as a bartender?"

"He doesn't know. Nobody knows who I really am, and yes, I talked to him."

"So how'd you pull that off?"

"I talked to him over the phone. Anyway, listen. This guy Dan Hiller, who worked in the banquet department, had what's being called an accident. They pulled him, or what was left of him, after the alligators finished with him, out of the swamp. Penny, I don't think it was an accident and neither was Quero's death."

I ordered more wine and filled Penny in.

"I think Barbara, Andre, and Diaz are involved in something. I don't know—maybe Dan was too."

The waiter cleared our plates. Penny eyed him as he walked away. Then she leaned toward me.

"So you think maybe Diaz had something to do with your father's death?"

"Carman says no."

"Let's say everything you've said is true, what do you want to do about it? You can't go raising holy hell with Carroll. You're not his boss anymore. In fact you work for him now. See—that's what I mean. This whole thing, working as a bartender—it's stupid. What if somebody recognizes you?"

"Nobody's gonna recognize me." I rubbed my chin.

"I'm incognito, and my name is James Anthony. Everybody calls me Jimmy."

She leaned forward and gave me that quarter-moon smile. "Well, I must say I almost didn't recognize you without the beard and mustache."

The waiter suggested dessert, some raspberry concoction with a foreign name. We passed. I paid the bill and we returned to the bar. I ordered two sambucas and two espressos. Three rounds later, the conversation was getting deeper. I decided we should leave when she started asking questions about women. I was about to tell her about Stacy, but thought better of it. Now was not the time.

We left Jason's at twelve-thirty. It was a beautiful evening. The traffic had died on the sidewalks and in the street. We grabbed a cab and took it to Penny's apartment. I wasn't ready to call it a night. I plopped myself on the steps of her brownstone. She sat down next to me.

"Frank, I know what you've been through this past year. Now you got this thing about Diaz that's come up. I don't know what went on between you and Carman today, but I always felt as much a daughter to your father as you and your brothers were sons. I miss him and at times I blame myself a little for what happened. But nothing we can do can bring him back now—or the business. You've got to put it all behind you and go on. Let it all go, Frank.

You'll see—in time, things will get better."

"Do you believe in destiny, Penny?"

"That's a big word, Frank. I don't think about it much. Why?"

"All the years, working in the business—you know—I never felt right. I didn't fit in. I wasn't comfortable. Even my marriage. I felt the same way about it. It was like I was forced into a situation where I didn't belong. Even after my father died, and we were running the business, I didn't feel right. My brothers talk about all the money we're gonna have. Well, money is not what it's about with me. Is money gonna help Angelo? I think having the business dropped in his lap after my father died might have been too much for him. Maybe that's why he's sick?"

"Anyway, as far as I'm concerned, it's not my money. My father built up the business and made the money. Me and my brothers have just been going along for the ride. They might be all right with it, but to me, it's phony. My father had nothing and look what he did. I can't float along on his coattails. I have to make my own mark. And believe it or not, this job has helped me."

"Oh, so what are you gonna do, tend bar at the Regency the rest of your life?"

She fingered through her pocketbook and pulled out a crinkled cigarette and a book of matches.

"Didn't you give those up yet?"

"I only smoke when I'm irritated. *You* are irritating me."

"No. I'm not gonna tend bar forever. That's not what I'm trying to say. What I mean is if my father hadn't died, the business would never have been sold and I'd still be there going through the motions and hating every bit of it. Don't you see? It was this last minute trip to Florida and this crazy idea of mine to apply for a job at the hotel that started it all. And look what I've found out since then! You see what I mean about destiny? And one more thing, just the other day, after me and Gino struck out at Diaz's suite, I was gonna pack the whole thing in and then you called. Explain that!"

She took a final drag before tossing the cigarette toward the curb.

"I don't know about destiny," she said. "But if you feel comfortable with what you're doing, go with it for now. Maybe it will give you some kind of closure and then you can go on with your life. Besides, if Diaz and Blanco had anything to do with your father dying, they should pay."

I was surprised by her objectivity, but seeing Diaz's picture in the paper must have aroused her suspicions. I think she was looking for answers and in her own way was telling me to find them.

"Listen. I'm beat," she said, "Why don't you come up, crash here tonight, and we'll have coffee together in the morning."

"No, thanks though. I'm gonna walk for a while."

Penny climbed the steps to the outside door of her building. She held the door open and called to me. I turned and looked up at her.

"Call the office tomorrow. Let me know what you're doing."

"I'll probably see you there. Oh...and Penny, thanks."

"Thanks? For what?"

"Just thanks."

I strolled along for five or six blocks then hailed a cab to my place.

Our long talk and the booze had completely unwound me. My head hit the pillow and I awoke to a ten o'clock summer sun. I still had one more question I needed answered and then it was back to Florida.

I called and reserved a one o'clock flight for the next day. After a quick shower and shave I grabbed a cab back to the office to see Angelo and Carman. I pushed open the glass doors. Penny was already at her post, hard at work.

"Morning, Penny."

"Morning, Frank. Did you sleep well?"

"Like a baby. Are they in?"

"Yep."

I headed down the hall and entered the office. There was a simultaneous click of the door and silence in the room as I entered.

"Morning, Frankie," Carman said.

I returned his greeting and turned to Angelo. The initial news about his condition had shocked me, but still I wasn't prepared for what I saw. *Oh God, where'd you go Angelo?* I thought. I wanted to put my arms around him. Instead I struggled not to stare. He said hello, teased me about my new look, but his voice was weak and raspy. His handshake was limp. He'd lost weight and most of his hair. He smiled at me with watery, bulging eyes. We embraced each other.

"How you feeling?" was all I could say.

"Better than I look. How you doing? How's Florida? I'm definitely coming down this winter. Carman says you're going back."

"Yeah."

"What are you gonna do down there?"

"I'm keeping busy. What am I gonna do up here? You guys seem to have everything under control."

"Sit down. I'll get us a cup of coffee."

He walked around behind the desk, pushed the intercom and called for three cups of coffee then sank into the chair. Carman centered himself on the couch and I took my seat in front of the desk.

"Carman tells me you ran into Victor Diaz."

"Yeah, that's right I—"

"Listen to me Frankie. I'm your oldest brother and you're like a son to me. Stay the hell away from Victor Diaz."

"Why wasn't I told about him, Angelo?"

"Pop said he didn't want you to know about Diaz coming to see us. We didn't question his reasons; we just did what he said. What's the sudden interest in him, anyway?"

"Wasn't this meeting you had with him just prior to Dad's death?"

"Yeah, so what? Frankie, if you think Diaz had something to do with Pop's death, forget it. We had it checked out. It was an accident. I don't know why you're starting up all this. It's all history. Put it behind you. You'll have the money soon and you'll be all set."

"This isn't about money, Angelo. So Diaz and Blanco wanted to buy into the business and Dad said no. Is that it?"

"Yeah."

"So if Blanco and Diaz were looking for a front and Dad refused, who did they buy into?"

"I don't know. Who cares?"

"Well, they tried Terry Donlin," Carman said. "But he turned them down too. He was getting his balls busted by that new attorney general in Albany. It's all over this bullshit about the mob and his disposal business. He almost made a deal with the Grano brothers, but that fell through too. I don't know why."

"Well, he must have made a deal with someone."

"Maybe not. Maybe he's still looking. Frankie, there are a lot of people out there that would or could front him. The thing is it's none of our business."

"I'm not so sure about that. Well, I have to go. I want to stop out and see Ma. I'll be leaving tomorrow."

"Tomorrow! So soon! Frankie, why don't you come back? Forget Miami and all this business and we'll be together *here*."

Angelo seemed earnest as he spoke, even a little urgent. Maybe he needed me and was too proud to ask. How could I say no, go back to Miami like everything was all right. But I was in the middle of turmoil myself. I needed time. But there didn't seem much of it left for Angelo.

"Yeah, Frankie, we're still a family," Carman added.

"I have to go back, there are some things I need to do," I said. "Let me think about it."

We shook hands and hugged each other. We were still a family but it would never be the same again. Not like before. Our father had held us together. We'd been a unit, a strong one I thought, that nothing could ever destroy.

But things were different now for me. I was, and always would be, just the kid brother to them. I was single and alone. I lost my family when I lost my father.

Was I being selfish? I thought of Angelo. He had his wife and kids to look after him and Carman could handle what was left of the business. How could I help them if I wasn't sure about myself? Once I got to Miami, I'd decide. Maybe it was time I got back to reality. After all, whose life is perfect?

Things were going well with Stacy. When I got back I'd tell her everything. Ask her to move back to New York. I'd get a "real" job. Try marriage again. Be there for Angelo. Who knew how much time he had left. When the end came, I'd want to be there.

"Take care of yourselves," I said. "I'll be in touch."

As the door clicked shut behind me, I wasn't sure my goodbye was more a melancholy farewell. Would we ever be together like this again? I felt the tightening in my chest returning. I lifted my head and walked down to Penny. I needed some things from her before I left.

"He's really sick," I said as I stood in front of her desk.

"Yeah, Frank. Even more than he wants to admit."

"Have you heard anything? What are the doctors saying? I mean, he looks awful."

She must have seen the fear and concern on my face. "That's because of the chemo. It happens to everyone. Once his treatments are over, his hair will grow back and he'll be back to normal."

We stayed silent a moment. Then I said, "I'm leaving, Penny."

"When?"

"Tomorrow."

"Why so soon? Don't you think you oughta—"

"I have things to do."

"Well, you're a working man now. When are you coming back?"

"I don't know. I need you to do something for me. Can you call someone and put my furniture and things in storage?"

"Storage?"

"Another thing. Those three companies we sold out to— I want copies of their corporate reports."

"We have them on file; it'll just take a couple minutes."

"No, I can't wait. Just make copies of everything, and I'll pick them up later. Also—can I borrow your car? I want to go see my mother."

She reached into her purse and pulled out the keys.

I stepped into the foyer and called to my mother. My father's hat was still hanging in its usual place, on a hook by the door. He'd never gone anywhere without that hat.

I moved into the living room, hearing the sound of my heels clicking on the gleaming hardwood floor. I stopped. The sound with its slight echo was familiar. I took two more steps. Images flashed through my mind. That clicking noise. And knocking. My mother standing at the door with the policemen.

Something brought me back. I found her in the backyard puttering in a patch of purple and blue flowers.

"Ma."

She looked up, her face brightening with delight. "Frank! You're back!" She threw her arms around me then pushed away. "Let me look at you. You finally shaved that awful beard, and your hair!" Her beautiful, deep blue-gray eyes were moist. Looking at her, I felt my eyes fill. "Come here and sit down."

She pointed toward two old green Adirondack chairs. I remembered those chairs. Dad picked them up on a trip one time. He loved those chairs. They were shiny now. A brighter green than I remembered. Maybe she had painted them.

"How are you, son?"

"I'm good, Ma."

"Are you eating well? You look well. Are you getting enough sleep?"

I'd forgotten how concerned she'd always been. Still wondering about what I'm eating. I wanted to tell her about Stacy, but I realized I hadn't really told myself yet. Didn't know what to say.

"I've been playing a lot of tennis, Ma, and I've met some new people."

"Well, you needed a little break. You've been working so hard."

"How are you doing, Ma? I mean *really* doing?"

"Me?" she paused. "I'm doing fine."

We were silent for a moment.

"Your father used to love to sit in these chairs. Sometimes he wouldn't say a word. Just sit."

"I remember. I couldn't play in the yard when he was out here."

I wondered if I should ask about the hat. Why hadn't she put it away? Maybe like the chairs, the hat kept his memory alive.

Our visit was short but uplifting. Her conversation was vibrant and positive, even when I told her about returning to Miami. I told her Angelo was coming down in the winter and suggested she come with him.

Her eyes turned moist again. "He hasn't been feeling well. The warm weather might do him good."

As for her, she said she'd think about it. I lingered a while longer sometimes just sitting. Finally I kissed her goodbye and she said, "Be careful, Frankie."

I knew I wouldn't be returning anytime soon, but she made it sound as if she were just shuffling me off to school. I left it that way.

It was four-thirty when I returned to my apartment. I called Stacy and asked her to pick me up at the airport. It struck me how much like two high school sweethearts we sounded. Giggling, interrupting each other. The sound of her voice made me miss her more. She said she had missed me. I couldn't wait to get back.

I called Penny and told her to meet me at Pellegrino's on Mulberry Street at seven. I had to pick up the papers and return her car. I thought we'd have dinner together again, and then I'd leave in the morning. Mulberry Street was still the same. One fabulous eatery after another. People crammed together at small sidewalk tables, cars parked on both sides of the narrow street, and a steady stream of traffic—in cars and on foot. It was like San Gennaro every night there in the summer. We had a great dinner. Penny offered to drive me to the airport but I decided to take a cab. She asked when I'd be back.

"Soon," I said.

I could see the doubt in her eyes.

My last night in the apartment wasn't restful. I was interrupted by images of Angelo, Diaz, my father, and a state of confusion over my future. I didn't completely agree with Angelo and Carman, but I had Stacy now. She was the first positive thing for me in a long time. Maybe it *was* time to let go of the past and look to the future.

I got up early to pack the few clothes I'd brought with me. With suitcase in hand, I opened the door, took a last look, flicked the light switch, and left. I had to be at the airport in two hours. I stopped for coffee then grabbed a cab to Kennedy.

Chapter Fifteen

I watched as the New York skyline disappear in the distance. I felt a kind of relief. It was easier to go back to my life in Florida than it was to explain it to my family and myself in New York. I checked my watch. I'd be with Stacy in three hours.

Unlike my first arrival when I walked aimlessly through the airport with nowhere to go and no one to be with, this time I walked into the terminal to find Stacy. I gave her a peck on the cheek and, arm in arm, we exited to her car.

"So, how was your trip?" she asked as we sped away.

"I'll tell you all about it," I said. I just had to find a way to explain it all to her. Until I thought it out, I decided to remain Jimmy for a while longer. We drove to her apartment and spoke about the last few days. I decided to wait a day before I called into the hotel to let them know I was back. A three-day trip to New York and back might arouse curiosity and, even though I didn't intend to continue my employment, I still wanted to remain anonymous.

The late afternoon turned into evening. Stacy put together a light dinner and we sipped wine and listened to "oldies" as we snuggled on her couch. The right moment came. Our eyes met, then our lips. We slid down on the couch, softly touching each other.

"So," I began, "is tonight the night I don't have to sleep on the couch?"

A look of surprise crossed her face, but then she smiled and moved to get us both off the couch. Without a word, she led me to her bedroom. "I'll be right in," she said and disappeared into the bathroom.

I got undressed, slipped under the blanket and waited. A moment later she appeared, wearing only a white tee shirt. She slipped into bed then, as an afterthought, reached up to flick off the switch on the bedside lamp. The room was dark except for a faint light from the parking area outside her window. I turned, put my arm over her, gently pulling her toward me.

Our lips met. First slow and soft then harder and faster. She stopped to pull off the shirt. I brought her thigh toward me. It was warm and soft. A rush of energy burst in my groin. I tried to control myself, not wanting to finish before her. I wanted to satisfy her. My hand stroked the soft places between her legs. She moved up and down on my fingers. She pulled me closer. I got on top and entered her slowly. She arched her back. We moved together until I lost control pushing harder and faster. Her deep breathing turned into soft moaning. She grasped my back. We exploded together. I stopped, let myself slowly down on her. My breath was still racing.

A moment later I was on my back next to her. She had curled up next to me, eyes closed. I looked at her, put my arms around her. Her eyes opened. She smiled. Such sweet contentment. Then she fell asleep in my arms. I lay in the dark.

It had been a long time since I'd felt this. A life I had once taken for granted had disappeared and returned. I couldn't sleep. In the glow of our loving, I was sure she felt the same. But who did she love? Not Frank D'Antonio the real estate mogul but Jimmy the bartender. I was pondering the sweet sincerity of it all, the strange security of it, when my eyes closed and I slept.

I woke to Stacy emerging from the shower wrapped in a white towel.

"There's coffee in the kitchen. You can drop me off at the shop and keep my car if you want. You gonna check in at work?"

"Yeah, I want to drop my things off at my place first."

"You should be getting a lot of hours pretty soon with that convention coming up."

I threw some water on my face, dressed, and joined Stacy in the kitchen. We gulped down the coffee and were on our way. I dropped her off and headed for my condo. I planned to call Gino, give him the news about my decision and take him to dinner with Stacy and me. I hoped to talk him into giving up his workout and beach time the next day to drive me around car shopping.

Mrs. Newman was busy washing her windows when I entered the courtyard. I waited till I had the key in the door. When I called to her, she turned and gave me a look as my screen door slammed shut.

I went straight to the bedroom, dropped my suitcase, shed my clothes, and jumped into the shower. I rubbed down my body with soap and tried to think of when I should terminate my employment and introduce Stacy to Frank D'Antonio.

The convention would make things pretty hectic in the beverage department. If I left now, Ted wouldn't be able to replace me until after the convention. I knew he'd need all the help he could get. I didn't have the heart to leave him. The job wasn't very taxing; I decided to stay until the convention was over.

Stacy was another matter. Telling her about who I really was wouldn't be easy. My sudden trip to New York didn’t go over very well. Now adding the hotel job, my obsession with Victor Diaz and Ricardo Blanco, how many tall tales could she take before the trust was broken?

I was still struggling with another dilemma. I needed to be sure Stacy cared for me as Jimmy-the-Bartender and not Frank-the-millionaire-entrepreneur. I decided to wait a couple more weeks before I unfolded the whole scenario to her.

I wrapped myself with the towel and moved back into the bedroom. My comb and other bathroom things were still in my suitcase. I tossed it on the bed and began pulling things out. On the bottom, with my toothpaste, deodorant, and cologne, was the yellow manila envelope with the information about the three corporations. It was odd, I thought. I never knew who bought our family business. I'd given up my crusade, but I thought I'd kill some time before I phoned Gino.

I pulled the pillows out from under the covers and propped them up against the headboard. I set the envelope on my lap and picked up the brochure labeled Holden International and scanned the first couple pages mainly journal form listings of assets and liabilities. Among them was the Regency, our Caribbean Cruise lines, our Dallas Regency, a chain of small hotels I didn't recognize, and our Atlantic City and Las Vegas Casbar Hotel and Casino.

I skipped the listing of assets and the annual report showing company earnings and went to the back of the brochure. I wanted to see the major stockholders and board of directors. The names weren't familiar to me. I flung it aside and picked up V.T.C. Corporation.

V.T.C. was a manufacturing company based in Chicago. Their main product was a line of candy bars. Our chewing gum factory in Pennsylvania was now one of their assets. I tossed that report aside and picked up the last one.

Paragon Incorporated was a land development company in Seattle. They were involved in commercial and residential property. Paragon had picked up all the New York properties including the Central Plaza. It was like reading an obituary of a dear friend. I flicked the pages to the back names. I scanned the list: a group of faceless people who now represented everything my father worked for.

Depression, like a cloud, hovered just above me. I was about to toss the last brochure when a name caught my attention. I threw down the brochure and picked up the Holden International brochure. I went directly to the names. I was right. Then I picked up the V.T.C. brochure. There was the name again. Richard White, II.

I was curious. Every time I tried to let go, something brought me back. I picked up the phone to call Penny.

“Frank? Where are you?”

"Back in Florida. Listen, I noticed something in these papers you gave me. Might be odd. All three companies have the same major stockholder. Richard White, II."

"So, what about it?"

"Doesn't it seem odd? The same person owns most of the shares in all three companies?"

"Oh, Frank! Not more of—"

"Do you know anything about him?"

"No."

"Well, do me a favor. Please."

"Another favor?"

She was impatient. Maybe I was pushing too hard, but I couldn't stop myself nor could I explain it to her.

"Call Schlenker. He handled the closing. He should know—"

"Frank—"

"Please, Penny. Just this last thing then I promise, I'm finished."

"I could more easily ask Carman or Angelo. They—"

"No! I don't want them to know."

"All right. It might take a day or so. You know how lawyers are."

"All right. Just call when you know something."

After Penny hung up, I called Gino, told him I'd decided to forget about Blanco and Diaz. I invited him out for dinner with Stacy and me and reminded him that I was still Jimmy. He agreed about Blanco and Diaz and laughed about Jimmy.

"I'll try not to slip," he said.

We made arrangements to meet at the Newport Beach Hotel on Collins at seven.

"One more thing," I said.

"Here it comes."

"What are you doing tomorrow?"

"My usual. Why?"

"You feel like going car shopping with me?"

"Not really."

“I'm buying tonight.”

“All right. As long as you don't make it an all-day thing.”

We hung up and I spent the rest of the day hanging around the condo, waiting for Penny to call. At four-thirty I checked in with Ted. He had a shift for me the next night at five-thirty.

I headed for the Regency to pick up Stacy. It was slow at the shop, so Stacy closed down as soon as I pulled up. I told her we were going out to dinner with Gino. She seemed pleased.

On the way I told her stories about the early days of the Newport Beach Hotel when Louis Prima was the biggest draw in its Seven Seas Lounge.

“Who's Louie Prima?” she asked.

Dinner was great. Gino entertained Stacy with New York stories about the two of us. He didn't slip once. I was Jimmy all evening. After dinner we had a drink in the lounge and then called it a night. Gino said he'd be over at nine to pick me up.

The next morning, though Gino was right on time, I answered the door half-dressed and told him to help himself to the coffee Stacy had made before she left.

“I think you hit the jackpot this time, Kid.”

He stood in the doorway to the bedroom with mug in hand.

“Yeah she's nice, isn't she, Gino?”

“I hope you don't fuck it up.”

“What do you mean?”

“I mean, I wouldn't wait too long before you give up your phony name and tell her who you really are. And quit this bartending thing you're doing.”

“Oh, that reminds me, I gotta work tonight.”

“See, that's what I mean. There's no reason for you to be doing this anymore. You're better off spending the time with her.”

“Gino, I can't let Ted down. If I quit on him now he won't be able to replace me until after the convention. It's a security thing. Next week's Fourth of July weekend. The convention's right after Labor Day. I'm gonna hang out till then. Besides it's not like I work every night. I haven't been there in over a week."

I slipped past him and he followed me into the kitchen where I poured half a mug for myself.

"I'll tell Stacy in a couple weeks."

"A couple weeks! Why so long?"

"I don't know. I guess I want to be sure she likes me as just Jimmy-the-Bartender before I tell her who I really am."

"Oh—she likes you all right."

"How do you know?"

"I just know."

"What—you a psychic now? Come on, let's go."

We hopped into Gino's Mercedes Convertible and were on our way.

"Did you buy this down here?"

"Yeah. We'll go look around some other places, then I'll take you over and introduce you to the guy who sold me mine. He's all right."

"Okay, but I don't know about a Mercedes. What's Stacy gonna think, me pulling up in a Mercedes?"

"What are you worried about? It'll be a great way to break the news to her."

We spent the rest of the morning between car lots. By twelve-thirty we were ready for a cold drink and some lunch. I told Gino to pick a place. The streets of Miami hadn't changed much over the years. The growth of the Hispanic population was obvious by the bilingual signs and ads. Some signs were written in Spanish only. We passed a billboard showing a Hispanic-looking man with a picture of the White House in the background. Underneath, the caption read: "Jose Ramierez. Hoy Congreso – Mañana La Casa Blanca."

"Christ, Gino, they're writing everything in Spanish down here."

"You're in Miami, Kid."

"Look at that sign," I said. "What's it say? My Spanish is rusty."

"That's for a guy running for Congress. It says, 'Jose Ramierez.

Today, Congress. Tomorrow, the White House.'"

Instantly it came to me: the Spanish word for "white" is "blanco," and "Ricardo" is Spanish for "Richard."

"What's the matter? All the Spanish got you confused, Kid?" Gino's voice interrupted my thoughts.

After lunch we dropped by the Mercedes dealership where I listened to another sales pitch. I didn't commit to anything. I was too distracted. I said I'd have to think about it. We drove back to my place. Gino dropped me off then went to his afternoon workout but offered to return and drive me to the hotel. I checked my answering machine, hoping there'd be a message from Penny. The red light wasn't blinking. I flopped onto the bed and dozed off.

It was five-thirty when Gino dropped me off at the parking garage in front of the employee entrance. I climbed the stairs to the security office and attempted to slide my I.D. card through the time clock. It didn't work.

"Hey, Howie, what's with the time clock?"

Howie Brady was a six-foot-two Irishman with a thick mustache, which, like his hair, had gone from jet black to mostly gray. Before taking early retirement, he had worked for twenty years on the New York City police force. We became good friends when he found out I was a New Yorker. He loved to talk about his days on the force, and I enjoyed listening.

"Hey Jimmy, you're back! Yeah, we started using the new I.D. cards the other day. Here."

He handed me a new laminated card with my picture and department name on it.

"Do me a favor. Keep this on after you punch in from now on. These government security guys are bustin my balls about everybody wearing one. They're even making Carroll wear one," he said with a smirk. "Can't wait till this fuckin convention is over. These government guys are a pain in my ass. All they talk about is Dan and the Colombian. Couple of em said if they had their way, they'd make the headquarters somewhere else. Between you and me, I wish they had."

"Hang in there, How. It'll be over soon."

I got off work at ten-thirty and called Stacy to pick me up. She had had a tough day on the courts and I was tired myself. We went right to bed.

The next morning I took Stacy to work and then headed for my condo to shower and change clothes. I liked spending most of my time at her place, but I didn't want to officially move in until she knew everything. Then I could move us both into my place and not worry about embarrassing encounters with Mrs. Newman.

I glanced at the answering machine on my way to the shower. No blinking red light.

The warm isolation of a shower gave me a chance to think. Was the Richard White/Ricardo Blanco thing a coincidence, or were they one and the same? I preferred coincidence, having lost some of my zeal for digging up the past.

My answering machine was blinking as I stepped out of the bathroom. Immediately I pressed the button. It was Penny. I grabbed the receiver and punched in her number.

"Yeah, Penny, it's Frank. So what did you find out?"

"Not much, Frank. Schlenker didn't know much about White's background. He's a semi-retired businessman who lives in Palm Beach."

"Did he have an address?"

"No, he just said Palm Beach."

"Okay, Penny, thanks."

"These favors of yours are really piling up. When's payback time?"

"I'll let you know. See ya."

Palm Beach. But where in Palm Beach? I dialed information for Palm Beach. There was a listing for a R. White on 2242 Ocean Drive. I had nothing planned all day. I decided to take a ride to

Palm Beach and check it out. I picked up the phone again and punched in Gino's number then hung up. On second thought, I better not get him involved.

Palm Beach was about an hour north on I-95. I'd been there before, but it had been a while. A small, posh town just over the bridge from West Palm Beach, it wouldn't be too difficult to find the address.

I drove for a while through finely groomed neighborhoods till I found Ocean Drive then headed north between palm trees lining both sides. I caught glimpses of the Atlantic between palatial homes on my right and yachts bouncing on the swells in the distance. I passed a couple Rolls-Royces parked off the immaculate street, but most of the homes were vacant. It was hard to believe these estates were vacant most of the year. What a waste.

I slowed down to see the door numbers. Most estates had no visible addresses, but I spotted a 2020 on my right, so 2242 was ahead on the same side. I drove for two blocks until the 2200s began. At the end of the block, a house number read 2244.

White's house was one house in from the corner. I took a left and used a driveway to turn around and backtrack to the corner where I parked under a palm tree. Two Mercedes were parked just to the right of the double doors on a pale-pink circular driveway.

I stared at the house. Should I just ring the doorbell and ask if a Richard White lives here? I wouldn't know Richard White from Ricardo Blanco. I needed a picture of Blanco. I could make like an ambitious realtor, interested in his home. It was farfetched, but it would give me a look. That's all I wanted.

I had one foot out of the car when another silver Mercedes pulled into the driveway. I pulled my leg back, slid down in my seat and looked on as the car parked behind the other two. Three men in suits emerged. I inched up for a better look and recognized Diaz, the guy with the scar, and his partner.

I watched as they entered the house. Sweat forming on my forehead. I wiped it with my arm and leaned back. No one had seen me. I could leave and let that be the end of it. I had decided to put everything behind me and move on. How could I walk away and plan my future with Stacy? I'd be haunted by uncertainty forever.

I'd made the trip. If Richard White was Ricardo Blanco, I wanted a look at him.

I couldn't knock on the door now. Diaz and I were old card game buddies now. A line of bushes separated White's house and the one on the corner. It was risky, but I could use the high-dense greens to spy on them. I crossed the street and crept past the corner house, thankful that the neighbors were snowbirds. I checked both sides of the street—no one in sight—and I slipped behind the bushes.

I worked my way back, periodically pulling apart the thick branches until I reached the backyard. A small structure like a gazebo centered the lawn. I made out four or five men sitting around a table. Skipping over Diaz and his goons, I tried to make out the others. Mostly I saw gesturing and the backs of their heads. In a rush of daring, I parted the bushes to get a better look. I could hear the murmur of conversation.

Two men were sitting with their backs to me. I focused on a man seated at the head of the table, wearing white pants and an aqua-blue short-sleeved shirt. His gray temples and pudgy cheeks suggested early sixties. He raised his hand and stuck a long cigar in his mouth. A huge pinky ring gleamed like a decoration in the bright sunshine. His complexion was dark. If that was Richard White, he looked more like a Ricardo Blanco to me.

I inched my way up closer to pick up bits of conversation, but as I did so a siren began blaring all over the property. Immediately the men dispersed and I raced for Stacy's car. I glanced at the house as I flung open the car door and jumped in. Diaz's two goons had come out from the side of the house and were rushing toward the street. I started the engine and screeched past them. The rearview mirror showed no one. Confident of my escape, I slowed to a casual speed and headed home. Thank God for tinted glass!

On the highway to Miami I had time to think and realized my fears about Blanco and Diaz were true. I was determined now to stop them. Not even Stacy mattered anymore. They were planning something and I was going to find out what.

It was two-thirty when I pulled up to my condo. Barbara had me working late for the next three nights. I needed some rest before I went in but first I had to talk to Gino. I'd tell him what I knew and ask for his advice.

I left a message for him to meet me at the Flamingo Club at midnight. I lay back and stared at my bedroom ceiling. The pieces were coming together. The nightmare mystery about my father's death was going to come to an end. I'd gotten this far and now I would deal with Blanco, Diaz, and the whole Colombian connection.

Stacy was busy on the courts when I dropped off her car. I told her I'd be late and Gino would pick me up. We were going out and I'd probably stay at my place for the night. “Boys' night out?” she called without missing a stroke.

I waved and headed for the beverage department. It was a long night. I couldn't wait to meet with Gino.

When I arrived at the Flamingo, Gino was waiting.

“Tough night on the job, Frank? What are you drinkin?”

“Johnny Red on the rocks.”

Gino ordered my drink and we made small talk for a while.

“When are you gonna get a car?”

“I have to decide soon. Stacy's going to the West Coast to play in some Fourth of July tournament in Naples this week and I'll be stuck. I think I'll just let your friend sell me one and be done with it.”

“He's all right. If Stacy's gonna be gone, just let me know and I'll take you around.”

"I took a ride to Palm Beach today."

"Palm Beach? For what?"

"Drink up, Gino. I've got things to tell you. Let's go to my place."

We downed our drinks and left.

"This better be good, Frank," Gino said as I ushered him into my condo. "I had my eye on one of those broads on the other side of the bar."

"It is. You want something to drink?"

I popped open two bottles of Heineken and handed one to Gino.

"I'll be right back," I said, and disappeared into the bedroom. A moment later I reappeared and took a seat next to him.

"Look at this, Gino," I said and opened the folder on Holden International to the list of stockholders.

"You see that?" I pointed to Richard White's name.

"So?"

"Just hold this, Gino." I handed it to him and picked up V.T.C. Corporation, fingering through the pages till I came to the stockholders page.

"Look at this," I pointed to Richard White's name again. Gino didn't say a word. I watched his eyes move back and forth from the two pages.

"His name's in this one, too," I said, holding up Paragon's folder.

"So, what about it?"

"Remember that sign on the billboard you translated for me? The guy running for Congress. What did it say?"

"I don't remember. Some campaign bullshit. Why?"

"Gino, it said 'today Congress, tomorrow the White House.' But it was written in Spanish."

"So?"

"So? Gino, how do you say *White* in Spanish?"

"Blanca."

"Or blanco. Right?"

"Right."

"And how do you say *Richard* in Spanish?"

"Ricardo! You think this guy is Ricardo Blanco?"

"No. I *know* he's Ricardo Blanco. Listen Gino, I called Penny when I noticed the name in all three files. She found out Richard White had a Palm Beach address. That's where I was today. I found his house and while I was watching it, who do you think pulls up?"

"You're kidding." A mix of amazement and fear crossed his face.

"Victor fucking Diaz in person. In living color. And he had his two goons with him, the ones from the club. Gino, you see? It all makes sense! My father wouldn't do business with Blanco way back when. He tried to get the Grano brothers and Terry Donlin in with him and they turned him down. That's why he had my father killed. He figured with him out of the way, he could trick Carman and Angelo into selling. Instead of taking a chance talking to them directly, he bought these three probably defunct companies for peanuts under the name Richard White. Then he approached Carman and Angelo as V.T.C. Paragon with Holden waving dollar bills in front of them. Maybe he even knew Angelo was sick."

"How sick is he, Frank?"

My throat tightened. "He's dying, Gino. He's got cancer."

The words left a bitter aftertaste.

Gino studied the floor a moment then looked at me. His voice was soft. "So, what will you do Frank?"

"I'm going after em, Gino. Those fucks killed my father. I think they're up to something again and it has to do with Luis Martinez and this convention. I've been reading it in the papers. This Luis Martinez is trying to make some deal with our governor here in Miami to crack down on the drugs coming into the country. Blanco's a drug dealer who just laid out a lot of cash to my brothers and me. Do you think he's gonna sit back and let somebody sabotage his business?

Gino got up, stroked his chin, and paced the room. Finally he stopped, looked at me, "Frank, I can't argue with you about what happened, but this thing about him and Martinez. I don't know."

"What's Diaz hanging around the hotel for then?"

"You said he's a PR guy for Blanco. Maybe that's what he's here for, to stroke Martinez. Make Martinez see it Blanco's way."

"That's what Diaz was doing with Pedro Quero—trying to make him see it Blanco's way. Look what happened to him."

I must have made an impression on Gino, because he was silent for a long time. After a gulp of beer, he said, "So, where do we go from here?"

"Will your car dealer friend loan me a car till they do the paper work on the one I buy?"

"Yeah, he'll let you use something. Especially this time of year. Business is slow. They'll do anything to make a sale."

"Then I'm calling Virginia Sullivan again. Try to talk to her."

"Be careful with that broad, Frank. She's Diaz's girl. Her loyalty is with him. If she thinks you're trying to screw him, she might rat you out. Then you're really fucked."

"Well, it's worth a try. You want another beer?"

"No. If I gotta play taxi driver tomorrow, I want to do it early so I can get to the gym in the afternoon."

"Okay, pick me up at nine. I have to work tomorrow night." Gino shook his head and took a last sip of beer. As we parted he threw me a smirk that gave me a confidence I hadn't yet achieved.

Chapter Sixteen

I filled out papers on a 500 SL silver Mercedes and the salesman was more than happy to loan me a car.

"How you gonna explain this to Stacy, Mr. Bartender?" said Gino.

"I told you...she's away this week. Besides, when she gets back, I'm gonna explain everything to her anyway."

We parted. Gino went for his workout and I drove back to my condo to call Virginia. Her voice was different. She responded curtly to all my questions. Something was wrong. She'd seized up on me. Out of fear for Diaz or contempt for me—I didn't know. She turned me down for dinner with a blunt "I'm busy." I persisted and she refused. It was not in our best interests, she assured me, to see each other again. She threatened to hang up, but I said I'd keep calling till she accepted. After a silence, she agreed to meet me next afternoon at a diner up in Hollywood. Abruptly she hung up.

Hollywood was a twenty-minute drive up I-95. I took a booth overlooking the parking lot. Ten minutes later she pulled up. I watched her strut across the parking lot dressed in faded jeans, sneakers, and sunglasses. Not her usual outfit, I guessed.

She scanned the room as she entered. I waited for her to look to her right then stuck my head over the booth. Our eyes met and she scooted down the aisle.

"Hi," I said as she slid into the seat.

"What's so important that you need to talk?"

"Are you hungry?" I asked.

"No."

“How about a cup of coffee?”

“No, listen. Let's get this over with. Okay?”

Our waitress approached. “Coffee for you, Ma'am?”

“Yes please,” I answered.

We waited while she filled Virginia's mug and zipped away.

“What happened to ‘Frank, you're a nice guy?’ Did I lose my charm that fast?”

She pulled off her sunglasses and looked at me. Her aloofness was gone.

“Look, you are a nice guy, Frank. I don't meet many guys like you.” She paused. “Well, I just don’t. And I got my own problems. I don't need more headaches than I already have. I gave you my number. That was a mistake. I'm sorry. There's plenty of girls out there; you won't have any trouble finding a date.”

“I'm not asking for a date. I need some help and I think you can help me. I need you to tell me about Victor. What's his business and why is he spending so much time at the Regency?”

“I told you—Victor doesn't tell me anything. All I know is he’s in the importing business.”

I leaned across the table until only inches kept us apart. I was trying to scare her, get her to say more.

“Yeah, he's in the importing business all right. I'll tell you what he imports. Drugs. He's a drug dealer, Virginia, a scum bag drug dealer—him and Ricardo Blanco.”

She looked surprised.

“Yeah, don't tell me you don't know. Your boyfriend's a killer, Virginia.”

She stared at her coffee mug.

“He wacked Pedro Quero and Dan Hiller,” I said.

“Who?” she looked up.

“Dan Hiller. He's a guy who works in the hotel.”

“Pedro Quero fell off that balcony,” she said in a manner more questioning than certain.

“Yeah, you keep believing that, that’s dangerous. One of these days it's you they'll be picking up off the cement."

She looked down again toying with the teaspoon in her mug of warm coffee.

"I'm sorry about your friend," she said, softly. "I—"

"Who? Dan Hiller? He wasn't my friend. I hardly knew him. But Victor, Blanco, and their friends—*they're* the guys. They don't do it directly, but they're responsible. And Quero and Dan won't be the last unless you help me. That's why I need to talk with you. What about that white shit they peddle? How many people does that kill? Look around you. Twelve and thirteen-year-olds overdosing or turning tricks to get a fix. Think of that the next time Victor buys you a dress or takes you to some fancy restaurant. Victor's money comes from some kid stealing or selling themselves to buy the shit."

For a moment, I thought she hadn't been listening. Then she looked up sharply.

"Do you know anything about me?" she said with a hint of defiance.

"I know you're Victor Diaz's girlfriend."

"Girlfriend! It must be nice not letting a little knowledge get in your way." She looked away, stared for a moment out the window then took a sip of coffee. "Do you know how I met Victor? Through my brother Billy. Billy Sullivan." She leaned back, wrapped both hands around her mug, glanced at me then stared at the table.

"I have—I *had*, a brother, but I thought you knew that. You seem to know everything about me." She gave me a bleary-eyed look then focused on her hands. "Billy came down here from our home in North Carolina. He and my father never got along. My father liked to drink. When he got drunk he'd beat my mother. Billy would step in and they'd go at it. He decided to leave and come down here. Make a new life."

She looked up again, raked her fingers through her hair and leaned forward. "Two years went by. Billy was doing great. He was writing, telling us about the condo he'd bought and the new car he was driving.

I decided to come down and join him. I wanted to get into modeling and maybe open up a boutique. Everything was going great. I took modeling classes in the day and I worked a couple nights a week waitressing though I didn't have to work, Billy was making enough money to support both of us.

Then one day Victor came to the house. I thought it was strange when Billy didn't introduce us. They talked for a while then he left. After that, Victor was coming to the house all the time. One day he asked me out. Before I could answer, Billy told him I was too busy working and going to school.

"After he left that day, Billy told me he didn't want me to have anything to do with Victor. I didn't care. I wasn't interested in dating. But Victor came over once when Billy wasn't home. Said he was supposed to meet Billy. I told him he could wait. It didn't take him long before he was all over me. Then Billy walked in. He was furious. He told Victor to stay away, threatened to kill him if he got near me again. A month later the police called to tell me Billy was killed during some drug deal.

It didn't take long before what money Billy had saved was gone. My two-night-a-week job wasn't nearly enough to keep up with the bills and I found out that Billy was sending our mother money every month. I didn't want to tell her what happened to Billy so I kept trying to send her money.

I quit the modeling school and started working fulltime at the restaurant. I still couldn't make it. The bills were piling up. I was nowhere when Victor showed up, offered to help me. All I had to do was go out with him. I asked him about Billy. He said he didn't know much about it...just that Billy was getting involved with the wrong people, taking too many chances.

He said I could go back to modeling school. That never happened. I threatened to leave once. He beat me and reminded me that there'd be no more money sent to my mother. I didn't care about me, but my mother...well."

She looked up and glared at me with watery eyes.

"So don't ever judge me, Frank. Ever."

"I'm sorry about your brother. I didn't know—"

"Yeah, you didn't know. What do you know about anything? Daddy's little rich boy, probably never worked a day in your life. I don't think much of Victor and what he's done. But when you're born into poverty, not knowing where your next meal is coming from and you have a chance to pull yourself out of that hole, you take it any way you can. What do *you* care about Victor, anyway? You're not a cop. Are you trying to cut in on his business? Go home to daddy." She was nearly yelling now, oblivious to her need for obscurity. "You got no business in our world."

I leaned forward, nearly putting my face in hers. "I can't go home to daddy," I hissed, "because Victor and Blanco had him killed. So you see, we have something in common. That's *my* interest in them. But I can't prove any of it. You know about your brother; I know about Pedro Quero, Dan Hiller, and my father."

I'd revealed so much it seemed foolish to withhold anything now. I told her about Blanco's attempt to infiltrate my father's business, which I believed led to his death. She went back to staring at the mug and listened as I unraveled my suspicions. When I finished she looked defeated, like someone who hasn't slept in days.

"I can't help you," she said.

Suddenly I felt shame. I looked into her fearful face, knowing I'd put her in danger by asking her to meet me. I couldn't involve her, I decided, any more than unloading my last year of life on her. I thanked her for coming and waited while she slipped out of the booth and to her car.

I gulped down the last of my cold coffee and watched her drive away. She was right. She had her own problems. How many Virginia Sullivans have there been and how many more would there be? With people like Blanco and Diaz around, it would be a very long list. I didn't expect to see Virginia again, but Diaz and Blanco were another matter.

Occupancy was up during Fourth of July week with mostly European tourists. Stacy was away all week and the banquet department was busy so Jimmy-the-Bartender went to work.

The atmosphere seemed to be changing in banquet beverage. Everyone was giving Andre the cold shoulder and Kevin was constantly scrutinizing his work. I hadn't seen John or Robin in a while. I asked Michele, who explained that Barbara and Kevin had their favorites. Seniority meant nothing. Barbara liked Andre and Robin wouldn't sleep with Kevin, so she and John didn't get called.

The favoritism and politics infuriated me. As my other self I'd have put Barbara and Kevin out on their asses but as Jimmy-the-Bartender, I could only fume. John mentioned that his daytime bank job didn't pay much, so he needed the bar shifts to make ends meet.

I was scheduled for the next two nights and I didn't really care about working, so I asked Kevin for John's number, called him and offered him my shifts. He said he didn't feel right taking my hours. I said he'd be doing me a favor, because I needed the nights off. He thankfully accepted.

A couple days later I called in for my hours. Barbara answered the phone.

"Did you tell John Palmer he could work your shifts?" she asked.

"Yeah I—"

"Since when do you make your own schedule?"

I wasn't used to being talked to like that and especially by someone like Barbara. I could feel the blood rush to my head and I desperately tried to control my anger. "John said he needed the hours and I needed the nights off so I asked him to work for me. Is there a problem with that?"

"Yeah, there is. Get this straight, Jimmy. I say who works or doesn’t work around here. You need a night off, you tell me. Now since you need time off, you got it. You’re off until next week.” Then she added, “And so’s John. Call in next week for your hours.” She gave me a defiant stare.

I tried to hide my rage. “Is that it?” I said.

“That’s it,” she replied then pretended to engross herself in some papers on her desk indicating the meeting was over. Without a word, I walked out.

There was also friction between Kevin and Barbara. He questioned every order she gave him and everybody else. His remarks reeked with sarcasm.

Once she gave her I’m-the-boss speech and you-do-this-or else warning. Kevin shot back. “Or else what? I take the midnight stroll through the swamp?”

Ted was caught between Kevin, his friend and underling, and Barbara, his assistant. I'd heard that Ted and Barbara were once romantically involved. She broke it off. Ted had turned to Kevin and Dan, among others, for comfort. Everyone told him to get her out of his personal and professional life. Barbara used Ted's infatuation with her to keep her job. Occasionally they'd been seen at the Dugout though they never left together.

Fourth of July came and went and I had one more day before Stacy returned. I'd met with Gino again and told him I'd struck out with Virginia. I was sure Diaz and Blanco were up to no good, and it all revolved around the convention and the Regency. Gino knew it too but with nothing to go on I decided to concentrate on explaining my life to Stacy. We had talked on the phone almost every day. I told her to come directly to my place on her way back.

It was late afternoon when she returned. I'd had some Chinese food delivered and we talked about her tournament over dinner and a bottle of wine. We bypassed the couch and went directly to bed. I don't remember ever wanting anyone more and the way she made love told me she felt the same.

After my week suspension I was back to work. I suggested to Stacy that we spend more time at my place. She agreed and for the next month we spent our nights together at my place. I still hadn't come clean with her.

I had two weeks until my farewell to Ted and the beverage department. I would give Ted my two-week notice and then I would unveil the whole thing to Stacy. As I'd anticipated, she questioned my choice in cars. I told her I bought it wholesale through a friend of Gino's, but she wasn't convinced and it remained a small tension between us.

On Stacy's day off we went to the beach. By four o'clock it was time to head home, shower, and go in for a five-thirty banquet. Stacy's lease was up at the end of the month. We were moving fast. She had one night at her place to pack up. She was moving in. I was elated.

The next day I arrived at work and saw three long tractor trailers backed up in the receiving dock. There seemed to be confusion at security as I entered and slid my I.D. card through the scanner.

"Hey, Howie, what's with the trucks outside?"

"That's your tax money at work, buddy. Fuckin politicians. They're delivering the shit for this convention. Banners, balloons, posters, all kinds of shit."

"Three truck loads?"

"Only in America. You working tonight?"

"Yeah, I gotta put my time in, you know."

"You'll be putting your time in after Labor Day with this convention. They got parties scheduled day and night. Yesterday we got a delivery of champagne for this thing. A whole truckload of champagne. I can't wait till this fuckin thing is over."

"It won't be long now, Howie. Hang in there."

Howie mumbled as I walked down the long corridor to the locker room where I changed into my black and whites. The elevator door opened on the banquet level. The sound of conversation from the office brought me to a standstill. From around the corner I saw light coming from the open office door. No one was setting up outside. Alone, it would be easy to eavesdrop.

"I came in early in case you needed any extra help, Barbara." I recognized the voice. It was Andre.

"Well, I don't. Just start setting up your bar."

"Screw the bar! I know what you—"

I heard a smack.

"Bitch! I'll—"

There was a scuffle. I started toward the open door, Barbara's voice stopped me.

"Go ahead. You gonna kill me like Dan, you creep. I agreed to put you here, even though you didn't know jack shit about bartending cause Diaz wanted you to spy for him. Nobody said anything about murder. Far as I'm concerned, you better just do your fucking job and I don't want to know about anything else. And if you ever put your fucking hands on me again, I'll have your ass thrown out of here. I don't give a shit what Diaz says. Maybe you can explain to him why I got you thrown out. Now get the hell out of my office and go do your job!"

"You're a lucky fucking bitch. If things were different, I'd wring your fucking neck and never give a shit about it. Don't flatter yourself, honey; you're not that good-looking, anyway. You think Diaz is gonna take care of you? He's just using you. You'll see. You'll be out on your ass!"

"I said get out!" She was screaming. Had she forgotten the door was open?

I used her last command as my cue and slowly started toward the office. Andre rushed by as I approached the office.

"Hi, Barbara," I said, pretending normality.

She looked up and made brief eye contact. Her rosy cheeks caught my eye. She ran her fingers through her hair and stepped behind her desk.

"You okay?" I said trying to act surprised.

"Yeah, fine. Let's get set up."

She picked up her purse and headed for the door.

"I'll be right back," she said. "If the phone rings, answer it."

Andre, Barbara, and Diaz. So it really was true. I had known it but coming upon stark evidence put me in shock. For a moment I had trouble pulling in a complete breath. Distractedly, I started setting up. A few minutes later, the two other bartenders arrived. The rest of the evening was quiet.

The green time clock read eleven forty-five when I slid my card through and exited. Fifteen minutes later I pulled up in front of my place. There were no lights on and I didn't see Stacy's car. My dashboard clock said two minutes after twelve. Stacy should have been back. I let myself in and phoned her place. Her "hello" was tense.

"Stacy? What are you still doing over there?"

"Jimmy," she said. Her voice was trembling.

"What's—"

"Jimmy, two men were here. They forced their way in. They asked me what I was doing in Palm Beach last month. I told them I didn't know what they were talking about. Then...then one of them whacked me across the face and knocked me down. He pulled out a piece of paper with my license plate number on it and asked if it was mine. He went on about snooping around his boss's business. Jimmy, I've never been to Palm Beach in my life."

"Okay, okay, please—just—be calm. What else did he say?"

"I don't know. I was so upset. The other guy went through my boxes. He found your pants in the bedroom, came out holding them up. The first guy asked whose they were."

"What'd you tell him?"

"I told him they were yours. He asked where you were. I told him you were working."

Stacy's terror nearly paralyzed me. I thought I'd gotten away that day in Palm Beach. I was wrong. I had to tell her everything now. I tried to calm her, told her to get into her car and come to my place immediately. She said she was too scared to move. I assured her. I would explain everything. She hesitated then agreed. We hung up. The clock on my kitchen wall read twelve-twenty.

By twelve-fifty, there was still no sign of her. I began pacing between rooms, stopping to look out my window, waiting for her to pull up.

At one-fifteen I decided to backtrack to her apartment. I'd made the turn onto the main highway that led to the causeway to Miami when in the distance, I could see flashing blue and red lights. My heartbeat raced. I pushed on the accelerator. As I neared the intersection before the causeway incline, I fell in line with backed-up traffic. The cars were creeping, taking direction from a uniformed officer in the road.

I edged closer to the flashing lights. It looked like an accident. At first I saw only a long tractor trailer in the middle of the intersection. Someone—probably the driver—was standing to the side. He was being interviewed by a policeman.

When I reached the rear of the truck, I noticed broken glass and metal debris scattered all over the road. Two paramedics pulled a stretcher away from another vehicle. Its front end was wedged underneath the rear end of the truck all the way past the front seat.

It was an obvious rear end collision. The car was mangled. I watched the paramedics slam shut the ambulance door and speed away with flashing lights and siren blaring. I looked back and noticed the plate number of the car. My heart sank. I stared. "LOVE-I." It was Stacy's car.

A horn blew behind me.

A policeman called, "Come on buddy, keep moving."

"Where's that ambulance going?"

"Dade Memorial, I think," the officer answered.

I hit the gas and raced up the causeway to the emergency room of Dade Memorial. Then I rushed down the hall to the nurse's desk. I had to catch my breath and get someone's attention.

"Excuse me, Miss? They just brought a woman in here, she was in an accident. I know her. Her name is Stacy Iseman. I need to see her."

"Are you a relative, Sir?"

"No,but—"

"I'm sorry, Sir, I can't give you—"

"*Please* Miss, I have to see her. She's my girlfriend."

All I heard was "sorry" and something about hospital rules. She said to wait in the waiting room.

"The doctor is busy right now. When he gets a minute, I'll ask him to come out and talk to you."

I got to the waiting room. The clock said two-thirty. Then three-fifteen. Finally a man dressed in a long white coat came out. Slowly I stood as he approached.

"Were you the man asking about the Iseman girl?"

"Yes, doctor."

"You're not a relative?"

"No. She's my girlfriend. She's gonna be all right? Please tell me she's gonna be all right."

"I'm afraid not, Sir. Miss Iseman passed away a few minutes ago."

My throat tightened and I swore my heart would burst out of my chest. My eyes filled up as I sank back into the chair. The doctor spoke. I couldn't hear him. I could see his lips move behind my tears. His face was blurred.

I can't remember how long I sat. A nurse came out and tapped me on the shoulder.

"Why don't you go home, Sir? Get some sleep. There's nothing you can do here."

Sleep, I thought. It would be a long time before I'd sleep normally again. I looked up and gave her a nod then slowly pushed myself to my feet and out to my car. Stacy was dead and it was all my fault. The reality of it was impossible to take. Diaz had robbed me again.

I stopped at the first bar I saw. A hole in the wall called the Brass Pelican. The barroom was dark. Cigarette smoke hovered around softball-sized white lamps that hung over the long bar. The room reeked of stale draft beer. I took a seat at the end. A bartender with poorly dyed red hair approached, chomping on a mouth full of gum.

"What'll you have, Sir?" I ordered a scotch. She returned and dropped the drink in front of me.

"Tough day, huh?" she said.

I didn't answer.

"That'll be three fifty."

I reached into my pocket and pulled out a crumpled fifty. Without saying a word, I dropped it in front of her. She took the bill and brought me the change. I never spoke another word to her. I was grateful that she respected my privacy and made herself known only to keep my ice cubes submerged.

I watched a young couple sitting in a far corner by a jukebox sharing a pitcher of draft beer. The jukebox glass was streaked: the dust and sweat of a thousand nights combined. No one had thought to clean it. I stared at the couple. They weren't newly in love. I could tell. But they loved each other. You could see that.

Stacy's face and eyes came sharply to mind. I ordered another drink. When the jukebox music stopped, there was only the soft slow hum of intimate conversation. My only interest was trying to expose the cubes in my glass as quickly as possible. I heard the clunk of coins dropping into the dusty music machine and Ronnie Milsap's voice singing "Almost Like a Song."

I downed what was left in my glass and quickly ordered another one. The rest of the night was a blur. Later I'd have no memory of going home.

Chapter Seventeen

The walls of my condo seemed to vibrate. I didn't move, hoping they'd fall and bury me under the blankets and pillows of my bed. I pulled them up to look around. The banging was coming from my front door. I lay back, wanting whoever it was to go away. My caller persisted and I made myself get out of bed, and go to the door. It was Gino. His voice was somber, his face long and drawn.

"I've been trying to call you all morning."

I left him standing in my doorway and retreated to my bed. I could hear him following me. He cleared my clothes off a chair next to the bed and sat down. I lay there motionless and silent. My eyes felt like holes stuffed with cotton. I could see enough to notice he was holding a newspaper.

"Frank, what happened?"

I couldn't answer.

"Come on, Frank, talk to me."

"Diaz and Blanco did it and it was my fault."

"What! What the hell you talking about?"

"Forget it, Gino. Go on home. Leave me alone. Please."

I buried my head under the pillows again. I thought I heard him leave. I didn't bother to look. I just wanted to go back to sleep. Guilt engulfed me as images from the night before returned.

I heard footsteps entering my room again. I pulled away the pillows and looked up. It was Gino again holding two mugs of coffee. Without saying a word, he held one out for me. I looked up at him, hovering motionless over me like a big bear. A friendly bear. Thank God for him. Slowly I sat up and took the mug from his hand.

"Thanks," I said.

We stayed silent for a while, both sipping coffee.

"The paper says it was brake failure," Gino said.

I didn't reply.

"What were you saying about Diaz and Blanco?"

"They did it, Gino."

"Frank. It was an accident, man. You've lost your mind. Her brakes gave out and she ran into the back of a truck."

"There wasn't anything wrong with her brakes. Diaz and one of those goons paid her a visit last night. They saw her license plate number when I drove away from Blanco's house."

I gave him all the details of the night before.

"Why don't you go to the cops?"

"And tell them what? I can't prove any of it. Did…did the paper give any details about—I mean what did it say about her?"

"Not much. Just that she worked at the Regency."

"She was the first positive thing that happened to me in a long time, Gino. We were really happy. She was gonna move in."

"I know, Frank, but you gotta snap out of it."

I repeated his words. Snap out of it. *Snap out of it?* His words seemed so unreal. Stacy was dead because I had brought her into my world. Snap out of it? How could I ever snap out of this?

"Oh, I'm gonna snap out of it all right. She had nothing to do with any of this, Gino! She was innocent and those fucks snuffed out her life like blowing out a match. Where does it end? How many people have to die? I'm gonna get em, Gino."

"How, Frank. You—"

"Whatever it takes."

I eventually convinced Gino I was all right but he wouldn't leave till I promised to call him later.

I spent the rest of the day in bed. I called Gino about seven o'clock. He offered to take me to dinner, but I wasn't in the mood to eat. I snatched a bottle of scotch from a cupboard in the kitchen and retreated to my bed. I knew I had to forget, but for the moment I needed help.

I gulped down two slugs of scotch, replaced the cap, and dropped the bottle to the floor. My head sunk into the pillow. I hoped the alcohol would chase the images of what had happened from my mind. It succeeded for a while. When they returned, I surrendered to the bottle.

When I lifted my head off the pillow again, I could see under the window shade that it was morning. On their way to the floor, my feet bumped against something. I looked down. It was the bottle of scotch. I picked it up and set it on the end table. I needed coffee and aspirin. I stood up slowly to stabilize myself enough to get to the kitchen, hoping the caffeine and aspirin would help me believe I wasn't going to die.

Somehow I managed to put together coffee, aspirin, and a cold shower. I didn't feel better in the way that really mattered, but I didn't feel I had to go back to bed. I called Human Resources and anonymously inquired about funeral arrangements for Stacy. I was told that cards and flowers should be sent to Fredricks Funeral Home in Salisbury, Maryland. I called the funeral home and learned that the funeral would be in two days. Immediately I phoned the airline and booked a flight.

I arrived in Salisbury behind schedule. I called the funeral home. A woman answered and told me the funeral procession had just left and was on its way to the church. I still had to rent a car. I knew I couldn't make the church, so I asked the woman for directions to the cemetery. Her directions were clear, but I got lost once anyway and when I got to the cemetery, the service had already begun.

A man in a black suit handed me a rose as I walked toward the small group of people surrounding the casket. I stood in the back and watched as a priest standing at the head of the casket recited prayers. The sky was gray, overcast. Thunder rumbled. He paused to glance at the threatening clouds, seeming to pick up the pace. Raindrops were falling as he said his final words. After a silent pause, the priest approached a man and two women dressed in black in the front row. I guessed it was her father, mother, and sister. The women's hair was auburn, like Stacy's.

I watched the man drop his single rose onto the coffin. The two women followed placing their roses more carefully than the man, paused for a longer moment then linked arms with the waiting man. They all walked away. I watched them walk to a waiting limousine. I wanted to talk to them. Tell them I was sorry. What would I say? How could I explain who I was? This would be my only chance. I reached them just as they were about to get into the car.

"Excuse me," I said "Wait. Please."

They stopped outside the limo door. The man turned and said, "What is it, Sir? Do I know you?"

"Uh, no you don't, Sir. I got here late and I wanted to express my condolences to you," I looked at the two women, "and to you too." I turned again to the man. "You're Stacy's father."

"That's right. Who are you?"

"Well, Sir, I'm...my name's Jimmy."

"I know who you are," said the younger of the two women.

We all turned and she came toward me. I recognized her almond-colored eyes.

"Stacy told me about you. You're from Miami, right?"

"Yes," I said.

"Ma, this is Jimmy—the guy Stacy was seeing."

I looked at Stacy's mother. She took my hand.

"She seemed so happy when we spoke, said you were a good man. You were nice to her."

"I was in love with her," I said.

"It was nice of you to come all this way."

"I wanted to be here."

"I don't mean to cut you short," her father said, "but it's really starting to come down, and well—we just want to go home. Come and see us tomorrow. Please."

"I'm leaving in the morning, but I'll call before I go."

"You can call the funeral home for our number," he said. Then they got into the limo and shut the door. I watched the car drive away.

I looked down at the rose still in my hand. I walked back to the coffin and set the solitary rose carefully on top. The rain was steadier now and made a tapping sound against the bronze metal casing. I pressed my fingertips against my lips then touched the top of her coffin. The metal was cold. I felt a chill run up my arm.

"Goodbye, Stacy. I'll always love you."

I pulled up my lapel and walked back to the car.

The next day I called Stacy's mother from my hotel room. We spoke for a short time. She said she was happy she had met me. I was happy, too. I gave her my number in Miami and told her to call if she wanted to talk. She asked me what had happened. I had to lie. I had to tell her it was an accident.

At the hotel the final arrangements were being made for the convention scheduled to start in a few days. The government people had literally moved into my pal Howie's office and taken over. Howie was caught up in the crossfire between his people complain-ing about the government boys stepping on their toes and the government boys complaining of lack of cooperation from his people. He'd sworn off drink fifteen years ago but he half jokingly insisted the stress was forcing him back to his old ways. Even Ted, easygoing as he was, had his patience challenged by the government security making its presence known in his office. We'd be busy moving out bars and they'd be asking why's and how's and why not's about things they knew nothing about. All this annoyance—and the convention hadn't even started yet.

The two floors set aside for the governor and Martinez were the most protected. No one but Martinez, the governor, and their immediate staffs were allowed on those floors. Guards were positioned at each staircase and elevator door to stop anyone from setting foot on the floor. Anyone doing maid service or room service underwent body searches when entering the floor and again when entering the individual suites.

The convention was scheduled to open with a large cocktail party in the main ballroom. We had planned for ten portable bars to be set up throughout the room. After an hour of reception, the speeches would start. This would be the moment everyone was waiting for. The governor would give his opening speech. If all the rumors were true about him and Martinez, everyone would know then.

The convention coordinators had requested that no beverages be served during the speeches to cut down on noise and confusion. Once the speeches started, we were told to wait quietly by our bars then push them down the hall past the kitchen and end up back at the beverage department outside Ted's office door.

Ted had scheduled a final meeting with us on Sunday afternoon, the day before the start of the convention. All ten of us, along with Barbara and Kevin, crammed into his office. When everyone had arrived, he brought us to attention from behind his desk.

"Well, this is it, guys. Tomorrow's the day. I know everyone's been under a lot of stress the last few months. A lot's gone on but this is where it comes down to individual departments. I'm not concerned about anybody else. I want our department to do its job with no screw-ups. If something's gonna go wrong, let it happen somewhere else. If anybody has questions, now's the time to ask them. If not, there's one more thing you need to know. Security has told me that after the reception and speeches are over they're gonna take Martinez and the governor back to their suites in one of the service elevators. Nobody knows which one. It could be this one outside the door or the two on the other end of the floor. We have to make sure the area outside my door is clear so they can pass through if they decide to use our elevator. Anybody have any questions?" He waited for a response. There were no questions. "That's it then. See you all tomorrow. Make me look good, guys."

Barbara opened the gray metal door and everyone filed out. John, Robin, Michele, and I walked out together.

"Hey Jimmy. Me, Robin, and John are going to the Dugout for a few beers. You wanta go?"

"I can't right now, Michele. I have a couple things to do."

"Okay, but tomorrow night we're all going out to celebrate—so no excuses."

"Sure. I'll be there tomorrow."

I really had nowhere to go and although the atmosphere around the hotel was festive, I was engulfed with Stacy's death and the frustration of knowing Diaz and Blanco were scheming something.

I'd heard people around the hotel mentioning Stacy, referring to her as the tennis pro and how terrible the accident was. But no one knew what I knew. In such a short time she'd given me something to look forward to and someone to care about. I'd forgotten my obsession with my two enemies and was looking forward to a new life with Stacy.

Everything I now loved, everything that newly mattered, died with her. Our relationship—the memory of it—I would keep deep within. I'd use it, as I had done with my father's memory, to give me strength and thrust me out into life. But I was so tired of memory. Mere memory. No—not mere. Memory was precious. But I wanted more. I wanted life to be okay and also last.

I spent Sunday night in my condo. Gino had called and asked if I wanted to go to the club for a few hours, but I couldn't concentrate on gambling. My mind was full of relentless confusion: What were Diaz and Blanco going to do?

I was lying on the couch, hands clasped behind my head, watching the white paddle fan on my ceiling turn when my phone rang. I reached behind my head and pulled the receiver to my ear. It was Gino.

"What's up, Gino? If you're calling to talk me into coming over there, you're still wasting your time."

"Frank. Who do you think I just run into here? That broad, Virginia. She says she's been hanging around the club every night hoping to see you. She wants to talk to you."

"What'd you tell her, Gino?"

"Zero. I said I didn't know where you were."

"What do you think she wants?"

"I don't know. Could be trying to set you up. If she told Diaz about you, you're fucked. I don't trust broads like her."

"Maybe I ought to come over there."

"No. Listen. I'm calling from Maxie's next door. Let me go back to the club and I'll call her over to the phone. We'll call you from there before she's got time to tell anybody."

"Okay, Gino. I'll wait for your call, but be careful."

"What? Just let them try something with me. That would make my day. I'll call you in a few minutes."

I didn't know if I wanted him to call back, but I waited by the phone. A few minutes later he did. He put Virginia on the phone.

"Frank? I bet you'd never think you'd hear from me again."

"Well, I am surprised. What do you want?"

"Well, I've been thinking a lot about what you and me talked about and the more I thought of it, the more I realized what a cold-hearted bastard Victor is. He's been using me like he uses everybody else. Victor's always gonna look out for Victor. That's not gonna change."

"Virginia, I don't want to cut you short, but what's this got to do with me?"

"I figure my days with him are numbered, so I thought maybe I could get some payback for me and Billy. I'm only gonna say this once, so listen. We were at a party in Palm Beach yesterday. Victor was talking to some men. They were laughing about this girl who was killed in a car accident."

I sat up on the couch.

"I said I thought it was sad, a young girl dying like that. Then he said, 'Accident? That was no accident, honey! That bitch put her nose where it didn't belong.'"

Rage ripped through me like a firewall. Virginia moved on, "At that moment I felt nothing but hate for him."

"Is that what Billy did?" I asked. "Put his nose where it didn't belong?"

"He said my brother Billy was a fool, that he tried to muscle him and he fucked himself. I'd always thought he'd had something to do with Billy's death, but that son of a bitch just about admitted to it. Later I overheard him, Blanco, Frederico, and Vincente talking about a guy named Martinez. He told Blanco their man was ready if the deal went through. I hope this helps you get what you want."

"It does. Thanks, Virginia. Virginia, now you have to watch out for yourself too. Watch your back."

"Don't worry. I won't be around long enough for him to find out anything. I'm leaving Miami. So long, Frank." There was muffled noise then Gino's voice.

"Did you get that, Frank?"

"Yeah, Gino. Look. Make sure she gets out of there all right then come over and we'll talk."

It was just past midnight when Gino knocked on my door.

"Well. What do you think, Frank?" I never heard him so agitated.

"I think if the governor announces a deal with Colombia, Martinez is a dead man. And I think I know how he's gonna do it. The way they got Bobby Kennedy. The same way."

"They got somebody on the inside?"

"Yeah. And I think I know who it is, Gino. Diaz did his homework. He's been planning this for a long time. Barbara and Diaz meeting in the parking garage. Then Andre, an inexperienced bartender, starts working there. He's a familiar face at the hotel now. Who would question him?"

“Yeah, but without any proof, Frank, it’s just talk.”

“I know.”

“So you can't go to the cops. What do we do?”

I looked up into determined eyes, then looked away, glad I wasn't alone.

“Well, one thing's for sure. You can bet Blanco's not gonna be anywhere near the hotel tomorrow. That leaves Diaz, and if I'm right, Andre. I gotta keep my eye on Diaz and Andre.”

“How do I help, Frank?”

“If something goes down, Diaz isn't gonna hang around.”

“He'll be long gone. Probably have one of his goons get him out of there. You know what they look like. Maybe you can hang around outside. Keep an eye out for Diaz's car.”

“What about Security? What if they see me hanging around?”

“Gino, there's gonna be so many people hanging around in front. Nobody's gonna question you. If Diaz comes out before the reception breaks up, you know something's going down. You can't let Diaz get away, Gino. You gotta stop his car somehow.”

“Okay. That all? I'll take care of it.”

“I guess the rest is up to me.”

“You sure you know what you're doing?”

“No, Gino, I don't. But it's been nine months since I left New York. I don't know if I'm going back, but this nightmare has to end. Until Blanco and Diaz are out of my life, I have no life. Tomorrow's my chance to get them.”

Gino left. I was too agitated to sleep. I kept turning, shutting my eyes then turning again on the couch. Some parts of the night I lost memory of. I must have slept in short intervals. Suddenly it was morning. Ted wanted us at work by noon. I fidgeted around the condo like an anxious bridegroom till it was time to go. I gave Gino one last call before I left and headed for the hotel.

Chapter Eighteen

A carnival atmosphere pervaded the hotel grounds as I drove onto the property. I slowed down to a crawl giving way to swarms of conventioneers. The shuttle area was packed with people waiting to hop a ride. A trio of musicians blasted out tunes from a far corner on the grass to guests mingling in front of the hotel. Stretch limousines were backed up out of sight dropping delegates at the front door.

At the parking garage, valets were hustling about, parking and retrieving cars. I didn't bother trying to find a space in front. I drove to the back and parked where housekeeping stored damaged equipment and furniture. I got out and walked between parked cars trying to focus on what was about to happen. If I was right and a deal was announced, Martinez would be assassinated. If no deal was announced, it meant Diaz and Blanco bought Martinez. Either way, Blanco wins. Unless Gino and I could stop him.

I passed security where Howie and three of his staff huddled over his desk discussing strategy. I changed into my black and whites and headed for the elevator. The door opened on the banquet level and I stepped off.

Immediately I found myself amidst mayhem. Bartenders were scrambling to set up their bars for the reception, now just a couple hours away. Ted was calm, treating the affair like any other function, but Kevin was pacing in the work area blurting out commands and checking the maze of bars across the room.

Barbara walked through wearing a clingy, cream-colored knit dress. A perfect choice, I thought, to impress political heavies attending the affair. Robin and Michele noticed too.

“Hey, get a load of her,” Robin said. “You think she's trying to hook one of those politicians?”

“She's been awfully quiet today,” Michele said.

“Yeah Michele, she's probably afraid if she speaks she might pop a seam.”

We laughed and I pushed my bar past Robin and Michele and parked next to Andre. He seemed very involved in his work.

“How you doing, Andre?“ I said.

“Uh. Oh, hi.”

“You think these people are gonna be heavy drinkers?”

He didn't answer. He seemed distracted, but I persisted. I wanted more conversation out of him.

“Andre?”

He squatted down to check the soda tanks beneath his bar.

“What?”

“I said do you think these people are gonna drink much?”

“I don't know. We'll soon find out, won't we?” He turned back to the tanks.

“You goin down to the cafeteria before we start?”

“Uh, no, I'm not hungry.”

“You don't have to rush setting up. We have lots of time.”

“Well—I just want to be ready.”

I went back to my work, but kept looking over at him. In no time he was done. He pulled a white handkerchief from his back pocket and blotted his forehead. After giving his bar a onceover, he stepped into the office. After a short conversation with Ted and Barbara, he came out and rolled out his bar.

“Where's he going?” I asked.

John Palmer looked up and gave Andre a glance.

“Oh Ted wants our bars in the room as soon as we're set up. He's no fool. The first ones out get the spots at this end of the room. If you get stuck at the far end, it's gonna be a bitch trying to push back here between all the people.”

"Pretty smart; you're right," I said.

My bar was only half set. I picked up my pace.

I didn't want to end up at the opposite side of the room, far from Andre. I was still gambling on my Andre-was-an-assassin theory. But there was nothing conspicuously peculiar or suspicious about the way Andre was acting. Sure he was in a hurry to get into the room but so was everyone else, including me. Ted said there were three possible routes for the executives. I had a one-in-three chance it would be through the beverage department. Even then I wasn't sure what I'd do.

I finished setting up and quickly pushed my bar into the massive ballroom. I headed straight for the back bar closest to Andre. I ended up halfway across the room from him. One by one, everyone took positions in the room then returned to the beverage office for a last minute pep talk by Ted. When the cocktail hour was over, we were to stop serving and stand at attention behind our bars until the initial speeches were over. At the proper time, Barbara would give the signal and we were to roll back our bars, break them down, and leave.

It was time. Ten of us filed out and took positions behind our bars. Fifteen minutes later the ballroom doors swung open and the conventioneers began wandering in. Between making scotch and sodas and gin and tonics, my eyes were on Andre. The conventioneers continued to file in and it wasn't long before all ten bars were three deep with impatient guests. I checked Andre at every opportunity, but all I saw was the backs of people clustered around his bar, waving and trying to get his attention. I took advantage of a short lull to check my watch. It was two-thirty. The speeches were scheduled to start at three.

The bar crowd thinned. I finally caught a glimpse of Andre between patrons. Hanging over the end of his bar was Diaz. I watched their lips move as Andre handed Diaz a drink, sending him on his way. Diaz disappeared in the crowd.

The program began right on schedule. At exactly three we

stopped serving. The mayor walked onto the stage at the far end of the room, stood behind the podium, and brought the convention to order. I watched Diaz walk through the crowd then I glanced over at Andre.

The mayor's voice was coming through the speakers. After a brief welcoming introduction, he turned over the podium to the governor amidst the cheers of the crowd. After beaming with self-confidence and letting the applause shower him, the governor raised his hands, signaling for silence.

As the crowd quieted, he began. “Thank you, Mister Mayor. It’s great to be here in Miami. We’re doing great things, not only here in Miami, but throughout our beautiful state of Florida. Touring our vast peninsula, I’ve seen prosperity and hope reflected in each and every face I’ve encountered. But there’s still much work to be done.”

It was a lackluster speech. The crowd listened restlessly as the governor outlined the agenda for the convention. Then came the awaited moment.

“At this time I’d like to introduce President Luis Martinez of Colombia.”

The room exploded with applause as President Martinez joined the governor at the podium. After an exchange of smiles and handshakes, Martinez took the podium.

“Thank you very much.”

His words silenced the crowd. Citing the drug issue as the cause of turbulent relations between Colombia and the United States, he thanked America for its financial aid.

“For the past six months the governor and I have been hard at work devising a plan that we feel will effectively crack down on the Colombian drug cartel and its American kingpins. I have pledged my sincere loyalty and support to the United States and to your great state of Florida to carry out our plan. But the cartel’s greatest weapon is its wealth. My government needs increased financial aid to combat the cartel’s inexhaustible source of revenue.

I ask for your support, and vow that within the next year, we can, through increased enforcement in my country and education through the media in yours, control the drug traffic between our countries."

He paused to let the crowd cheer then continued to outline the program.

As he finished his speech, the governor joined him at the podium. They joined hands and raised them in unity. The entire ballroom cheered. I felt a lump in my throat. Martinez's announcement was bad news for Victor Diaz and Ricardo Blanco. I was scared for Martinez, scared for me. I could sense something was going to happen. Somehow I had to stop it.

"Okay, Jimmy, we're out of here." Kevin whisked by like the Roadrunner.

I quickly packed up and started pushing my bar. I had to keep close to Andre. He had positioned himself at the far end of the work area. If the entourage came through, it would pass him first. Michele Walker had reached the room before me and pulled up next to him. All I could do was take my place next to her. Everyone began unloading their bars.

I fiddled with mine, afraid to leave in case the entourage appeared. I checked Andre. He didn't seem to be in a hurry either.

Kevin came out of the office and went down the line of bars, inspecting our progress.

"Andre. What the hell are you doing? Let's get going."

Andre didn't respond. He was bent over his bar.

"Andre! Come on! Let's go!"

Andre gave Kevin a blank look and continued working.

He seemed calm, calmer than he needed to be. Except for Robin's babbling, the room was calm too. I could hear my heart pounding as the moments ticked by. Nothing was happening. I was torn and frustrated. I hoped for Martinez's safety, but an attempt on his life was my only way to expose Diaz and Blanco. It seemed too much time had passed. The entourage must have used one of the other routes. I'd stalled long enough. I made a trip into the office and unloaded some canned soda and juices. Michele reminded me about getting together when we finished as I followed her out of the office.

We reached the door. I glanced down the corridor. A crowd emerged. Michele said something. I was out of position. Andre was at his bar watching as the entourage headed toward us.

"Hey! Look! Here comes the governor!" Robin said.

Everyone stopped to watch. I passed Michele and quickly attempted to take a place behind her bar.

"Hey Jimmy, that's my bar," she said.

I slipped out and returned to mine.

Ted, Barbara, and Kevin stood in the doorway. The entourage was close now. I could see Martinez and the governor amidst five bodyguards. I stiffened as they approached. I checked Andre. He looked flushed and preoccupied. In a blur of slow motion, the entourage entered the work area. Barbara, Ted and some of the bartenders watched from inside the office door. One of the guards had split from the crowd and headed for the elevator. I focused on Andre, trying to concentrate on him. He was still hunched over his bar as the entourage passed.

"Come on. Just a little farther," I said, mentally urging them on. The celebrities drew everyone's attention. They passed Andre then Michele. I was next. My back stiffened, my eyes fixed on each movement. A hand on my shoulder startled me.

"Isn't this cool?" It was Michele's voice.

I glanced at her but didn't respond.

She moved in to get a better look, putting herself in the space between my bar and hers. The shift in position annoyed me. I gave her another look. Over her shoulder, I could see Andre coming around his bar into the aisle behind the crowd. Still unsure. All I could do was wait.

Andre's eyes had a vicious glare. He drew near the rear of the entourage and slipped his hand under his jacket. My chest tightened. I couldn't take my eyes off his jacket. His hand pulled out a pistol. My heart jolted.

Screaming, "Look out!" I pushed Michele aside and burst toward him.

The attention then shifted to me. I focused on Andre. His glare held a hint of surprise.

Our eyes met as I lunged at him, knocking his arm upward. The gun went off. Fragments of ceiling tile fell to the floor. Robin and Michele screamed. Everyone scattered. Grabbing his wrist with both my hands, I bulldozed Andre into the wall. He fought to shake his hand free. I could feel my fingers separating. Seconds later the bodyguards overtook Andre and shoved him face down to the floor.

Diaz! I thought. He was probably getting away. In a frenzy I started down the hall, hoping to get lost in the confusion, but a security guard's voice halted me. "Hey! Where do you think you're going?" He made a hand motion directing me back. "Nobody leaves this area."

"Listen," I said as I approached him, "let me go please. The guy you really want is getting away right now! You gotta believe me. Let me go before it's too late!"

"What are you talking about? A bartender! What do you know about this?"

Everyone's attention focused on me. Ted intervened.

"What's going on here, guys?" he asked.

"Your bartender here says he knows who's behind this."

The seconds were ticking by. I didn't have time for explanations. Ted turned to me.

"What's going on, Jimmy?"

"I don't have time to explain now, Ted, but one of the brains behind this is getting away right now. She's involved too."

I nodded toward Barbara.

She turned to me with raised eyebrows. Her cheeks were red. "What are you talking about? You jerk! How dare you! You'll never work here or anywhere else in this town again!"

"Okay. That's enough everybody," the guard said. "Let's just settle down. Paul Carroll's on his way with the cops." Turning to me, he said. "You can tell him your story."

"You don't understand. I gotta—"

"I said nobody leaves."

All I could feel was frustration. I waited helplessly while Barbara glared at me. Ted looked on, disappointed and confused.

The guard had left his post at the elevator when the ruckus began. He and another guard quickly escorted the two dignitaries from the scene. The door was still open. I couldn't wait any longer. I was standing just past the office door a few yards from the elevator. I noticed that one of the bars was pushed to one side. Ted, Barbara, and the others were frozen, still in shock. I grabbed the bar and yanked it across the floor, momentarily blocking me off from the others.

"Hey, what the fuck are you doing?" the guard shouted. Everyone turned to see me racing for the elevator. The guards rushed toward me but the elevator door closed just in time.

"I'll explain later!" I screamed against the door.

Suddenly time was precious. I had to find Diaz before the police and Security found me.

The news of the attempted assassination hadn't reached the main floor yet. I entered the lobby and quickly scanned the room for Diaz. Through the crowd I caught sight of him casually exiting the front door.

Anxiously I edged my way through the swarm of people. I glanced behind me. The door swung open and Howie and two guards entered the lobby, their eyes darting in every direction. One of his men moved in on me. I froze for a second. Our eyes met. He pointed toward me. I turned to the front door and forced my way toward Diaz, now outside waving to his left.

I reached the front doors, shoved them open, and burst out. I heard him call, "Frederico!" He was looking to his left. I slowed down to check where he was looking. It was Gino standing by the open door of Diaz's car. He had Frederico pinned to the hood of the car. I noticed blood running down his cheek.

"Diaz!" I screamed.

He turned to find me coming at him in my black and whites. With Freddy out of commission and security now blocking the front entrance he began running toward the back of the property. I took off after him.

He raced to the boardwalk where a shuttle was leaving with a group of passengers heading to the beach. He ran up alongside the shuttle till he reached the front. Before the driver knew what was happening, Diaz grabbed him from behind, yanked him from the seat, and took the wheel. He slammed the pedal to the floor and headed for the beach. The full load of passengers screamed and flung themselves to the far end of the shuttle, jostling and crushing each other to get away from Diaz.

I threw myself onto the rear of the car just in time and worked my way through the terrified passengers toward the front.

Diaz looked frantically over his shoulder then swung the steering wheel back and forth in an effort to shake me off. Adrenalin pumped through me. The first jolt of the car took me by surprise. I stumbled sideways between the seats and felt a sharp pain as my head banged against the metal frame. I grabbed the back of the seat and pulled myself up. Gripping the seat-backs stabilized me. One by one, I used them to pull me toward the front.

When I got to him, he looked up and swung at me with his right arm. I ducked to avoid the blow and fell on my back. Pain surged through me but rage kept me going. On my feet again, I rushed at him and threw my arms around his neck, trying to yank him from the seat, but he kept his hands clasped tight on the wheel. Suddenly it pulled sharply to the right throwing the shuttle into a fishtail.

Passengers were screaming. Diaz was like a lead weight in the seat. Gripping his neck, I struggled to reach the brake pedal with my foot. He shoved his elbow into my diaphragm. The blow dazed me. For a second my arms went limp. He butted me with his shoulder, knocking me backward over the passenger seat. I caught my breath and lunged back at him. The momentum knocked his hands from the wheel and we wrestled in the seat. I took a blow from his right fist which dazed me.

The shuttle was meandering. Diaz was desperately trying to push me over the side. I was right on the edge and felt myself falling. As my body dropped, I grabbed Diaz's neck and we both landed onto the wooden slats of the bridge overlooking the swamp. The shuttle sped out of control, crashing to a stop against the side rail at the far end of the bridge.

I was overcome by rage. I felt unstoppable. I wrestled him to the edge of the wooden planks. I pinned his face over the edge of the small bridge. Alligators floated in the waters below. Furiously I smashed his face against the wooden plank.

"How's it look, Diaz? Is that what Dan Hiller saw before he died? And Pedro Quero and Stacy Iseman! You took my business! You destroyed my name with your drugs. You killed my father, you bastard!" With nothing helping but my adrenalin, I flipped him over and glared at him.

"It's over, you son of a bitch."

Diaz was gasping for breath. "Who are you?"

"I'm Frank D'Antonio, you cocksucker. Joseph D'Antonio was my father and Stacy Iseman was my girlfriend."

I beat him over and over against the wooden slats. I was out of control.

"Stop. Police!"

I looked up. Another shuttle carrying police and security approached with pistols pointed at me. Exhausted, I released Diaz and struggled to my feet.

"Raise your hands so we can see them." A voice came from the shuttle. My arms felt like dead weight. Slowly I lifted them shoulder high. Another voice screamed, "Look out!"

I turned to find Diaz's hands going for my throat. Frantically I tried to pry his hands loose but his grip was too much. I was too weak. I was gasping for air. I tried to bulldoze him backward with my body.

From the corner of my eye I could see the police rushing toward us. He held in his grip and the momentum sent us catapulting against the rail. With one last surge of energy, I broke his hold and pushed him away. He rushed me again, his outstretched hands grabbing my shirt. Sheer instinct saved me. I shifted to avoid him. Instinctively I went for his chest trying to push him away. I shifted my body again. The combined force lifted him and sent him over the rail. He let out a scream that faded as he plunged into the water below.

I caught a glimpse of his face, eyes wide bulging. His hands slapped at the water, fighting to stay up. Into the thrashing waters, alligators pulled him under, their backs turned to mere ripples, remnants of the final struggle.

I felt a grip on my wrists and watched in relief as one of the officers fit me with matching silver bracelets. I didn't resist.

I was relieved, exhausted, but to be totally free I had to go after Blanco. It wouldn't take long before he learned who had sabotaged his plan and killed his partner. He'd come after me with all he had. But for today victory was mine.

I was transported back to the hotel where a plainclothesman waited in Paul Carroll's office. Barbara, Ted, and Howie were standing there. They looked grim and wouldn't meet my eye. Two security guards from the beverage department were there too.

"I'll take your statement downtown, but right now I just need some general information." The lieutenant was speaking to me.

"I—"

"He said he knew who was behind this!" It was the security guard.

"Yeah, and he accused me too!" Barbara said, glaring at me.

Turning to Ted and the lieutenant, she said, "He works for the union. They know we've been bought out. They think they can take advantage to try to organize the help, making us look bad to the new owners."

She turned to me, arms crossed, haughty and confident: "Well, it didn't work."

"Is that why you had Diaz send two of his boys to beat me up in the parking garage? Did Diaz tell you if you play along with him, he'd take care of you? Maybe give you Ted's job? Or maybe it's Paul's you're after?"

Ted and Paul turned to her. Her confidence visibly collapsed. Her arms dropped.

"That's a lie! I don't know what he's talking about."

"I saw you talking to Diaz in the parking garage months ago. Just before Andre started working. Diaz told you to convince Ted to hire him, didn't he?"

Ted's face turned stone-gray. He looked at Barbara, waiting for an explanation.

"Don't believe him, Ted."

Ted folded his arms over his chest. She moved toward him until the lieutenant's voice brought her to a halt.

"Okay. Everybody shut up!" he said. Then turning to Barbara he barked, "You sit down."

He glanced at Ted. In a calmer tone, he said, "You too, Ted." He scanned the room, making eye contact with each of us. "Now, may I continue?"

Then he turned to me. "Okay, Sir. What's your name?" Again Barbara blurted out, "It's James Anthony."

"Lady—another word—I lock you up."

"My name is Frank D'Antonio."

I looked up at a stunned Paul Carroll.

"What—? That's impossible. Frank D'Antonio was my— I know he has a—" Incredulously he raised his hand to his cheek, staring straight at me.

"I shaved, Paul."

"Wait a minute. Who's Frank D'Antonio?" the lieutenant asked.

"Frank D'Antonio. The D'Antonio brothers from New York. They owned this hotel up until about a year ago."

"Yeah, they own a lot of property in the city," Howie added. He and Paul gaped at me in disbelief.

Barbara's rage turned to fear as everyone looked at me.

"Is that who you say you are?" The lieutenant asked.

I thought of Stacy. If only this had happened before she had to die.

"That's right."

"He's lying!" Barbara said.

The lieutenant turned again to Barbara. Before he could utter a word, Ted said, "Barbara, shut up!"

"I just talked to Frank D'Antonio not long ago. He's in New York," Paul said.

"I was calling from here, Paul."

"Okay, what did we talk about?"

"I asked you to get me the report on Pedro Quero's death. Remember?"

Turning to the lieutenant I said, "I think Diaz had Quero killed along with my father, Dan Hiller, and...well, he works for Ricardo Blanco."

"Blanco! You're dropping a lot of big names here."

"Who's Ricardo Blanco?" Carroll asked.

He is the biggest drug lord in the world," the lieutenant answered.

"That's right," I said.

"Of course you can prove all this," he said.

I hesitated. "Quero, Dan, and my father's murder, no. But you have Andre for attempted murder. With Diaz dead, he'll probably tell you everything you want to know, including her part in this," I threw Barbara a look.

"I want to call my lawyer," Barbara said and stood up.

"I'm warning you, lady. Sit down! You'll have time to make phone calls when I'm done. No one leaves till I say so." Then he turned to me. “What about you? Can you prove who you are?”

I looked over at Paul’s confused face.

“Paul, call Penny in New York. She'll verify everything.”

“Miss...Anderson?”

“Yes, Paul. Miss Anderson.”

Immediately he picked up the phone. He stared at me with disbelief as I recited the number. I motioned with my shoulders. “Go head, Paul. Dial.” Slowly he punched in the numbers then raised the receiver to his ear.

After a short conversation with Penny, he looked down at me and cleared his throat. “She wants to talk to you, Sir.”

I made a gesture behind me and Paul put the receiver to my ear.

“Frank!—What—?”

“Just tell these people who I am. I'll call you later when I can explain. I'm a little tied up right now.”

Penny confirmed my identity and the police took the bracelets off. The lieutenant read Barbara her rights then placed her in the cuffs he’d just taken from me. Two uniformed officers led her away. She gave Ted a teary look, hoping, I think, he'd come to her rescue. He glanced at me and Paul then watched her walk away.

“I could use a drink,” he said. “Can I get you something, Jim? Frank, I mean. Sir?”

“Good idea, Ted,” Paul said. “What would you like, Sir? Anything at all.”

I asked for water, which Ted brought to me. I noted a new solicitousness. He seemed almost to hurry. I vouched for Gino, who was being held outside.

“We’re gonna have to take him downtown for questioning,” The lieutenant said, then added, “You too.”

After we’d had our drinks, the lieutenant drove me down to the precinct. He asked if I wanted to call a lawyer. I declined. Then he and another plain-clothed detective listened as I disclosed everything, including names and places. They interrupted periodically to challenge some of the details, but they seemed to find my story credible. I used my family's name and reputation to persuade them that I wasn't a flight risk. The lieutenant reluctantly agreed but demanded I keep in touch.

After two hours they released Gino and me. The lieutenant offered to have us driven back to the hotel, but we opted for a cab. On our way out I caught a glimpse of Andre, Barbara, and Freddy being led into a room.

The cab dropped us off at Gino's Mercedes. From there we went to my place.

I left Gino in the living room and walked into the bedroom. There were two messages on my answering machine: one from Penny, the other from Angelo. Immediately I called the office and explained what had happened. Penny asked what my plans were. I said I didn't know. "Is Angelo there?" I asked.

She said he'd gone home. "Let me know what's going on," she said and then we hung up.

I paused a moment, staring at the phone. Finally I dialed Angelo's number. The phone rang twice before he answered.

His voice was raspy but frenzied. I repeated what I'd told Penny, assuring him everything was all right. "I guess I better come home," I said.

"From what you've told me, it looks like Blanco's going to be looking for you," he said.

We stayed silent a moment. "Maybe I ought to get lost for a while."

He paused a moment then said, "Maybe."

My throat tightened. "I'll keep in touch," I said.

"You better not. I'll fix things with Ma so she doesn't worry."

"I'll call."

"You can't call or write, Frankie. Blanco's got a lot of resources."

Again we stayed silent. "Well…" I felt my voice start to crack. "Take care of yourself, Angelo."

His seemed to quiver. “You too, Frankie.”

We lingered a few minutes more until finally I said, “Maybe we’ll get together this winter?”

“Yeah… maybe.”

Tears filled my eyes. “I’ll see you.”

“Yeah… I’ll see you.” I heard a click then I hung up.

I inhaled deeply, swiped my eyes with my palms then returned to the living room. Gino sat patiently on the couch. He looked up when I entered. “What are you gonna do, Kid?”

“I gotta get out of town for a while, Gino.”

“Good idea.”

“Give me a few minutes. I want to pack a few things. Then I’ll need a ride to the airport.”

“Where you goin?”

I glanced at the phone in the bedroom then looked at Gino. “I'm not sure.”

He looked at me. I wondered if he’d heard my conversation with Angelo.

I disappeared into the bedroom. Fifteen minutes later I appeared, suitcase in hand. “Let’s go,” I said.

We passed Manatee Park on the way to the airport. I caught a glimpse of children playing behind the rusted fences. When things cooled down I’d try to get the city to resurface the courts. I knew when the story hit the papers, the D’Antonio name would have a new celebrity, but at that moment I felt more like a fugitive. When the time was right, I’d use my new celebrity status along with our family name and some money and give the kids a nice place to play.

An hour later Gino pulled up in front of the terminal. I grabbed my bag and jumped out.

“Gino, one more thing. See that Virginia gets this.”

I tossed an envelope on the front seat. We shook hands. I

slammed his door shut and headed into the terminal. I'd walked ten feet when I heard Gino call me. I went back and stuck my head into his passenger side window. He looked at me. I felt tears spring to my eyes but I couldn't let him see.

"Watch yourself, Frank." Like my dad's words. I paused then nodded slightly and turned away.

An airport again. A marquee announcing excursions to Key West loomed in front of me. I'd been there before. It was as good a place as any.

Airline attendants had been eliminated on puddle-jumpers and fewer than ten passengers had booked this flight. A recording recited the preflight instructions. I fastened my seatbelt and waited for the move down the runway.

An old couple sat two seats from me but the other passengers were spread out, each traveling alone like me. A mix of relief and comfort settled over me. The plane didn't feel so empty. I imagined a story for each traveler. Maybe some had no clearer destination than I did. But I was myself again—and comfortable sitting here. It was a new feeling. Things had changed—I had made things change. I could make my life different now. Life would be different now. I hoped eventually to get back to New York. It was there I belonged. Sabotaging Blanco's drug business had put me temporarily in danger, but if I could elude him I had a plan to get back our holdings.

I thought about Gino. I hoped he'd remember to deliver my note to Virginia. She'd told him she was moving to Atlanta to open a boutique. Her life could be different now as well. In the envelope I'd put the names of friends I had in Atlanta and a short letter introducing her as a friend. She wasn't really a friend, but she'd done a good thing and I wanted to help her. My friends in Atlanta would help her get started.

Images of Stacey entered my mind. I was reluctant to let them stay. I wanted to remember her smiling, happy. She had not died smiling. I wondered what had she been thinking in her last moments of terror. Had she thought of me? Had she an inkling of the web of greed and evil that had caught and held her life? The doctor assured me she had died with no awareness. But how could he be sure? I pushed aside these thoughts, but I knew I would carry them with me forever.

Acknowledgements

I wish to thank the following people for their editorial help and dedication: Nina Alvarez, Jean Wood, Janine Warsaw, Portia Weiskel and Victor West.

To Dick (Ricardo) Brown, Tony Tracy, Marshall Loeb, Sharon Cuschieri, thank you for your support, friendship, and advice.

CPSIA information can be obtained at www.ICGtesting.com
Printed in the USA
LVOW12s1022030414

380176LV00001B/2/P